The Management of Technical Change

The Management of Technical Change

Automation in the UK and USA since 1950

Alan Booth

First published 2007 by
PALGRAVE MACMILLAN
Houndmills, Basingstoke, Hampshire RG21 6XS and
175 Fifth Avenue, New York, N. Y. 10010
Companies and representatives throughout the world

PALGRAVE MACMILLAN is the global academic imprint of the Palgrave Macmillan division of St. Martin's Press, LLC and of Palgrave Macmillan Ltd. Macmillan® is a registered trademark in the United States, United Kingdom and other countries. Palgrave is a registered trademark in the European Union and other countries.

ISBN-13: 978–1–4039–9174–4   hardback
ISBN-10: 1–4039–9174–X   hardback

This book is printed on paper suitable for recycling and made from fully managed and sustained forest sources.

A catalogue record for this book is available from the British Library.

A catalogue record for this book is available from the Library of Congress.

10   9   8   7   6   5   4   3   2   1
15   14   13   12   11   10   09   08   07

Printed and bound in Great Britain by
Antony Rowe Ltd, Chippenham and Eastbourne

*This book is dedicated to the memory of my father,
Albert Edward Booth (1920–1993), for the encouragement
and support that he unfailingly gave to both his sons.*

Contents

List of Tables

List of Figures

Acknowledgements

This book has been a very long time in the making. Over such a long period, many intellectual debts are accumulated and I would particularly like to thank Jo Melling, Jim Tomlinson, Nick Tiratsoo for their helpful comments on my work over the years and to Mike Anson, Mark Bufton and Andrew Jenkins for stimulating conversations when the germ of this project was hatched. None of them should be blamed for what follows; my obstinacy is legendary. More generally Jeremy Black has been a rock of support and encouragement. Above all, I should like to thank Louise Hill Curth for her enthusiasm for and assistance with all things academic. I have also accumulated debts to many archivists, from whom I would like to single out Edwin Green and Sara Kinsey at HSBC Group Archives, London, Beth Kaplan and Carrie Seib at the Charles Babbage Institute and Susan Hengel, Lynn Catanese and Marge McNinch at the Hagley Museum and Library. At various times, this work has been supported by the Hagley Institute (with many thanks to Philip Scranton, Roger Horowitz and Carol Lockman), the British Academy (research grant LRG 37246), the (then) Arts and Humanities Research Board (research leave grant number RL/PID11476/AID18709) and the University of Exeter for a period of study leave. I am especially grateful to all four institutions for their generous and flexible support.

For permission to use and quote archival material, I am grateful to the following: Graham Goulden (Fujitsu Services for the Fujitsu, formerly ICL, Archive), Edwin Green (HSBC Group Archives, London), Helen Langton (British Bankers' Association Archive) and Philip Winterbottom (Royal Bank of Scotland Group Archives, London), Professor Stephen Broadberry, Cambridge University Press, The National Institute of Economic and Social Research and Professor Karel Williams. Every effort has been made to contact all copyright holders of material reproduced in this book. If any have been inadvertently overlooked, I apologise and will attend to the matter at the first opportunity.

Acknowledgements

1
The Political Economy of Technical Change

This book focuses on the management of technical change in the British economy since the 1950s, with US experience as the reference point. It employs the well-known device of looking at crises, in this instance the "technology scares" that have erupted in twentieth century Britain. They began with "national efficiency" concerns, flowing from the demonstration of US and German productive power in late-Victorian and Edwardian Britain.[1] During the First World War, the threat of postwar German industrial competition briefly gripped British political and business leaders, but did not penetrate far beyond that (Cline 1982). There was a low-grade technology scare in interwar Britain around the impact of rationalisation, but was rather small beer when compared to the intense concern in Germany during the 1920s and in the USA in the 1930s.[2] In fact, the US debates of the 1930s were so powerful that they coloured the attitudes and expectations of American producer groups into the 1960s (Bix 2000).

In Britain, the pace of technology scares quickened after 1945. The first, lasting more than a decade after 1945, turned on how best to cope with the US technological lead at a time of growing liberalisation in world trade and payments. For reasons sketched in the next section, we will concentrate primarily on the automation scare of the mid-1950s. Confidence in British industry returned for a few years of "You've never had it so good", but technology worries returned in the debate over "What's wrong with Britain?", linked indelibly with the Wilson government's efforts to bring the white heat of the technological revolution into British industry. Britain's own problems were submerged in the global downturn of the 1970s and early 1980s, but as relative stability returned, Britain, like much of the developed world, became pre-occupied with the threats from microelectronics and "Japanisation".

1

In every case, it seemed that technical progress had created global excess capacity, and Britain's slowness to modernise had left it uncompetitive in the new international order. In one sense, therefore, technology scares are merely part of "the pathology of decline" (Tomlinson 1996). Indeed, the most lasting image of 1950s automation in Britain is of automobile workers striking against new technology.[3] In the USA, on the other hand, the classic image is the Ford cylinder block machining line, with queues of work-pieces waiting their turn to be machined automatically by one of a large number of linked cutting, boring and milling machines. These images, although literally snapshots, are important in that they have been moulded by, and in turn shape, national attitudes. Whether they contain a kernel of truth is a question for this study.

Automation and the power of American industry

Although the British may believe that technology scares are uniquely domestic, the previous section has indicated that even the most powerful economies have experienced the same pain and introspection. The most protracted and bitter scare occurred in 1930s America, where mass unemployment, increasing job insecurity and debates on the social ethics of industrial innovation scarred the national conscience. These fears abated at the end of the decade: "With national security possibly at stake, production technologies suddenly acquired new meaning. To the extent that mechanized equipment could help manufacture weapons and military supplies while releasing manpower for other vital functions, it became invaluable. In the Depression labour-saving machines seemed to present a threat; in a time of global crisis, they came to represent a virtue" (Bix 2000: 232). The successful alliance of science, technology and industry during wartime strengthened these opinions. Research and innovation were considered the keys to US economic and political supremacy and by extension, as the Cold War progressed, the foundation upon which the capitalist world would be built; hence the US decision, simultaneously generous and self-seeking, to supply financial aid and technological support to selected overseas countries (McGlade 1998: 23).

From these liberal international intentions came an "extraordinary array of programmes aimed at European financial reform, technical modernisation and the revival of business activity" (McGlade 1998: 24). The most eye-catching were the "productivity missions" from Europe (and later Japan), brought to witness and report on the US system of production and distribution (see Barjot 2002). Their reports were often technically astute and wide-ranging, with 66 reports from the Anglo-American Council on Productivity (the forum for UK productivity missions). These were, however, highly "political" texts, having been compiled (in the British case) by mixed teams of employers and employees, occasionally after fierce disputes over the exact composition, usually with a keen eye on the allocation of "blame" for domestic "inefficiency" (Tiratsoo and Tomlinson 1993: 136). In these circumstances, interpretation of the results has been contentious, both at the time and subsequently. Broadberry and Crafts (1990: 387; 1996: 83–5) have emphasised the over-manning and restrictive practices revealed in the reports; Carew (1987: 131–57) has pointed to the vague social-psychological elements and the promotion of US-style scientific management. Tiratsoo and Tomlinson (1993: 139), by contrast, have emphasised reports of managerial deficiencies. Both Tomlinson (1991b: 84–5) and Carew (1987: ch. 9) have noted the carefully crafted and sanitised picture of US industry presented to foreign productivity teams. This was best practice, with its less attractive elements (cartelisation and confrontational industrial relations) obscured. There are obvious dangers in comparing best practice in one country with the average in another, yet historians seldom make allowances.

Fortunately automation generated more effective comparisons in the mid-1950s. The productivity missions and the US Technical Assistance and Productivity Programme (TAPP) that underlay it were worthy but dull, operating behind the scenes. Automation, on the other hand, presented a more public and populist picture of Americanisation in the mid-1950s. It pivoted on very powerful images of the immense productive power and technological sophistication of US manufacturing. The seed was planted in a special issue of *Fortune* on the automatic factory (Leaver and Brown 1946). The central article described a "workerless" factory, capable of continuous operation and overseen by a handful of managers and an engineering and technical staff. The special issue was deliberately controversial, and disagreement soon erupted (Noble 1984: 67–71). Most significantly, in a series of publications the pioneer of cybernetics, Norbert Wiener (1947; 1950), explored the (adverse) social consequences of computer control of industrial processes (Heims 1980: 175–7). He feared that Cold War militarists and reactionary businessmen would use these control technologies to attack labour unions. In 1949–50, he alerted Walter Reuther, head of the United Automobile Workers of America (UAW) and the most impressive union leader of the time, about the threats of automation to organised labour (cited by Noble 1984: 74–6).

By this time, however, automation was becoming a more explosive public issue. The business press continued to show interest in the automatic factory (*Business Week* 1951; 1952a; 1952b; *Scientific American* 1952). A new group of self-publicising, young business analysts became closely associated with automation.[4] In this context, Ford presented its new engine plant at Cleveland, Ohio, as a major step towards the automatic factory (Nevins and Hill 1962: 355), a step forward from the famous A.O. Smith factory (which in the 1930s produced 10,000 car body frames per day with a staff of 600 engineers and 200 mechanics and supervisors, a feat that formerly needed 2,000 men) (Bix 2000: 151) and towards the completely automatic Rockford munitions plant (*Business Week* 1952a; NAM 1954; US Congress 1955: 564-71). Ford claimed that one of its own engineers, Del Harder, had created the term "automation" (Nevins and Hill 1962: 354). In engineering terms, the cylinder block line was breathtaking spectacle, albeit one that had experienced "tremendous growing pains" (Hounshell 1995: 71–5). The line took a rough cylinder block casting and machined it in 530 different operations without human intervention, with automatic handling and positioning between machining processes and selection so that the different cycle times of cutting and milling processes were balanced. In effect, the whole line acted as a single machine (Bright 1958: 61–2). The most favoured image was undoubtedly the "electronic brain" controlling the line, usually with a convenient human brain – approximately one-tenth the size – in shot. Other publicity photographs presented the line without a single worker, or possibly with a single worker in a prostrate position. But the "spin" of the publicity department was still more breathtaking. This "workerless factory" actually employed 2,700 production operatives and 4,500 employees in total; even the cylinder block line required 36 operatives and 11 inspectors per shift (Davis 1955: 56–7; Bright 1958: 60–1). As for the claim to have coined the word automation, Harder's mysterious Automation Department, allegedly created in 1947, appears in none of the organisation charts in Ford's archive (Hounshell 1995: 63, 82n).

Ford's publicity coincided with renewed insecurity about employment. The first postwar downturn occurred in 1947–8 and, although recovery resumed with the Korean War, there was another downturn in 1953–4 when industrial output fell by 7.5 percent and unemployment rose, raising concerns about the impact of automation on the labour market.[5] Reuther and other critics of automation illustrated the threat of unemployment, using Ford's publicity. Stung by the first postwar recession, the UAW had been bargaining vigorously over the terms of automation, not least because "speed-up" was generating friction, both with employers and within the UAW (Lichtenstein 1986: 132). Ford was in his sights. He had already used the reductions in cylinder-block cycle times (the centrepiece of Ford's publicity) to campaign for a shorter working week and the right to inter-plant transfers for any worker of a multi-plant corporations displaced by automation.[6] The UAW also demanded higher rates for those working on automated jobs, and used automation to press long-standing demands (made, needless to say, to Ford) for the guaranteed annual wage (GAW).[7] The GAW had been on the agenda of the UAW and other strong Congress of Industrial Organisations (CIO) unions since 1950, but new threats to blue collar employment gave added impetus.

Conservatives among management were horrified by demands that appeared to undermine the commercial viability of innovation, especially against the background disturbed industrial relations.[8] The leading business interest group, the National Association of Manufacturers (NAM), launched a vigorous counter-attack, much of it directed personally at Reuther, seen by some business leaders as the Devil Incarnate.[9] They rejected institutionalised joint consultation and the GAW as threats to the American system and reacted vigorously against the shorter working week on the grounds of cost.[10] More moderate voices, who considered that industry would gain by limiting the seasonality of demand, were drowned in the fear that Reuther would win a precedent for the entire workforce.[11]

Management fears, and labour's defensiveness, were accentuated by the Cold War context. With the Korean War having only recently ended, the US establishment monitored the Soviet bloc very closely and became very concerned that the US lead in industrial efficiency was being overtaken. Much was made of the number of Soviet engineers graduating each year, far in excess of US output.[12] Business conservatives used these fears to denounce any labour encroachment on the rights of employers to innovate.[13] During the 1950s, business conservatives clawed back much of the ground they had lost to labour in the New Deal era (Boyer and Morais 1955: 371–3). On the other side of the fence, US labour leaders queued up to express, almost in formulaic terms, labour's support for rapid technological progress, provided that the burdens of adjustment were spread evenly. Reuther (1955: 117–20), for example, gave unequivocal commitment to the military-strategic importance of automation; but his colleagues, before a more partisan audience, could strike more aggressive postures (CIOCEP 1955: 55–6, 70–1).

Automation comes to the UK

British unions followed US technological developments very closely. Britain's leading metal-working union, the Amalgamated Engineering Union (AEU), for example, had good links with the UAW and publicised the UAW's bargaining tactics (Priest 1955). The major articles on automation in the AEU *Monthly Journal* during 1954–5 leaned heavily on UAW experiences (Conway 1954; Kent 1955; Dinning 1955; Carron 1955; Smith and Allaun 1955). The AEU *Monthly Journal* regularly aired British concerns about the apparent irresistibility of US competitive power (Smith and Allaun 1955: 308). However, not all British reactions to US developments were quite so pessimistic.

Surprisingly, the British economy suffered no adverse reactions to the US downturn in 1953–4 as industry surged ahead, and both exports and Britain's gold and dollar reserves rose.[14] The Chancellor, R.A. Butler, held out the prospect of doubling British living standards within 20–25 years, if only more resources could be freed for investment and industrial modernisation.[15] To hasten the pace of technological change in Britain, ministers commissioned the Department of Scientific and Industrial Research (DSIR) to undertake a detailed study of automation in British industry. The DSIR prompted employers and unions into action. The employers began to assemble material on "the automatic factory" from August 1954, and the TUC's production department opened its file on automation at approximately the same time (July 1954), exploiting its contacts with US unions.[16] Individual British unions had their own links with US counterparts, and the first comments on the impact of automation in the UK were filtered through US experience.[17] At this stage, the response to automation was mixed.[18] Unions of technicians saw benefits from automation both for themselves and the national economy.[19] Unions of industrial workers also regarded automation as inevitable but thus far containable.[20] Many manual unions reported that job losses from automation had been more than offset by the general increase in production.[21] Some unions recognised that British firms would need to innovate to survive in competitive markets, and that the key was the right to negotiate over the introduction of new technologies.[22] The most pessimistic replies came from the service sector, and particularly from banking.[23] The National Union of Bank Employees feared that computerisation, already under discussion in British banking, would create mass redundancy among routine clerical workers (see Chapter 6).

Meanwhile the aggregate economy began to overheat but, for political reasons, the Treasury allowed the economy to boom until after the 1955 general election.[24] There were profound consequences for industrial relations. Inflationary expansion encouraged leap-frogging wage claims and a rash of unofficial strikes in mid-1955, making industrial relations a matter of public concern (Davis Smith 1990: 122–3). Overheating also brought an exchange crisis after the election. In a classic "stop" of the stop-go cycle, the Treasury tightened credit policy and increased purchase tax sharply in July–October 1955.[25] The combined effects of the hire-purchase restriction, tighter credit and increased purchase tax cut demand for consumer durables, especially motor cars, where Turner *et al.* (1967: 105–6) estimate that demand fell by 20 percent in 1955–6. When the Suez crisis in autumn 1956 brought a big increase in petroleum tax to conserve fuel imports, demand for new cars slumped (Dunnett 1980: 61–2).

In the early 1950s, UK motor producers had invested heavily in automation (Turner *et al.* 1967: 77–80). But the 1955–6 credit squeeze hit domestic demand for cars, leading quickly to layoffs and strikes (Church 1994: 44; Dunnett 1980: 61–5). First to feel the pinch was Standard Motors. This company has attracted business historians because of its innovative, automated production systems and its uncertain labour and financial management (Tiratsoo 1995). Between 1945 and 1955, the company had instituted several bouts of short-time working, redundancy and major work restructuring, but ran into real difficulties in 1956. Standard wanted to lay off approximately 2,500 workers while re-tooling (which included the introduction of Heller ATMs) took place for a new tractor.[26] Shop stewards wanted the firm to retain the entire workforce by short-time working but, while the talks continued, trading conditions for Standard cars deteriorated, and the number of layoffs rose to 2,900, or one-quarter of the workforce. By early July, the management stopped talking and put *all* its workers on a three-day week.[27] Although automation was only a peripheral issue in the dispute (as was confirmed to the Ministry of Labour by the firm's production engineer), the press made it the centre of attention. The *Daily Herald* chose to describe it as "the men against robots strike" in which "automation firm sacks 2,600 men" and the *Daily Telegraph* claimed to have found evidence of activity by the Communist Party, in its fight against the productivity drive and automation.[28] Other newspapers, while noting that short-time and redundancy were the main issues, could not resist the automation angle.[29] Only the authoritative industrial reporting of the *Daily Worker* and the local knowledge of the

Coventry Evening Telegraph were immune to the "automation bug".[30] British newspapers had been primed by the US experience to look for automation and technological unemployment. During the Standard dispute, George Varnom, president of the Birmingham Trades' Council, warned of 20,000 possible layoffs in the Birmingham and Coventry vehicle firms and his remarks were widely reported, especially in those papers emphasising automation in the Standard strike.[31] Major redundancies were in prospect, but more as a result of the slump in car demand and intensifying competition in the market for tractors than any reorganisation of production.[32]

Other volume car producers found the motor industry slump of 1956–7 difficult. The expansion plans of the British Motor Corporation (BMC), formed in 1952 by the merger of Austin and Morris, were disrupted. Below-capacity working raised unit costs and profitability, always BMC's weakness, was hit (Williams *et al.* 1994: 137, 142–3). Management needed drastic workforce cuts and, having seen Standard's attempts to proceed by agreement, chose instead to make 6,000 workers (one-eighth of its workforce) redundant without warning in late June 1956. This provoked a major dispute with the workforce, upset the Engineering Employers' Federation and embarrassed the government (Wigham 1973: 181–2; Tolliday 1985: 130–1). BMC made enforced concessions. It gave *ex gratia* payments to redundant workers in the face of threats from the Transport and General Workers' Union, which led the dispute on the union side, to disrupt the docks and transport (Lyddon 1996: 191–2). BMC's Longbridge factory was technologically advanced, giving the press another opportunity to present cyclical adjustment in motor manufacture as evidence of union Luddism. Thus, in Britain automation was synonymous with redundancy and worker resistance.

The automation material

The discussion above has given a good indication of the press interest, both daily and weekly, in automation. This was, however, merely the first instalment of the automation literature and was followed by more weighty and authoritative studies. The decision by the US Congress to hold its own inquiry was highly important in signalling official recognition and focusing attention towards four discrete areas of technical change: automatic transfer machines in engineering;[33] computer controlled (N/C) machine tools, also in the engineering industries;[34] the use of closed loop control mechanisms in continuous flow industries;[35] and computerisation of routine clerical tasks. The Senate Committee on automation (US Congress 1955: 4–5) established these definitions in its report and this agenda was widely accepted (see Moos 1957). In the USA, rapid technological progress and relatively high unemployment continued into the 1960s, prompting more official reports and a gradual relaxation of the definition of automation (US Congress 1956; 1957; 1960; USPAC 1962). This continuing preoccupation with automation culminated in a second major investigation by the Johnson administration (USNCTAEP 1966 – report and six volumes of appendices). Throughout this lengthy period, the US Bureau of Labor Statistics produced a string of detailed, empirically-grounded investigations of the impact of automation on a wide range of industries (see Weinberg 1955; Paschell 1958; Freedman 1966). The intense public interest prompted a number of major US universities to investigate. Harvard, Yale, MIT, and many state universities launched research projects into various aspects of automation.[36] Management groups quickly published practical guides drawing on accumulating experience (see AMA 1956), and more polemical pieces making the case for accelerating automation (see Terborgh 1965; CCUS 1965). Unions countered with their own perspective (AFL-CIO 1956; 1962). A new breed of specialist, the "automation expert" contributed massively to the literature (for example, Fairbanks 1956; Hugh-Jones 1956; Buckingham 1961; Schils 1963; Diebold 1959). This brief review can give only a glimpse of the range of material.

The volume of publications in the UK was equally impressive. The explosion of press coverage in 1954–6 was remarkable. There were also national surveys of automation (by the DSIR, the Board of Trade, the TUC and the Federation of British Industries) that were at least as good as anything produced in the USA. Just as in the USA, new journals in automation and industrial control were established in the UK.[37] The DSIR's work on automation and the human factor in industry prompted an explosion of research on technical change and its management, though a disappointingly large proportion did not reach publication.[38] Simultaneously, the European Productivity Agency and the OEEC organised comparative studies. These were based on direct questions to or observation of practitioners in industry at a single moment in time and mainly focused on specific technologies.

The largest single study of automation anywhere in the mid-1950s in any country was the Board of Trade's questionnaire to British businesses on the use and planned implementation of the four "automation technologies"; transfer machines, computer controlled machine tools, closed loop feedback controls, office computers. It asked about the reasons for purchase, the country of origin of the equipment and expectations of the impact on capital expenditure and demand for labour. It also asked the machine tool and computer manufacturers about their products and customers, making cross-checking possible, and the results inspire confidence; consumers and suppliers can be matched.[39] The realities of corporate politics and commercial sensitivities meant that the questionnaire went to trade associations rather than individual companies, but with the close contacts between Whitehall and industry of the 1950s it is possible to find company-level data in the Board of Trade files.[40] This material also gives confidence that officials were attempting to monitor economic trends rather than give ministers quick but superficial answers.[41]

Japanisation and the second industrial divide

Automation lost its political resonance in the UK by the late 1950s and disappeared more slowly in the USA. Technology scares continued, especially in the UK, but the huge international boom beginning in the late 1960s seemed to promise expanding markets for all. In retrospect, this increasingly inflationary boom inaugurated more than a decade of great economic and financial turbulence in Britain, the USA and, more generally, in the international economy. When more settled economic conditions returned in the 1980s, the international economic order appeared very different. The US economy, which had been the model since 1945, was palpably in difficulty.[42] The number of workers in the US automobile industry fell from 802,000 in December 1978 to 487,700 in January 1982, during which time the US producers' share of both the domestic and the world market fell alarmingly. Similar stories were evident in other mass production industries: transistor radios, cameras, binoculars, sewing machines, colour televisions, VCRs, compact disks, glass, and tyres. The same symptoms presented themselves in other sectors. The workforce of the US steel industry almost halved between 1977 and 1988. The machine tool industry was badly undermined until it could agree import quotas. The position in high-tech sectors seemed even worse, with the US electronics industry, especially in defence contracting, increasingly dependent on Japanese components and nationalist Japanese were ready to explore the strategic bargaining opportunities this implied (Holland 1989; Ishihara 1991). Confidence in US managerial systems collapsed and FDI from Japan was welcomed to re-invigorate US management (Locke 1996).

The British position was equally dire in the early 1980s. This crisis, following from the deeply disturbed conditions of the 1970s, was widespread but the symptoms were most acute in exactly the same industries as in the USA. The back cover of Keith Smith's (1984) Penguin on Britain's economic position trumpeted: "Why do many experts now believe that the British economy is on the brink of a full-scale collapse?" Smith called upon government and employers to introduce Japanese corporatist methods rather than to pursue monetarism and aggressive industrial relations policies. Politicians were deaf, but business leaders had already begun to turn to Japan. As in America, Britain saw rising volumes of Japanese FDI, building upon the firm foundation already long established in consumer electronics. The British were accustomed to see their domestic systems of industrial management and labour relations as problematic and major British firms began to explore Japanese methods from the early 1980s (Dunning (1986); *Industrial Relations Journal* (1988); Oliver and Wilkinson 1992: 81–131; Owen 1999: 276–82).

The evident problems of European and North American mass producers and the vigorous expansion of Japanese enterprise into export markets led many commentators to identify a major break in trends in the international economy during the 1970s. At one level, there was renewed interest in the economic theory of long waves and debates on the possibility of a Kondratiev slump in the world economy (Mensch 1979; Freeman *et al.* 1982; Freeman and Perez 1988). Social and political theorists, especially the radicals, preferred to explore the notion of a crisis in "Fordism", with the emergence of a "new age" in which technological, market, institutional and social forces were very different from those that had dominated the postwar world economy until the 1970s. The key contribution to this analysis was the work of Piore and Sabel (1984) on a conceptual distinction between two modes of manufacture. The first, "mass production", was characterised by the use of specialised machines, semi-skilled workers, extreme division of labour and Taylorist management of the workforce to create huge quantities of standardised consumer goods. The second was "flexible specialisation", characterised by general purpose machines, skilled workers with some autonomy at the workplace creating a much wider variety of customised goods.[43]

Throughout the nineteenth century these two types of production co-existed but were in collision (Piore and Sabel 1984: 35–48; Sabel and Zeitlin 1985). Mass production came to dominate at the turn of the twentieth century and limited the further growth of more flexible methods (Piore and Sabel 1984: 49–104). Buttressed by Keynesian macro-economic management to sustain consumer demand, mass production was taken up by emulators after 1945. It ran into difficulties in the 1970s, however, as markets for standardised consumer goods became saturated and unstable and the institutions of Keynesian management (the Bretton Woods system of international finance, for example) broke down in waves of inflation and bitter class conflict. A "second industrial divide", or gateway for changes in the path of technological development, thus opened in the later 1970s. Piore and Sabel (1984: 281–308) indicated that the new economic conditions would favour a more flexible production system capable of satisfying the strongly growing demand for non-standardised, better-quality, short shelf-life goods. They suggested that the falling prices of computer-controlled equipment and more flexible work practices would reinforce the advantages of flexible specialisation. However, flexible technology needed reinforcement and they pointed to the advantages of organic, co-operative links between firms, local and regional government and educational and research institutions to supply the skills, credit facilities and information needed to respond to rapidly changing markets for high quality goods.

Piore and Sabel had in mind the potential of prosperous industrial districts like the machine tool producers of Emilia-Romagna in northwestern Italy, but it was easy to see how the obituarists of Fordist mass production should see the essential characteristics of flexible specialisation in the Japanese enterprise system. It is useful to begin with technology, especially in automobile production, since so much of the aura of Japanese manufacturing reflects from the major car assemblers and particularly from Toyota. Although the use of industrial robots for body-welding and other tasks was pioneered by General Motors, the intensive use of computer-controlled robots in stamping, welding and painting and computer control of machining in engine and gearbox production was one aspect of the Japanese system discovered by management specialists in the 1970s and 1980s (Foreman-Peck *et al.* 1995: 122–3). Computer controls helped to reduce cycle time and the unproductive time in switching from one model to another, allowing increased flexibility, enabling producers to work on a multi-model or mixed model basis.[44] These productive interventions were however the least distinctive features of the Japanese approach to automobile assembly; the Japanese system of management caught most attention from contemporaries.

Three areas were particularly attractive to western observers; the system of labour management, and the relations between major firms and their suppliers, and the relationship between business and the state. Western firms were immediately taken by the Japanese approach to employment and training. Lazonick (1990) stylised US management as "taking skills off the shopfloor". Typically, US firms employed deep managerial hierarchies to control of the pace and content of work following Taylorist principles and replacing manual skills by heavy investment in machines, fixtures, jigs and special purpose tools and semi-skilled workers. The Japanese system, by contrast, could be described as "building skills on the shopfloor", with firms giving lifetime employment to core workers, in return for lifetime training and retraining and great flexibility in work tasks. Furthermore, Japanese firms harnessed the mental skills of shopfloor workers by encouraging them to suggest ways of saving costs and improving quality in production. Whereas US management incentivised and disciplined workers on an individual basis, Japanese managers utilised teamwork extensively. It is easy to see how this sat easily with the notion of a "second industrial divide" in which traditional "Fordist" and "Taylorist" methods had run their course.

Similarly, western commentators saw very different systems in the Japanese supply chain. Piore and Sabel (1984: 28–31, 286–95) had emphasised the importance of collaborative relationships between firms within "industrial districts". This concept, derived from Marshall, describes an area where a dominant industry encourages the development of interrelated technologies and products, methods of organising work and business structures in linked industries (Zysman 1994). Toyota, in particular, seems to fit this pattern. In 1980, Toyota controlled ten important subsidiaries and had 220 primary subcontractors. Approximately 80 percent of this supply chain had plants within the boundaries of Toyota City, and in turn were supplied by a huge network of secondary and tertiary subsidiaries, most of whom were located within the engineering complex of this part of east-central Honshu (Cusumano 1986: 241–61; Kenney and Florida 1988; Oliver and Wilkinson 1992: 59–62). The relationship goes far beyond physical proximity, with Toyota having a minority equity stake in many of its subcontractors and frequently supplying know-how, managerial and shopfloor expertise, raw materials, integrated planning with Toyota's own forward strategy and support in times of downturns in demand. At the most developed extent of these relationships, the principal firms contract predominantly with suppliers from the same *keiretsu* group (*keiretsu* firms being the smaller firms controlled by the industrial giants or major bank). These high-trust, mutually interdependent contracting relations are again consistent with the "flexible" alternative to mass production sketched by Piore and Sabel and have been identified as the foundation of the Japanese industrial system.[45]

Finally, many commentators on the Japanese system have identified a close relationship between industry and the state. The most celebrated study, by Chalmers Johnson (1982: chs. 5–9), almost argued that industry was organised by the most powerful ministry in Japanese economic affairs, the Ministry of International Trade and Industry (MITI). Some of the subtlety of Johnson's argument was missed by those who used his work, and subsequent research has demonstrated the ability of Japanese firms to ignore MITI's plans to reshape and control a number of key industries (Yamamura 1982; Dore 1986; Samuels 1987; Calder 1988: chs. 4, 7, 11; Okimoto 1989; Katz 1998). But it is undeniable that the Japanese state has influenced leading firms, whether directly or indirectly through intermediate organisations, tax and subsidy regimes, special loans, aid to industry research organisations, government purchasing, tariff and quota protection and other short-term support (Abé 1997: 37–9). Thus, there were apparently excellent grounds for associating the unmistakeable rise in Japanese industrial strength from the later 1970s with the ability of Toyota, Nissan, Honda, Sony, Hitachi *et al.* to exploit the new consumer demand by using more skill-intensive, flexible and collaborative methods of production. Business schools were particularly impressed and unleashed a stream of publications that placed Japanese systems of manufacturing and enterprise management on a lofty pedestal as an example for the rest of the developed world.[46]

The classic veneration of the Japanese system occurred in the generously funded project based at MIT to research the international automobile industry. The International Motor Vehicle Project (IMVP) gave birth to two major studies in the business school approach; *The Future of the Automobile* (Altshuler *et al.* 1984), which was billed as "the most comprehensive account ever conducted of the world's largest industry", and *the Machine that Changed the World* (Womack *et al.* 1990), "a popular business book that became an international best seller" (Williams *et al.* 1994: 4). The authors claim that Japanese lean production methods permitted a substantial efficiency lead over traditional US methods and that this productivity advantage was the result of superior Japanese management (Womack *et al.* 1990: 79–88). Other management consultancies subsequently embellished this conclusion. Thus the Anderson Consulting (1992) report on lean production claimed that "world class plants", by which they meant Japanese "lean production", had a 2:1 productivity superiority and 100:1 quality superiority (see also Harbour and Associates, Inc. 1992).

This sort of management literature does not claim scholarly authority but it certainly helps to mould popular opinion. The course of the Japanese economy since the bursting of the bubble economy in 1990 and the subsequent difficulties of its major companies, even in automobile production, has in turn burst the bubble of Japanese superiority, and has produced a much more sober and balanced assessment of Japanese industrial organisation. There has, thus, been an element of myth making in the literature on Japanese management methods – "Japolatory" according to some commentators (Williams *et al.* 1994) – just as was the case three decades earlier with automation. Similarly, the notion of a "second industrial divide", though still very powerful in the USA, has received extensive criticism from European scholars (see Amin 1994). The strongest strand in this criticism has been the polarisation of styles of production ("mass production" versus "flexible specialisation") that are not only caricatures (a rigid past versus a flexible future, unskilled Fordism versus highly skilled flexible specialisation) but also are blind to the enormous diversity within volume and specialty production. To assess the lessons of "Japanisation" and the "second industrial divide", we need an approach to the literature that is as critical and discriminating as is necessary to understand the significance of automation. In general terms, the skills to assess this evidence are those at the heart of the historical method: where and in what context was the evidence assembled, by whom and with what purpose? How reliable are opinions and estimates? What sort of cross-checking of opinion and evidence is possible?

A framework of organisation

This section attempts to build a framework with which to study technical change in the second half of the twentieth century. The descriptive chronologies in previous sections hint that twentieth century technical change has involved both economic and political dimensions, with "economic" defined as involving the allocation of resources and choice of technique and "political" as concerned with power relations and bargaining. It should also be obvious that there are different spatial levels, roughly falling into three, which for analytical convenience can be termed the international, national and enterprise strata. Simplifying heroically, we can image a three-by-two matrix, into which can be fitted substantial themes in the literature on postwar political economy. This is a framework to organise the flow of an argument rather than to build a model for empirical testing. Neither the economic nor the political can claim analytical precedence. Economic theorising is essentially a method of investigating in a closed world the impact of specific changes on patterns of behaviour *when all other influences are held constant.* Where questions of national economic performance are concerned, it is difficult to see how this *ceteris paribus* condition can be observed, especially over a long span of years (Gould 1969). Even at the enterprise level, business historians have been divided on the utility of economic theory as the primary method of interrogating performance.[47] It is equally plausible to claim analytical precedence for politics, especially where, as in the case of this study, power relations and bargaining over change are fundamental to the inquiry. A recent history of trade unions has claimed: "The traditional essential subject of history is politics, for it is through politics that change takes place, it is through politics that change in other realms, economic, technological, social is mediated" (McIlroy *et al.* 1999b: 10). However, this was not a call for fundamentalism but "for a multi-layered concern with social and economic, as well as political, factors. We are looking for a totalised approach, a return to the broad vision of political economy" (McIlroy *et al.* 1999b: 9). McIlroy and colleagues may not approve of the analysis below, but it is conceived within the same spirit.

At this stage it is appropriate to put more flesh onto the bones of the basic matrix described in the last paragraph. Beginning with the economic sphere and the international level, much has been written about international technology transmission in general and even more about the "Americanisation" of European industry after the war. The foundation must be the convergence literature pioneered by Abramovitz (1986) and Baumol (1986), which saw the postwar period as a phase of rapid catching up to the technology of the lead producer, the USA, by "follower" nations that had sufficiently plastic institutional and policy arrangements to facilitate learning from abroad. Three important qualifications to the convergence approach deserve mention. First, there are profound sectoral complications. Early convergence theorists implied an economic model in which manufacturing drove the economy and aggregate leadership rested primarily upon leadership in manufacturing. Denison (1967: 218–24), Feinstein (1990), Broadberry (1997b; 1998) and Temin (2002) have demonstrated, on the contrary, that the most important influences on aggregate convergence have occurred outside manufacturing. Second, the

"Americanisation" literature has been divided between those who believe that the US lead stemmed from systemic advantages (in other words, the benefits of "Fordism" as a *system* of mass production, management and distribution) and those who argue that the American lead rested instead upon a portfolio of management techniques from which followers might select and which were unrelated to the scale of production.[48] Third, there are disagreements about whether the followers should copy the leader's methods or adapt them to local conditions. Business analysts have polarised between those who have advocated imitation of the successful (Porter 1990; Chandler 1990: ch. 1) and those promoting adaptation (Kay 1993: 1–124; Hamel and Prahalad 1996). Despite the pressure to imitate during technology scares business historians have begun to see the benefits of adaptation and the creation of local hybrids from the mix of cultures and ideas (Kudo *et al.* 2004b: 22–5; Zeitlin 2000a: 34–50). Certainly the recent literature on Americanisation and Japanisation has suggested that "cross-fertilisation" and "intelligent learning processes" are much better terms than "transfer", "diffusion" or "transplantation" (Zeitlin 2000a: 42; Gemelli 1998; Lillrank 1995). Finally, it is hard to see how discussion of international technology transfer can avoid mixing international and *national* levels of analysis.

In convergence literature the pace of catch up by diffusion depends upon the interaction of the size of the "productivity gap" (international) and the "capability for convergence" (national). To complicate matters still further, the literature on the diffusion of innovations has identified a series of influences that can apply to the international, national and even enterprise levels. In the "social capability for convergence", the convergence literature has identified the conditions by which knowledge is diffused and circumstances that influence both the speed of structural change and the ability to generate funds for investment (Abramovitz 1986: 390). The diffusion (and the Americanisation) literature has pointed to methods of judging the appropriateness of innovations to local circumstances, the channels through which ideas are communicated, the extent to which potential innovators participate in wider national and international communications networks and the activities of "change agents" (Bjarnar and Kipping 1998; Rogers 1995: 17–19, 281–334; Kipping 1997; 1999).

At the enterprise level, there has been an explosion of research in business studies in recent years on the innovating firm (for a good introduction, see Fagerberg *et al.* 2005). We are not, however, interested in the aspirational literature to guide Chief Executive Officers towards world leadership in their industries, but rather in the conditions that enable the more typical firm to react positively to new ideas and new forms of competition. At its most basic, innovation entails learning by the organisation and the creation of knowledge that enables the firm to raise its efficiency (Kogut and Zander 1992; Grant 1996). The literature, borrowing from earlier work in philosophy, tends to distinguish between two dimensions of knowledge, that which is "explicit", can be codified and circulated in written texts and that which is "tacit" and resides in practical skills (Nonaka and Takeuchi 1995; Brown and Duguid 2001; Ryle 1949; Polanyi 1966). In the period covered by this volume, it is usually assumed that two, polarised methods of organisational learning have predominated; the "Fordist/ Taylorist" method of concentrating on the production of explicit knowledge in a deep, stratified managerial hierarchy and the "Japanese" method of harnessing the tacit knowledge of shopfloor employees (Lazonick 2005). However, these are not the only possibilities. The literature also points to the value of networks that extend beyond the boundary of the firm to facilitate the processes of organisational learning (Biggart and Hamilton 1992; Powell and Grodal 2005). These may be loose "communities of practice" in which organisational learning is concentrated (Lave and Wenger 1991; Brown and Duguid 1991) or may be little more than contacts with the "change agents" mentioned in the previous paragraph.

Although recent literature has concentrated heavily on knowledge as a resource for the innovating firm, finance should not be forgotten. Indeed, in both the "automation" and "Japanisation" scares, innovation has implied heavy investment in often complicated machinery. Lazonick's (2005: 50) study of innovating firms since the British industrial revolution has emphasised that "ploughed back" profits have been the most fundamental source of new investment. Thus, profitability and product market pressures are important considerations when examining innovation at the enterprise level. More basically, relative factor costs are important as automation invariably implied the substitution of labour by machines, which focuses attention on the firm's labour market; firms with elastic labour supplies are unlikely to invest heavily in labour-saving automation. Thus, the economic sphere at the enterprise level embraces traditional views of the firm as profit-maximiser and the more recent "knowledge-based" theories.

In the political sphere, it is possible to identify a "politics of production and technical change" with three interrelated strata; global, national and enterprise. While it may appear fanciful to propose a global politics of production and technology, there is no doubt that Cold War tensions coloured US attitudes to automation in the 1950s and fears of the loss of its leadership in high technology, defence-related industries profoundly shaped its attitude to Japanese competitive pressures in the 1980s.

The computer and N/C machine tools were developed for defence purposes during the Cold War (Flamm 1988; Noble 1984) and significant work on the theoretical and practical advance of closed loop feedback controls was undertaken during the Second World War (Dorf 1989: 4–6). For Britain, Cold War pressures were real but perhaps less severe than in the USA, but its world role depended critically upon mobilising US support for the international use of sterling (Strange 1971: 48–70) and Britain's commercial policies (Milward and Brennan 1996: 37–129; Schenk 1994: 12–15, 65–87, 119–23). American support was never unequivocal, as Suez demonstrated (Kunz 1991, but see Schenk 1994: 6–11), and could be very manipulative (see Chapter 2). The failure of the external position to improve as fast as policy-makers hoped left British governments with little alternative but to pressure employers and unions to improve productivity and competitiveness, albeit within confines dictated by party politics (Tiratsoo and Tomlinson 1993; 1998b) and institutional configurations (Middlemas 1986; 1990).[49] Postwar British governments thus had enormous incentives to create effective national frameworks to accelerate productivity growth, increase export competitiveness and introduce new cost-saving technologies.

The notion of a national politics of productivity and technical change is now well accepted, especially in the British case. Tomlinson (1991a; 1997b: 85–90, 295–9) and Middlemas (1986) have explored the debates between peak level representatives of government, industry and labour over national economic policy. This work reflected a growing interest in the impact of institutions among social scientists more generally. From this work a number of simple propositions emerged (notably that the continuity of institutions and their structure had a major impact on the pace of national economic growth) and received fierce criticism.[50] At a more sophisticated level, Eichengreen (1996) argued that the nature of national institutional bargaining was a major determinant of variations in national rates of productivity growth in postwar Europe. He suggested that an effective national politics of production will encourage both employers and employees agree to defer current consumption in return for future gains from the faster growth generated by higher current investment. Using game theory, he suggests that such bargains are most likely when monitoring, commitment and co-ordination mechanisms are available to give both parties confidence that agreements will be kept.[51] However, Eichengreen's analysis is set firmly within the manufacturing-as-leading-sector approach to convergence and makes no allowance at all for the more sophisticated understanding of how convergence operated in the work of Broadberry and Temin cited above. In general, the institutional literature has found it very difficult to classify interest groups on a single structural dimension when the interrelations between management and labour in modern societies are so complex (see Bufton 2004: 4–10). We are left with the strong likelihood that bargaining over new technology and work arrangements at the national level is important, that there is no simple relationship between institutional structure and the results of negotiations over new technology, and that there is no agreement among social scientists on the optimal configuration of national negotiations to facilitate change. The minimalist position is that the national politics of productivity is helpful if it can build consensus between capital and labour (because conflict must both delay and raise the costs of change) and if it can, when necessary, control recalcitrant lower-level officials/members if that consensus is threatened.

Finally, we reach down to bargaining over new technology at the enterprise level. The issues concern authority, power and control. The classic work from the 1970s on the management of labour and the content and pace of work in the twentieth century claimed that the logic of capitalist enterprise was to "de-skill" work by pressing the division of labour ever further, through mechanisation and automation with the point of extending managerial control over the pace of work and how it was performed (Braverman 1974). Refinements to this picture have identified many control strategies, in addition to the direct controls of "scientific management" on "Taylorist" lines, as emphasised by Braverman. Edwards (1979) has argued that employers experimented with a number of strategies – welfare schemes and company unionism – in addition to scientific management, and when, these failed, resorted to more structural forms of control. These are embedded in the physical structure of the workplace, rather than dependent upon the authority of the employer and his managers. They include technical control, as for example the assembly line and other aspects of mechanisation and automation. After this came bureaucratic control, through institutional hierarchical command built upon systematic and highly stratified job descriptions and promotion procedures. These initiatives were necessary because of effective worker resistance to control strategies, a theme that has emerged strongly in other post-Braverman writing (see Thompson 1989: 122–52). It is also apparent that workers and their unions in many industries have come to accept employer control. Thompson (1989: 130–1) notes a

> tendency for unions to try to incorporate phenomena such as scientific management within a collective bargaining framework. This has certainly been the trend at shopfloor level after the Second World War in Britain. Resistance to work study and other managerial methods continued, but largely as a means of extracting the highest rewards through controlling the conditions under which scientific management is utilised. The existence of the methods themselves is reluctantly accepted as a basic fact of industrial life.

Nor should we assume that management and labour were monolithic entities. The firm's ability to control its labour force must be related to the *external* (national) labour market(s). When national unemployment rates are high, managers can use the threat of redundancy to persuade employees to accept new methods of working. When national unemployment rates are low, as they were during the 1950s and 1960s especially in the UK, workers may feel that they can move easily to new jobs or bargain more vigorously to resist new work methods or demand higher rewards for compliance. However, we also know that firms in the UK developed strategies to fit the worker's skills to the specific needs of the firm and other methods of making "quitting" more costly to the employee. Control was undoubtedly a major issue for employers in both the Americanisation and Japanisation programmes but we should be wary of accepting either that automation increased control by de-skilling work or that tight external labour markets handed control of the labour process to the workgroup during the long postwar boom. Authority, power and control over the pace and content of work were contested terrain, and we should not overlook that these contests also occurred within management and labour. Haigh (2001) has described the efforts of "systems men" to use their understanding of computers to raise their status within the managerial hierarchy. Technical workers were generally more favourably disposed to automation than the semi-skilled. Automation exposed divisions within and between capital and labour.

Drawing this material together, our matrix for studying the management of technical change is given in Table 1.1. The main themes in the literature for each element have now been stated, but it should be obvious that the interconnections may be complex and that discussion may be unable to observe a rigid distinction between the "economic" and the "political" or between the three spatial levels. To repeat, this is a framework for ordering thoughts rather than for empirical testing.

The structure of the book

The practical difficulties in executing the model outlined in Table 1.1 are evident in the organisation of the book. Chapter 2 was originally intended to focus only on the global level (boxes 1 and 2 of Table 1.1), but international technology transfer is so dependent on the national capability for convergence and related issues (box 3) that they are also included. Chapter 3 examines only the national politics of productivity and technical change in the two countries (box 4). The next four chapters focus on the management of technical change at the enterprise level and take in as much of the agenda of boxes 5 and 6 as is relevant to each case study. Chapter 4 considers the two automation techno-

Table 1.1   Matrix for studying the political economy of technological change

	Economic/Industrial	Political/Bargaining
Global	1. Transnational dissemination via "catch-up" mechanisms; copying versus adaptation.	2. Extent to which "national politics of production" is coloured by global political (Cold War) or competitiveness rivalries.
National	3. National "social capacity for convergence", including financial, educational and entrepreneurial dimensions; activities of "change agents" and other channels of communication.	4. Institutional configurations and capacity to forge "productionist" alliances with monitoring and reinforcement mechanisms.
Enterprise	5. Incentives and resources from firm's product and labour markets for new technologies; knowledge-based resources of the firm and its networks to innovate.	6. Frontier of control over the labour process; ability of managements to make technological choices and to work this technology to capacity; relative power of workgroups, national unions and managers; divisions within these groups.

logies most closely associated with metal-working, automatic transfer machines and N/C machine tools. The period covered is that of the classic automation scare from the mid-1950s to the early 1960s and the industries most concerned are automobiles and aircraft manufacture. Chapter 5 moves the spotlight to the continuous flow industries, and to the use of feedback controls. In this instance, the perspective stretches beyond the classic automation scare, in large part because the pace of technical change soon moved rapidly from the closed loop feedback systems that attracted so much attention in the 1950s to computer-controlled operations that spread rapidly during the 1960s and beyond. Chapter 6 is the first of two dealing with office automation and looks at the introduction of computers into routine clerical work. Again, the pace of change was so rapid and extensive that there is little real point in narrowing the perspective to applications developed during automation scare. In many cases, the real story of office automation came later, first, when bigger, more powerful machines allowed real-time, multi-tasking and on-line processing and subsequently the development of the PC and the spread of desktop work processing. In truth, the management of automation in office work is an extremely difficult topic to research adequately because of the fragmentation of the clerical workforce and the wide variety of work environments in which clerical work is undertaken. Any treatment must therefore be partial and incomplete, and the solution has been to include a separate chapter (Chapter 7) on the management of computerisation in the high street banks, again from the mid-1950s to the main developments of the 1990s. Chapter 8 returns to the metal-working industries to discuss the impact of "Japanisation", which in its technological context involved the use of computer-controlled machine tools (industrial robots) more extensively in branches of engineering. But before examining the enterprise level, the discussion in Chapter 8 returns to the matrix developed above and discusses the global and national context of Japanisation. The volume ends with a brief chapter that makes some comparative conclusions about the management of technical change in Britain and the USA since the mid-1950s.

2
World Roles and International Technology Transfer

As noted above, this chapter addresses the world roles of postwar Britain and America and the question of international technology transfer from the USA to the UK. In order to complete the latter, it is necessary to examine aspects of the British economic and social systems to judge the openness to new ideas and the speed of communication among firms. The chapter begins with an assessment of the impact of Cold War tensions on the development of US technology and its willingness to communicate innovations in technology and management to other nations. Attention is then turned to the impact of Britain's world role in shaping the domestic politics of productivity and technical change, paying particular attention to the role of government. Finally, the focus is switched to Britain's incentive and capacity to absorb innovations from the technological lead nation, the USA.

The Cold War context in postwar America

The foundations of the Cold War lay in interwar geo-political analyses of the ways in which nations mobilised their capabilities, acquired additional strategic resources and combined them with new forms of transport and weaponry to pursue power politics (Leffler 2001: 22–3). During the Second World War, US strategic planning crystallised around the notion of defence in depth, with elaborate plans for a network of overseas bases from which US military power could be projected quickly and effectively against any potential adversary (Leffler 1984; 1992; 1994; 2001). At home, the primary need was to preserve after the war a capacity for rapid mobilisation, mainly in relation to missiles and air power (Noble 1984: 4). It was agreed in the autumn of 1945 that there should be a major change in US defence posture – US planners were convinced that they needed a policy of active defence and that the USA should, in effect, become the world's policeman (Sherry 1977: 201–5). Indeed, Roosevelt's thinking on the use of the atomic bomb from late 1942 implied a much more active postwar world role for the USA (Sherwin 1973).

Decisions to continue the high state of military preparedness and the rapid development of strategic technologies thus pre-date the Cold War, as conventionally understood. In 1945–6, sensing the national war-weariness, US military and political leaders gave priority to the creation of a progressive liberal international economic and political order. However, Stalin's announcement in February, 1946 that he wanted to rebuild not upon the principles of international co-operation outlined at Bretton Woods and in the United Nations, but upon the "Soviet social system" gave anti-Soviet conservatives renewed impetus (Leffler 1992: 3–24; Gaddis 2001; Hogan 1987: 21–2; McGlade 1998: 19–20; 2000: 54–7). The decisive shift in US foreign policy came after the Soviet blockade of Berlin in 1948, the Russian atomic bomb test of August 1949 and the Communist victory in China in the same month. The outbreak of the Korean War and the subsequent entry of the new Chinese leadership into the conflict seemed to prove the idea of an international communist conspiracy against the "free world". Not surprisingly, the temperature of Great Power relations affected spending on military technology, research and development, what Hogan (1998: 18–19) has called "a capital-intensive strategy of containment". Three industries claimed the lions' share of the growth of military spending – electrical and electronic equipment, aircraft and machine tools. The first and the last have immediate and direct implications for automation in the 1950s.

The computer is the most obvious case (Flamm 1987; Cohen 1988; Edwards 1996). The ENIAC (Electronic Numerical Integrator and Computer), developed by a team led by Eckert and Mauchly at the University of Pennsylvania's Moore School of Electrical Engineering, was the first fully electronic digital computer and was developed to calculate mathematical formulae (Stern 1981; Tomayko 1983). ENIAC and its immediate successors were designed to undertake the complex computations required for missile trajectories and the physics of the atomic bomb. They had limited input-output facilities and even less versatility. Eckert and Mauchly, however, believed that computers could be adapted to process business data and in 1946 established their own company to build a commercial computer (Stern 1982: 570–3). The path of development from calculating machine to office automation was short and direct. Despite severe financial problems, Eckert and Mauchly's first UNIVAC (UNIVersal Automatic Computer) began its acceptance tests for the US Bureau of the Census in March 1951. This first business computer performed the same work as punched card office machines only faster and at much higher cost. It took a lot of government money funding a series of defence projects to increase the potential of computers in civilian work.

The story began during 1943 in work to develop a universal flight simulator in MIT's Servo-Mechanisms Laboratory and progressed via two extraordinarily expensive air early-warning initiatives, Project Whirlwind and the SAGE air defence system. After the first Soviet nuclear bomb test in August 1949 and appraisals of the USSR's strategic bomber capability cost was not an issue (Smith 1976: 457; Redmond and Smith 1980; Noble 1984: 106–13; *Annals of the History of Computing* 1981; Campbell-Kelly and Aspray 1996: 157–69).[1] All three projects required massive and rapid computing power to analyse complex data in "real time", in turn demanding advance in memory and control systems. However, it took much longer than anticipated to develop fast, reliable computing power; SAGE entered service when missiles rather than bombers were the strategic threat. Thus,

> [t]he real contribution of SAGE was not to military defence, but through technological spin-off to civilian computing. An entire sub-industry was created as industrial contractors were brought in to develop the basic technologies and implement the hardware, software and communications. These contractors included IBM, Burroughs, Bell Laboratories and scores of smaller firms. Many of the technological innovations that were developed for SAGE were quickly diffused throughout the computer industry (Campbell-Kelly and Aspray 1996: 168).

Among the spin-offs were core memories, printed circuits, mass storage devices, CRT graphical displays, digital communications and networking technologies and wide-ranging software expertise, with IBM the major commercial beneficiary.[2] But electronics was not the only sector of the economy to benefit from prodigious state support for military research.

The machine tool industry also "enjoyed" unstinting state support thanks to its role in manufacturing military aircraft. As the strategic role of air power increased, the sophistication of aircraft design surged ahead and the emergence of the jet engine posed vast new theoretical and engineering problems. As Noble (1984: 8) notes, "As designs grew more sophisticated and complex, so too did tooling and production methods. As designs changed rapidly with advances in engineering, and with an escalating arms race, the need arose for more versatile and flexible methods, for special machines and special tooling to accommodate rapid redesigns and short production runs". Pre-flight engineering time in production was 27 times longer in 1953 than in 1945 and the development processes in aerodynamics, metallurgy, electronics and engine design were underwritten almost entirely by the military (Hanieski 1973; Hunsacker 1955: 270). The complex machining required for the new aircraft designs made skilled workers potentially a strategic bottleneck.

The producers themselves had devised ways to simplify or automate complex machining processes but, according to Noble, citing the case of the Parsons Corporation, their practical solutions were overtaken by more theoretical approaches.[3] Parsons sought help from the MIT Servo-Mechanisms Laboratory in developing automatic machining of helicopter rotor blades. MIT saw the problem as part of the general issue of computer-controlled machinery and saw a role for their real-time computer, part of Project Whirlwind (Smith 1976: 457). In MIT, research concentrated on powerful machine tools to produce complex shapes from the difficult materials needed for jet engines and fighter aircraft and its prototypes eventually had capacities and prices beyond most machine shops' reach.[4] To make these machines attractive to users, MIT created a programming system (APT – Automatic Programmed Tools) that would be both universal and infinitely adaptable. The USAF funded this work and had to subsidise users of these very expensive, complex machine tools, but on condition that those seeking air force supply contracts had to use N/C technology. In turn, these features limited diffusion: "[MIT's machines had] high system complexity (and thus unreliability), prohibitive cost, and excessive maintenance, programming, computation and other overhead requirements. The very aspects of the technology that made it suitable for Air Force needs tended to render it inaccessible to those firms outside the circle of government subsidy" (Noble 1984: 220).

The computer and computer-controlled machine tools indicate the opportunities and pitfalls of US technological development during the Cold War. There were ample funds for projects with military potential and intellectual interest to academics, but the commercial consequences were unpredictable. Defence funding accelerated the evolution of the digital computer in ways that enhanced its commercial potential. In the

1950s, IBM's computer sales were concentrated in the aircraft industry of southern California and IBM's computer sales teams channelled information on customer needs back to the research division (Akera 2002: 782–4). However, ample research funding and close links to academic science helped shunt numerically controlled machine tools into a *cul de sac* of excessive technological complexity and high cost. Both projects were highly publicised as triumphs of US inventiveness but, for machine tools at least the military-academic-industrial complex undermined the industry's commercial edge.

Of course, this capital-intensive policy of containment had implications far beyond extravagant support for defence-related industry at home. As hinted above, after 1947 US foreign economic policy was concerned above all with the containment of Soviet expansion. It took the form of generous flows of funds to the market economies of Western Europe, Latin America and the Far East, bolstered by a programme of technical assistance (the TAPP briefly mentioned in Chapter 1) and more direct methods of supporting strategic industries overseas through the "Off-Shore Procurement" programme (OSP) when the Cold War was most intense. As McGlade (2000: 72–3) notes "vast tides of US money and support" went towards the larger European firms for production and research in a wide range of military-related industries. This interpretation of the nation's mission as the containment of communism also had profound implications for the conduct of policy-making towards and within domestic industry, but these are more properly considered in the next chapter.

The UK's "world role"

Global pressures on the British were equally powerful, but came as much from the efforts to re-establish Britain as a global economic and political power as from the Cold War more narrowly defined. British governments emerged from the Second World War with a seriously weakened external financial position and severe shortages of consumer and producer goods. The capital equipment of many consumer industries was depleted, but new markets in Europe beckoned, albeit for an uncertain period (Broadberry and Howlett 1998; Milward 1977: 329–65). The external problem had two elements, an enormous reversal in Britain's assets and liabilities (Matthews *et al.* 1982: Table 5.2) and a huge current deficit that would only continue to increase until the economy could be reconverted to a "normal" peacetime footing (Cairncross 1987: 3–10). British policy-makers had recognised from an early stage in the war that they would need substantial postwar financial assistance from the USA but it was also clear that financial assistance would have strings that would tie Britain into America's vision of a postwar liberal international order (Sayers 1956: 405–13; Tomlinson 1997b: 24–5). But it was also clear that Britain's postwar *domestic* settlement, and in particular the commitment to postwar full employment, also implied the creation of a liberal, expanding world economy (Booth 1989: 139–47). The alternative of Britain seeking to restore her external position without US assistance implied extreme privations for the British population, more severe than experienced during wartime, and were judged politically impossible even though the cabinet had reservations about the terms of the *pax Americana*.[5]

This is not to imply that Cold War tensions were unimportant in the UK. The Foreign Office saw Germany, South East Europe, Greece, Turkey, Persia and the Far East as areas in which Soviet policy threatened British interests (Watt 1984: 57). Bevin distrusted Soviet intentions after his experiences of negotiations with Molotov in the Council of Foreign Ministers (Bullock 1983: 159). Bevin, thus, played a pivotal role in encouraging the USA to supply Marshall Aid and the US commitment to defend Europe in the NATO treaty (Bullock 1983: 393–427, 614–82; Milward 1984: 61–9). He also fought tenaciously for an aggressive military defence of British interests in the Mediterranean and the Middle East to defend British interests as a global and imperial power, despite the enormous external costs of military bases overseas (Carr 1993: 139–41).

Simplifying heroically, we can identify a number of consequences for productivity and competitiveness policies of this foreign policy that saw Britain presenting itself as a key ally of America while simultaneously seeking to become a global power in its own right. The dependence on US financial support left Britain vulnerable. Dobson (1986: 189) cites a memorandum by a White House aide who backed postwar financial support to Britain: "Marlborough once remarked that in every alliance one party wears the boots and spurs and the other the saddle ... we are obviously wearing the boots in the Anglo-American Alliance. If we want to stay in this fortunate position, we have to find some way to feed the horse". The feeding regime worked out in the US Treasury during wartime was to provide Britain generous assistance, but then to manipulate the details so that Britain's external account remained weak. Thus, Lend-lease contained Britain's huge problem of paying for wartime imports, but the US Treasury trimmed the coverage at any signs of improvement in Britain's dire reserve position (Dobson 1986:

159–84). The supply of carefully controlled assistance continued into peacetime. The US Loan gave Britain a substantial support to its reserves on more generous terms than offered to any other country but with strings that would impose full convertibility of sterling before Britain's balance of payments could possibly take the strain.[6] Similarly, after the 1947 convertibility crisis Britain was allowed to discriminate against imports from the USA and re-invigorate its imperial commitment (Cain and Hopkins 1993: 278–9), but the US administration put limits on the extent of this neo-mercantilism and pressed for the devaluation of sterling and liberalisation once the crisis had eased.[7] Neo-mercantilism and liberalisation co-existed uneasily into the early 1950s, but the trajectory of liberalisation under US tutelage, with strong support from elements within the British Treasury (Booth 2001), was not in doubt. British politicians could argue about the number of controls they needed for domestic economic management (Rollings 1994), but, by carrots and sticks, the US Treasury led their horse towards liberalised world trade and payments.

However, this slow transition from neo-mercantilism to the US vision of liberal internationalism left the UK with structures and policies that left the economy fragile and exposed. The costs of acting as a bulwark against communism across the globe imposed burdens on the current balance of payments, as did the neo-mercantilist policy of developing the sterling area. The sterling balances, the large debts run up during the war to countries of the sterling area to finance the war in the Middle and Far East, were neither reduced, as Keynes had suggested (Moggridge 1979: 281–2, 385–9) nor cancelled as proposed by the US team in the 1945 US Loan negotiations (Cairncross 1987: 90–9). The Attlee government had pragmatic reasons to retain the balances and encourage the holding of sterling, which the Conservatives used as a step to re-establish sterling and the City's role in international finance (Tomlinson 1997b: 46). The huge overhang of debt and (mistaken) market perceptions that the balances were volatile and reserves weak left sterling vulnerable to small shifts in market confidence for much of the 1950s and 1960s (Schenk 1994: 17–53). The slow retreat from the world role failed to repair the situation as new sources of difficulty appeared in the 1960s. Competitiveness deteriorated in terms of both prices and non-price factors (delivery dates, after-sales support and the like) and the increasing instability of the wider Bretton Woods system added its own acute complications (Posner and Steer 1978; de Vries 1987). Accordingly, British governments could not take the balance of payments for granted. They needed constantly to remind both sides of industry to improve competitiveness and productivity. In short, they needed a vigorous politics of productivity and technical change. The extent to which they succeeded will be a focus of Chapter 3.

International diffusion of new technologies

When American industry began to lose its markets to Japanese competitors, US management science became very interested in "national systems of innovation" (see Nelson 1988; Freeman 1988; Porter 1990). This literature was principally concerned with policies and institutional structures to promote international competitiveness rather than the more limited task of absorbing new ideas from abroad, which is more directly addressed in the concept of "convergence". As noted in Chapter 1, international technology transmission from the lead nation to the followers occurs when (i) the size of the "productivity gap" (interpreted at the sectoral rather than the aggregate level) is substantial and (ii) when "social capability" is well-developed. Table 2.1 shows Anglo-American productivity gaps by sector for the period 1937–90 in the form of relative levels of US output per worker. In each year, the output of the average British worker in each sector is 100, so in 1937 the average US agricultural worker produced slightly more (103.3 percent of

Table 2.1 Time series extrapolations of comparative US/UK labour productivity levels by sector, 1937–90
(Output per US worker; output per UK worker = 100 in each year)

	1937	1950	1960	1968	1973	1979	1990
Agriculture	103.3	126.0	153.1	156.7	131.2	156.1	151.1
Mining	232.1	376.5	618.4	700.9	668.0	156.6	119.1
Manufacturing	208.3	262.7	243.0	242.8	215.0	202.6	175.2
Construction	107.8	177.6	235.5	204.5	146.6	129.7	98.5
Utilities	359.3	573.4	719.9	767.9	590.8	523.9	389.8
Transport/ Communication	283.4	348.4	318.8	336.8	303.3	302.7	270.5
Distribution	119.8	135.2	143.2	147.9	149.6	153.8	166.0
Finance/Services	96.1	111.5	112.3	121.3	118.0	118.3	101.0
Government	100.0	116.2	110.2	104.4	101.7	96.5	93.2
Total of above	132.6	167.2	163.4	159.1	144.3	139.4	128.3
Whole Economy	132.6	166.9	167.9	164.2	152.3	145.5	133.0

Source: Broadberry 1997b: 7.

the average British agriculturist) and the average US worker in the utilities produced very substantially more output (359.3 percent more than the British average). To some extent, the widest "gaps" represent different natural resource endowments, but manufacturing is more of a problem to explain and has dominated the discussion on Britain's relative economic decline, as noted in Chapter 1.[8]

Given the size of the manufacturing productivity gap, there were very high incentives for British industry to import US ideas and methods. Using the same methodology, Anglo-American productivity gaps *within* manufacturing also varied extensively, as is evident in Table 2.2.

Engineering, chemicals and metals had the lowest relative efficiency in 1950. The first two made big inroads into the US lead by the mid-1970s, whereas metals did not.

As far as the "social capability" for convergence is concerned, Abramovitz (1986) emphasised the supply of investment, appropriate labour skills, risk-taking managers and openness to new ideas. The literature on diffusion of innovations has produced a subtly different list of determinants. Rogers (1995: 207), for example, has listed the following influences: the perceived attributes of the innovation, the type of "innovation-decision", communication channels, the nature of the social system of those seeking to adopt innovations, and the extent of the activities of "change agents". Clearly, there are elements common to both lists, but both also contain factors that have been identified as important at the enterprise level. For the sake of convenience, therefore, this discussion will focus on Rogers' agenda and leave relative factor costs, the supply of investment funds and attitudes to the

Table 2.2   Comparative US/UK labour productivity in manufacturing, 1950–75 (Output per US worker, output per UK worker = 100 for each year stated)

	1950	1967/68	1975
Chemicals & allied	356.4	281	226.8
Basic metals	274.4	294	251.1
Engineering/metals	337.3	294	190.6
Textiles, leather, clothing	197.9	225	222.8
Food, drink, tobacco	215.3	246	208.4
Other manufacturing	284.7	276	274.8
Manufacturing	273.4	276	224.7

Source: Broadberry 1993: 786.

enterprise case studies. It is, of course, impossible to assess the extent to which British conditions satisfied Rogers' requirements without also considering company case studies. Accordingly, this section concludes with an examination of how representative these case studies might be of the wider population of British firms.

Attributes of innovations

There is not much doubt that progressive British firms had looked to their American counterparts as the source of new ideas on products and processes from the late nineteenth century onwards. Kudo and colleagues (2004b) have argued that Japanese and German companies experienced waves of interest in Americanisation that broadly match the British "technology scares" listed at the start of Chapter 1. This implies a long-standing interest in US technology among many British (and German and Japanese) firms. But it was also common for new relationships to be forged during the automation period to try to exploit the obvious technical leadership enjoyed by American firms.

The computer industry provides an excellent illustration. English Electric Computers (EE) fortuitously acquired an information-sharing agreement with the Radio Corporation of America (RCA) when it acquired Marconi in 1945.[9] This agreement had originally concerned technical information on radio valves and had been mutually beneficial. It provided each side with access to product information (all technical reports, results of research into new products, software for computers, etc.) and full details on manufacturing processes (technical drawings, know-how, etc.). Both sides were obliged to provide any information requested though not to volunteer it mechanically. The balance of the information flow is evident from the different contact arrangements. EE had a permanent representative with RCA, but the head of RCA computer research visited the UK once a year for this purpose. Accordingly, EE paid an annual "balancing payment" of £45,000 in the early 1960s in recognition of the one-sidedness of the information flow. EE had taken the full design of its highly-rated KDP 10 computer from the RCA 501 and "anglicised" the circuits (re-specified them for components, transistors and diodes from UK sources) but the exploitation of the agreement by the newly merged EE-LEO Computers reached new levels. Before the merger both EE and LEO had lost orders because they could not offer random access memory and when the new company was formed their first thought was to send a team to the USA to get technical details of RCA's work in this area.[10] Campbell-Kelly (1989: 240–1) recounts the slightly later episode when EE-LEO, lacking development time and resources to develop a rival third generation computer (see Chapter 6 for an explanation of "generations" of computers) to compete with the IBM System/360 range, sent a team to acquire the technical details of RCA's own third generation machines, the Spectra 70.

Of course, computers may be unrepresentative of British industry. Tiratsoo and Tomlinson (1993: 150) have argued that in the 1940s "many British industrialists were sceptical about the relevance of the American model to British conditions". Their reservations rested on the scale of investment required to introduce US mass production and the inappropriateness of US mass production to more fragmented British and imperial markets. There was also suspicion of the rhetoric of both the centrality of competition and human resources management within Americanisation (Tiratsoo and Tomlinson 1998b: 97; Kipping 1998: 64–5). The formation in 1948 of the Anglo-American Council on Productivity and its metamorphosis into the TAPP was designed to calm these fears and similar reservations on the part of labour. However, the reports of the AACP and the dissemination of the results through meetings, conferences and similar activities produced mixed results. The inherent message in this activity that American industry possessed unique qualities of hard work and enterprise created opposition and antagonism (Carew 1987: 144; Clark 1999). But there was also an enormous amount of detailed information on technological developments and managerial innovation.[11] Indeed, Tiratsoo (1999; 2003; Tiratsoo and Gourvish 1996; Tiratsoo and Tomlinson 1997; 1998a) has shown that publicity for a whole range of discrete managerial innovations from America gathered momentum in the 1950s, only to have relatively disappointing results in the 1960s. The picture of US technology circulating in Britain from the later 1940s was thus mixed and confusing. In part, the picture was of an alien, almost irresistible industrial system that threatened British systems of production, but British business leaders would have been perverse indeed to have concluded that US technological and managerial innovations were entirely inappropriate to British conditions.

Innovation-decision types and communication channels

Rogers' second major influence on the speed of innovation, the type of "innovation-decision", relates to the number of persons involved in making the decision, and need not detain us further, but the question of communication channels does merit comment. Research has shown that information received from mass media is perfectly adequate to encourage adoption of relatively simple technologies, but interpersonal contacts are much better when the innovation to be adopted is more sophisticated. In the context of automation in the 1950s, the sheer range of Anglo-American communications channels is staggering. It was evident from Chapter 1 that there was enormous British interest in American automation technologies and this was stoked by both the mass media and interpersonal contacts and that more technically complex literature soon appeared in the UK. Interpersonal contacts are more difficult to monitor, but the automation literature can give some insights into the range of contacts. The PEP (1957: 17, 39–40) study, for example, described in detail three automation projects, and in two regular contacts between British and US firms was an important element in the decision to innovate. The first case described, the introduction of an Assel mill by Tube Investments [TI], followed the visit of three executives to the USA in August–September 1950 to assess technological developments in the US steel industry. On the basis of their reports, TI decided to adopt this technology and sent two engineers to spend six months in the USA with both the producers of the equipment (the American firm Aetna Standard) and the patent holders (the Timken Roller Bearing Company of Ohio). The second example, the LEO computer, grew from a more complex pattern of interpersonal relationships. The bakers and caterers, J. Lyons, fearing that costs were getting out of control as the firm expanded after the First World War, employed a Cambridge mathematics graduate, J.R.M. Simmons, to develop a system of management accounting. Simmons in turn recruited a second Cambridge mathematician, T.R. Thompson, and they gradually established a management accounting department in the early 1930s (additional details from Hendry 1987: 74–6). They made periodic visits to the USA to monitor the most advanced methods of clerical management and in the first postwar trip, made by Thompson and Oliver Standingford in 1947, they met Herman Goldstine, who had been involved in the development of the successor to ENIAC, on 12 May, 1947. Goldstine explained how the computer worked and put them into contact with Douglas Hartree and Maurice Wilkes, who were working on a computer to US specifications at the Mathematical Laboratory in Cambridge. Just like Eckert and Mauchly, Thompson saw the potential for a computer in office management and his visit to Cambridge in July–August 1947 provided enough information to merit a paper for the Lyons board on the developments that would be needed to utilise computers in the office. Taken together (and with the examples cited in the case studies in following chapters), it appears that the larger British firms of the early postwar years already had, or could develop, rich personal contacts specifically oriented towards technological learning. The question of diffusing this knowledge to other British companies is the focus of Rogers' fourth element, the nature of the social system.

Characteristics of the social system

The characteristics of the social system that Rogers (1995: 24–6) identifies as important in the speed of diffusion are the formal and informal patterns of interaction and communication, embracing the norms, or established behaviour patterns, and the network interconnectedness of the society. Whilst this agenda was devised to explain diffusion of new innovations among micro-social groups, it can be applied equally to the national context. A number of strategically-placed observers suggested that this was an area of real failure in the UK. Goodman (1957: 195–6), for example, argued that:

> In many firms which could use the knowledge [about new production processes], there is no staff to review scientific literature, to find out what is relevant, or even to appreciate the significance of relevant material when it is brought to their attention ... The real problem is the lack of realisation on the part of some managements of the need for scientific and technical staff or the effective organisation of such personnel. It was found in a Birmingham survey, that the managements of a large number of firms did not realise that they had a responsibility for innovation. Many had a lack of interest in new ideas.

The 1950s saw a number of initiatives to improve British performance in this area by trying to establish networks at the local level to broadcast new ideas more widely and rapidly. The AACP productivity teams laid the foundation, which was bolstered by the British Productivity Council (BPC). It established local productivity associations and committees to disseminate knowledge of best practices. Potentially, the most effective method was the "productivity circuit", which involved taking industrialists into each other's factories to see and appraise methods of production and organisation. Bufton (2004: 156–7) has related both the great difficulties in establishing these networks, because of commercial sensitivities, and the great benefits accruing to managers in the scheme.

At the end of the decade another version of this idea came to the minister responsible for science, the Lord President. In March 1959, Michael Fraser floated the idea of a "College of Automation", possibly based on the Cranfield Institute and aimed at recruiting representatives from the electronic and engineering industries.[12] The Lord President was advised not to become involved in negotiations that had already begun spontaneously and independently between the interested parties.[13] In the event, the college was not created and the effort to improve communication networks within these two diffuse industries petered out, but the ideas launched a major reappraisal of science and technology policy across the political spectrum.

During this process, the main aim shifted from diffusing innovations more rapidly to expanding the research and development activity by the larger industrial firms (O'Hara 2002). In 1957, Aubrey Jones, Minister of Supply, had proposed the creation of a Ministry of Technology to develop civil contracts for research and development parallel to those used in defence (Vig 1968: 30). The initiative was rejected but a Conservative Party Science and Industry Committee report of 1962 emphasised science policy as the core of economic policy and called for funding to be concentrated on activities with commercial potential (Tiratsoo and Tomlinson 1998b: 158). The expansion of funding occurred however under the Wilson government, especially under the aegis of the Ministry of Technology, and simultaneously the ministry attempted to shift the bias of government-funded research and development from military to civilian projects (Edgerton 1996a: 60–5). Beneath these very prominent activities, Mintech also undertook the familiar task of speeding diffusion of advanced technologies through personal and institutional contacts. Coopey's (1993: 120) assessment of these measures is, however, depressingly familiar: "Technologies often proved unamenable to general industrial dispersion, and industry itself frequently reluctant to respond to initiatives on offer". For completeness, we should also add that the view within both government and Whitehall of the experiments to cut back defence-related research to free resources for civilian R&D was equally disappointing; Labour came to doubt whether British industry was in fact short of civilian R&D (Edgerton 1996a: 81). The notion that British industry had a well-networked head of efficient producers but a (long) tail of firms who were either "out of the loop" that discussed improved methods or, more probably, deeply resistant to change is a point to which we will return.

Activities of "change agents"

The final element of Rogers' diffusion process is the activity of "change agents", among whom we must number propagandists for automation, management consultants, US transplant firms and the sales teams of US machinery and office machinery companies in the UK. We examine the roles of each in turn, beginning with propagandists. Chapter 1 suggested that US expert opinion was on automation was sharply divided between "optimists" and "pessimists" but British scientists, on the other hand, were generally happy to work with government to speed the take-up of new scientific ideas by industry (Vig 1968: 7–33; Wilkie 1991: 42–3; Horner 1993). The nearest British equivalent of John Diebold, the young US business analyst who published a number of studies of automation, was probably Frank Woollard. Woollard was at the other end of his career, having retired as director of two engineering companies in the Birmid Industries Group in 1953. His main connection to automation was as a champion of flow production in the automobile industry. He had been director and general manager of the engines branch of Morris Motors when it built the first ATMs ever made and was president of the Institution of Automobile Engineers in the later 1940s. After retirement, he produced his classic work on flow production techniques (Woollard 1954) and lectured extensively on automation (see Woollard 1955; 1956). Slightly closer to Diebold in age was John Sargrove, an electronics engineer working in the radio industry who developed the first printed circuit board (PCB) and automatic machines on which to produce it in volume. He was an active publicist for this and other automatic manufacturing and inspection machines (Sargrove and Huggins 1955; Beauchamp 1981) and, despite its commercial failure the PCB venture featured extensively in the automation literature (see Diebold 1952: 39–41). Thus, Britain had its share of pioneering propagandists for automation among its production engineers, allowing the concept to be at least partially domesticated.

Management consultants have become recognised recently as important "boosters" in the international diffusion of American management techniques. American management consultants had been very active in Britain in the interwar years and helped to bring versions of F.W. Taylor's approach to shopfloor management, initially to US multinational transplants and subsequently to the larger British industrial companies (Kipping 1997: 71–3; 1999: 199). American consultancies and their British off-shoots grew rapidly during the 1930s and still faster in the 1940s and early 1950s against the background of labour scarcity and official propaganda for the adoption of American methods of labour management (Ferguson 2002: 72–120). The second generation of US management consultants, like McKinsey, A.T. Kearney and Booz, Allen and Hamilton, which specialised less in labour management and more in organisational and strategic issues, came to the UK in the mid-1950s, with remarkable impact on Britain's largest companies, as Chapters 5–7 will suggest. This second generation invariably established their first European office in London and helped transform the older British management consultants into more Americanised organisations (Kipping 1999: 209–17). These US consultancies expanded rapidly by bringing well-networked British personalities into the organisation and relying on reputation to spread from this base. For this reason, their clients included the largest companies, especially British-based multinationals, and the more venerable British institutions, like the BBC, that were struggling to control costs and impose an agreed management strategy. Management consultants were in the vanguard of office mechanisation and computerisation from the later 1950s. A move of great symbolic significance was the creation in 1958 of Urwick Diebold, a joint venture by the British management consultants, Urwick, Orr and Partners, and John Diebold, the American automation expert who has figured prominently in the story so far, to identify processes ripe for computerisation within client firms (Ferguson 2002: 211–12).

The British offshoots of US multinationals could become "change agents" by acting as a bridge for the transfer of US management "know-how". In many ways, Britain was the most fortunately placed European economy to receive such benefits because it received the lion's share of US manufacturing FDI in Europe at least until the mid-1960s (Wilkins 1974: Table 13.3). The most thorough assessment of the impact of US multinationals in transferring new ideas on production and organisation to domestic firms during the early 1950s was Dunning's (1958) study, based on interviews conducted in 1954–7. He noted that US transplants operated in the middle ground; with lower levels of labour productivity than their US plant but higher than British firms in the same industries. Significantly, the strategies and policies of competing UK firms adapted to American competition and raised British manufacturing productivity growth. He produced a long list of stimuli to higher productivity among British firms and emphasised the impact on British suppliers of flows of technical information from the US multinationals. On returning to this work in the 1990s, Dunning (1998a: 262–3; 1998b: 88–9) concluded that the vast quantities of literature that had been published since the late 1950s on the impact of FDI offered new theoretical approaches and techniques of empirical analysis, but none of this would change the broad thrust of his earlier conclusions.

Finally in this section, it is worth examining the impact of American firms in machine tools and office machinery, as these two industries "carried" technical change to the manufacturing and service sectors. The Burroughs Corporation offers an excellent example of an office machine supplier helping to diffuse advanced office mechanisation in British financial services. Burroughs was one of the first US office machine suppliers to locate a subsidiary in the UK when it established in the UK in 1895, opening its first non-American factory at Nottingham three years later (Cortada 2000: 38–9). Its calculating machines were prominent throughout British financial services in the interwar years but the company's trajectory changed significantly after 1945, when it embarked upon a vigorous programme of expansion and development. In part, this represented a move into electronics, by recruiting the head of research at the University of Pennsylvania's Moore School of Engineering (see above).[14] At approximately the same time, Burroughs opened new factories in the UK, taking advantage of regional incentives to locate in Scotland and transferring the entire production of adding machines from Detroit to Strathleven.[15] The next key step was the establishment (and "de-bugging") of the production of "Sensimatic" accounting machines in the UK and the introduction of "Sensitronic" ledger posting machines.[16] The "Sensimatic" had been launched in 1950 as the first accounting machine with a programmed control panel, which Burroughs promotional literature presented as the greatest advance in accounting machines in 25 years and "Sensitronics" five years later, with the promise that they could double the productivity of staff in this task.[17] The latter came to the market just as British banks embarked upon a drive to mechanise ledger posting (see Chapter 7 below) and Burroughs mounted a very strong sales drive on both sides of the Atlantic. Like many producers of electronic machinery, Burroughs employed sales teams that blended engineering and commercial skills, and the group dealing with Williams Deacons, the small Manchester-based bank, helped to advise the board on customising the hardware and the bank's own management systems and reported on production and management methods elsewhere in the British financial system.[18]

Burroughs had a distinctive sales strategy, seeking to target their efforts on specific sectors rather than spread their activities to office machine users in general. The Sensimatics and Sensitronics were aimed primarily at financial services in both the UK and the USA and Burroughs was anxious, perhaps over-anxious, to pioneer automation in this sector. When the British Bankers' Association wanted to see examples of the computerisation of bank services in the USA, they were shown a promotional film from Burroughs with equipment that had not yet been patented in the USA.[19] It showed an electronic cheque-reading and sorting machine linked to a Burroughs "Visible Record Computer", which could select a ledger card containing account details and posted details of the cheque transaction to the appropriate account card. In fact, the hardware was regarded by many of Burroughs engineering staff as a dud, and it made no market penetration when in the 1960s British banks nervously embarked on the first round of computerisation (see Chapter 7).[20]

However, by the mid-1960s Burroughs had developed a much more impressive central processing unit for data processing applications, and re-entered the British market in 1965, with two medium-sized machines the B2500 and the B3500. The big step occurred in early 1967, when it launched the B5500, which had multi-programming and real-time potential for large systems.[21] When the B2500 and B3500 were launched, Burroughs created a "London-Banks" office by splitting and expanding its City of London sales office.[22] The sales team began intensive efforts to persuade British banks to change commitments to existing suppliers, using price competition, reference to the proven service of B5500s in American banks, and increasingly by referring to the potential of its terminal computer unit, which would work most effectively with Burroughs central processors.[23] Nudged forward by the competition between Burroughs and IBM for hardware contracts, with communications firms like Plessey and the GPO insisting that secure remote communications were technically feasible, British banks put themselves at the technological frontier of on-line, real-time large-network computing in the later 1960s. It is highly unlikely that this would have occurred without the vigorous sales efforts of the US firms, and as examined in Chapter 7 the banks were extremely uncomfortable in this exposed technological position. But the episode shows the enormous potential impact of sales activities on the pace of diffusion of new processes.

Limited diffusion and the "British disease"

Thus the conclusion to this section seems to be that the larger British firms were generally open to ideas from the USA, but small and medium-sized companies were much less so. It was the larger firms that had long-established links with US firms in the same or related industries, often through personal contacts, and were more likely to come into contact with the "change agents", such as industrial consultants. The larger firms were increasingly the targets of the TAPP and OSP programmes. The literature suggests that British manufacturing industries had a distinctively long tail of inefficient producers (see Broadberry and Crafts 1990; Crafts 1988; Davies and Caves 1987: Table 7.4). By implication, deficiencies in Britain's national institutional structures caused innovations to diffuse slowly beyond the largest firms. The list of ultimate causes of limited diffusion is almost as long as the list of causes of the "British disease", and includes: a weak competitive framework (Broadberry and Crafts 1996; 2001), unprofessional management that preferred to lead by personality rather than by developing technical competence (Tiratsoo 1995; 1998; 1999), obstructive labour (Pratten 1976), crushing institutional structures that have failed to adapt to new economic conditions (Lazonick 1990: 181–212), misplaced economic policy priorities (Barnett 1986; 1995), and inadequate research and development activity at the level of the firm (Peck 1968). However, like so much of the literature on British industrial performance there is an element of "declinism" (Tomlinson 2001: 21–6) in these studies and the productivity record of British manufacturing was much better than customarily supposed, at least during the long boom (Booth 2003). Thus, it is worth exploring whether the head of Britain's efficient firms is so small and the tail is as comparatively long as the critics suggest.

There are some hints that the distribution of efficiency in the UK might not be as distinctively poor as is commonly believed. The case for an excessively long tail of underperformance is most frequently based on industry-level comparisons, using material from the censuses of production in Britain and America. Unfortunately, the two countries used different industrial classifications for much of the postwar period and industry-level studies can be extremely unreliable. There is the further knotty problem of valuing the output of one country in the currency of another, while taking account of differences in quality between countries. There are two ways around this. The first is to look at the distribution of efficiency growth rates in other countries. The evidence of the Bureau of the Census to the automation inquiry of 1955 found that about half of the 152 industries for which indexes of physical output per hour worked could be calculated had annual rates of growth of between 1 and 5 percent per annum in the period 1947–52. Slightly more than one-quarter had average productivity growth rates between plus 1 and minus 3 percent per annum. The remainder (slightly less than one-quarter) showed annual gains of more than 5 percent and this group contained a small number of industries with gains of more than 10 percent per annum (US Congress 1955: 318). US data thus also reveal a substantial tail of relatively poor performance. The second method is to construct "manufacturing footprints" (Booth 2003: 15–17). The footprint first divides total manufacturing output by that produced in establishments of different size (which can be standardised between countries). The next step is to compare the efficiency of each establishment size with the average for manufacturing as a whole in that country. The manufacturing footprint will only compare differences in the *distribution* of productivity performance within each country, not differences in the *absolute level* of productivity.

With these provisos in mind, the figures in Table 2.3 tell an interesting story. They compare British and American manufacturing footprints in the census of production years 1954 and 1967/68. In the former year, the output of the average US manufacturing worker was 2.51 times higher than that of the average British industrial worker. In the latter years, the average American manufacturing worker produced 2.43 times as much as the British counterpart. The literature implies that American producers were especially good (and the British were rather bad) at Fordist mass production and that their productivity lead was concentrated in this area of large-scale production in large establishments. The manufacturing footprints suggest, however, that American productivity was superior across the board. In 1954, both countries produced roughly one-fifth of total manufacturing output from firms of the largest size and in both countries establishments of this size produced roughly 10 percent more per worker than the sector average. In 1954, in both countries the largest single share (approximately 30 percent) of manufacturing output came from firms employing between 100 and 499 workers, and in both countries productivity in establishments of this size were fractionally below average levels for manufacturing as a whole. Interestingly, the similarity remains in the later 1960s and the subtle shifts in the footprint show up equally in both countries. There is a small fall in the proportion output coming from and relative productivity of small plants (50–99 employees) and a relative rise in the proportion of output and the relative productivity level of the largest establishments. In summary, American manufacturing had a huge productivity lead over its British counterpart in the 1950s and 1960s, but there is no indication that the British were especially poor at large-scale production, nor is there any real indication of a long tail of inefficiency in the UK.

Table 2.3 Manufacturing footprints, UK and USA, 1954 and 1967/68

	Size of establishment (number of employees)						
	10–49	50–99	100–499	500–999	1k–2,499	2.5k+	All
1954							
UK relative productivity	85	89	96	105	111	110	
Share of total net output from UK manufacturing	9	9	32	14	17	19	100
US relative productivity	82	87	96	105	113	112	
Share of total net output from US manufacturing	11	9	29	14	17	21	101
USA 1967	1–49	50–99	100–499	500–999	1k–2,499	2.5k+	All
US relative productivity	86	85	92	103	115	118	
Share of total net output from US manufacturing	12	8	29	13	15	23	100
UK 1968	1–49	50–99	100–499	500–999	1k–1,999	2k+	All
UK relative productivity	88	83	91	105	112	116	
Share of total net output from UK manufacturing	11	7	28	15	15	24	100

Note: See text for an explanation of the meaning of "UK/US relative productivity"
Sources: 1954: US Department of Commerce 1954: vol. 1, 203–1; Board of Trade 1956: Table 10.
1967: US Department of Commerce 1971: General summary, Table 4.
1968: DTI 1971: Table 2.

This conclusion should not be so surprising. Phillip Scranton (1997) has argued that the role of the mass producers in the trajectory of US economic development has been exaggerated and the role of "specialty production" has been undervalued. Equally, Diebold judged that the average batch size in US manufacturing during the mid-1950s was relatively small: "Most of American industry ... depends upon relatively small runs of product. About 80 to 90 percent of American production is in lots of less than 25 individual pieces" (US Congress 1955: 7). It was widely agreed that the production of an extremely long run of standardised products was a special case in the US economy of the 1950s (Buckingham 1961: 40–6). This might suggest that the balance between the head of efficiency and the tail of inefficiency was not so very different in Britain and America, though whether other European economies and Japan shared this distribution is a question for future research.

Reverse flows

Thus far, we have not questioned the assumption in the convergence literature that there was a one-way flow of technical ideas from the lead nation, the USA, to the followers, such as Britain. However, we should be wary of such simplifications. Chapter 4 below examines the rather ambiguous parentage of the automatic transfer machine, one of the central technologies of the automation scare of the mid-1950s. The idea was born in the UK, but somewhat prematurely in view of the unreliability of the control technology on which it depended. The machine grew up in the USA, but experienced a turbulent adolescence until it re-crossed the Atlantic and was re-engineered for maturity by the French and British. This mature technology re-shaped American ideas. This general point was reinforced by Dunning (1998a: 242): "The flow of research, development and managerial expertise, though primarily from the parent company to its British subsidiary, is by no means solely in that direction. The fact that important technological and other gains have accrued to American firms as a result of their UK interests is not always publicised as well as it might be". He mentions manufacturing knowledge on diesel engines and turbines from AEI to International GEC and aspects of harbour radar that were pioneered by Sperry in Liverpool for application in California. New knowledge was also passed back to the USA in the chemicals and materials handling and Britain offered a number of US companies the opportunity to experiment with new industrial processes on a smaller (and hence cheaper) scale than would have been required in the USA. These examples were minor when compared with the flow from the USA, but this is scarcely surprising – the huge majority of products and processes that characterised the postwar world were of American origin (Edgerton 1996b: 65). A study of 110 significant innovations from 1945 to the early 1960s revealed that 74 were American, but of the remainder 18 were British, 14 German and two French (OECD 1970: 198). Indeed, British firms were leaders in patenting activity in the USA in the 1950s and even in the early 1960s Britain and Germany dominated US foreign patents, until both were overtaken by the meteoric rise of Japan (Pavitt and Soete 1980: 40–3). The technological dependence implied by the convergence hypothesis needs some qualification.

Conclusion

Cold War fears pushed Washington into lavish funding of strategically important technologies that had potential for take-up by "ordinary" American industry and to undertake a vast programme of technical and material support for industry in the market economies. These fears made US government extremely concerned about the management of production and technical change in key strategic industries, initially at home but increasingly in the wider US orbit. Paradoxically, beyond the defence sector it left conditions of production to managers and workers in domestic industry but elements within the US administration continued to worry about the general levels of (civilian) industrial efficiency in countries sheltering under the US security umbrella. For as long as American industry remained dominant in world markets the administrators of the TAPP campaigned both directly and through the OEEC for greater take-up of American methods by industry in Europe and Japan (McGlade 2000: 68–73).

Thus, British governments would have come under pressure to develop policies to accelerate productivity growth and technical change. However, there were even more powerful "domestic" reasons for British governments to push in this direction. The wartime impoverishment of Britain's external position combined with the postwar domestic and external settlements gave governments limited scope to rebuild Britain's external assets and fulfil its self-appointed role as a second-tier world power. The vision of Britain as the head of a global commonwealth of nations faded only in the early 1970s (Cain and Hopkins 1993: 281–5). The costs of this role were substantial and induced British policy-makers to take short-term risks (the failure to formalise the working of sterling balances, exporting capital to develop the sterling area countries in the later 1940s and the intermittent dashes towards sterling convertibility in the 1950s) to reap the longer-term rewards of the full array of overseas earnings of the City of London. The postwar balance of payments was thus always frail, despite the relatively healthy state of the current account. In this context, British governments could not allow managements and unions free rein to decide pay, effort and the technical conditions of production. The constant refrain from government was that bargainers needed to take account of "the national interest" in their negotiations. Governments always needed faster productivity growth, higher competitiveness and more technically efficient production to strengthen the external account and limit the recurrent crises of confidence. The extent to which postwar governments succeeded in defining a national interest and persuading bargainers to abide by its priorities is the subject of the second part of the next chapter.

In one important respect, however, British governments could feel reasonably satisfied, if somewhat perplexed. There is every reason to suspect that the larger British firms were well-informed, largely from their own efforts, on relevant new technologies in the USA. The channels of communication between British and American industry (and labour) were diverse and sophisticated, and were boosted by a substantial and varied cast of "change agents". The perplexing factor was the failure of the Anglo-American productivity gap in manufacturing to fall more rapidly. There is no doubt that the rate of manufacturing productivity growth was faster in Britain than in the USA from the early 1950s until the mid-1970s (Broadberry 1997a: Table A3.1c) and fractionally below the pace achieved in Germany from 1952 until the OPEC crisis of 1973 (Booth 2003: 7). However, manufacturing productivity growth rates were faster in France and the Netherlands and much faster in Japan during the long boom (van Ark 1993: Table IV.4). This is a mixed record, but by the time that it was becoming clear that British productivity levels had been overtaken the culture of decline had become well-established and British policy-makers were beginning their efforts to reform the domestic politics of productivity (see the discussion towards the end of the next chapter). Thus, the subtleties of the situation were missed and British policy-makers committed themselves more fully to reform the domestic politics of productivity and technical change, the theme of Chapter 3.

3
National Politics of Productivity and Technical Change

To complete the examination of the global and national levels set out in Chapter 1, this chapter concentrates on the national politics of productivity and technical change (box 4 of Table 1.1). The agenda comprises institutional configurations and the content of national bargaining over pay, effort and the choice of production technique. The discussion in the previous chapter set out the context within which this national bargaining took place. In America, great power rivalries led government to create conditions under which production of defence materiel could be expanded rapidly both at home and in other countries under US protection. But the productivity leadership of American "civilian" industries allowed government to concentrate on liberalising world trade and payments. Suppliers of raw materials were encouraged to emerge from discriminatory blocs to make their commodities available to American industry. Richer nations were encouraged to open their markets to American manufacturers. Britain, on the other hand, did not enjoy the luxuries of the industrial leader. As will be seen below, industrialists, trade unionists, and many policymakers would have preferred Britain to follow the American government's *laissez-faire* attitude to negotiations over pay and conditions. However, the recurrent external crises gave British governments no real alternative. Their authority was eroded by the regular jitters of foreign exchange markets.[1] British governments had to steer the industrial relations system towards agreements that would not upset foreign confidence in sterling. Thus, this chapter compares a fundamentally decentralised politics of productivity in the USA with a British system of multi-level bargaining in which "concertation in crisis" became a regular feature. We begin with the centrifugal trajectory of US bargaining.

The politics of productivity and technical change in the USA

In the 1930s, US society was bitterly divided about technological change (Bix 2000: 80–235). Trade unions, backed by sympathetic intellectuals, felt threatened because they saw machines displace workers. They recognised the importance of technical change in the capitalist economy, but considered the social consequences of redundancy, mass unemployment and community upheaval excessive. The National Association of Manufacturers (NAM), the Chamber of Commerce and the Machinery and Allied Products Institute, on the other hand, proclaimed the benefits of mechanisation in lower prices, rising consumer demand and thus more jobs – at least over the long run. Scientists and engineers supported business but popular culture remained sceptical.[2] However, as the international situation deteriorated in the later 1930s, the potential of machines to produce both more consumer goods and defence materiel subtly changed the tone and balance of the discussion. Inventiveness, innovation and new technologies were seen as the main hope for survival and US opinion took comfort in the idea of native technological brilliance.

The dramatic surge in output from 1939 to 1943 was accompanied by a large, government-financed expansion of research, especially in the largest manufacturing companies and elite universities, and the continuation of this military-industrial-academic-complex seemed the key to America's strategic future (Rockoff 1998: 93–4; Kevles 1975). Unfortunately, the tightening wartime labour market generated conflict, which usually took the form of short-term, unofficial strikes at shopfloor level and occurred against a background of high absenteeism and rising labour turnover (Renshaw 1991: 53–8). The key problem was that prices and profits grew faster than wages under wartime regulations (Boyer and Morais 1955: 339). Roosevelt's government restricted the right to strike and drew labour leaders into policy-making but with no noticeable impact on strike levels (Lichtenstein 1982; Tomlins 1985:252–6; Renshaw 1991: 84–6). The industrial situation deteriorated further in 1945–6, with the biggest strike wave in US industrial history. The main issue concerned workers' efforts to make wages catch up with wartime inflation against fears of a return to mass unemployment (Rayback 1966: 388–96).

Employers, moving rapidly to the right, campaigned for full and rapid de-control of prices and a watering of the Full Employment Act of 1946 to make it more of a rhetorical aspiration than a blueprint for actual policies (Soffer 2001: 781). Business conservatives argued that organised labour had become too strong. As early as 1946, Charles E. Wilson, President of General Electric, noted that "The problems of the United States can be captiously summed up in two words, Russia abroad, labour at home" (Boyer and Morais 1955: 345). Led by the large-scale corporations and supported by the NAM and the Chambers of Commerce, business sought to regain ground lost under the New Deal. Union leaders expected a business counterattack (Harris 1985: 184–5; Tolliday and Zeitlin 1986c: 108–9). The AFL craft unions were generally more confident of holding wartime gains than the industrial unions organised by the CIO (Richter 1984: 40). The latter's efforts to prolong wartime corporatism to protect against the anticipated employer backlash failed in the face of AFL apathy and employer insistence on the rights of postwar management to manage (Brody 1980: 82–110; Carew 1987: 51–2). The large corporations began their fightback in the automobile industry, where the major firms insisted on the inclusion of clauses underlining management rights in settling the 1946 disputes (Tolliday and Zeitlin 1986c: 108). Ford and Chrysler also secured disciplinary measures against employees who participated in unauthorised strikes, forcing much stronger central control in the UAW, which had hitherto depended heavily on shop stewards for organisation and defensive capacity (Lichtenstein 1983: 300–3; 1986: 125; Herding 1972: 30).

The disputes in the automobile industry at the end of the war helped consolidate the rise in the US labour movement of Walter Reuther, who became President of the UAW in 1947 by narrowly defeating the Communist-backed coalition that had run the union since 1940. Reuther brought a distinctive vision to US industrial relations; a combination of traditional tactical business unionism, the political economy of Keynesianism and the social vision of business welfare (Lichtenstein 1986: 122). Reuther saw his union as the vanguard shaping postwar America. By bargaining with the prosperous automobile corporations, he identified companies that faced steeply rising demand and were wealthy enough to conclude ambitious collective bargains, which might be used as patterns for the rest of manufacturing. In the process, Reuther's UAW led the anti-Communist drive in the CIO, which gathered momentum as the Cold War intensified and the domestic political climate became more conservative.

The passage of the Taft-Hartley Act by a Republican-dominated Congress in 1947 brought the issues to a head. Title I, *inter alia*, required unions to file non-communist affidavits from their officers to qualify as certifiable bargaining agents and followed Truman's insistence on loyalty checks on public employees, firing those belonging to "subversive" organisations (Tomlins 1985: 284; Renshaw 1991: 100–24). The anti-communist faction in the CIO, led by Reuther, had few qualms about these provisions, even though they wanted Taft-Hartley repealed in its entirety.[3] The purge on communist officials began in 1948, gathered momentum at the 1949 annual convention at Cleveland, where the CIO revised its constitution to make communists ineligible for executive office, and reached its high point in 1950 when the CIO expelled the United Electrical Workers, the biggest communist-led union, and ten others. When appearing before the Congress hearings on automation, Reuther prefaced his evidence with a ringing endorsement of the Cold War context: "We have said many, many times that the struggle in the world between our way of life, between the forces of freedom and the forces of tyranny, on the other hand, is more than just a struggle for geography; that it is essentially a struggle for men's minds and their hearts and their loyalties" (Reuther 1955: 117–18). Thus, the radical vanguard of organised labour in the 1930s became firmly hitched to the *status quo* and its bargaining strategy became equally conservative.

The consensus forged by Reuther with the automobile producers rested primarily upon bargains struck with Ford and GM in the late-1940s. As noted above, employers sought formal union recognition of the rights of management to manage and compensation for unauthorised actions by union members. In return they gave substantial wage increases. Reuther's famous deal with GM in 1948 comprised a two-year contract that included an automatic cost-of-living adjustment (COLA) triggered by rises in the general price index and an "annual improvement factor", under which wages rose by an extra 2 percent to reflect labour's contribution to rising productivity. Two years later GM offered an even more attractive package, with a $100 per month pension, an improved COLA and annual improvement factor and an extended five-year contract to give the company predictable labour costs and confirmation of managerial rights during its phase of rapid expansion (Harris 1982: 139–43). This "Treaty of Detroit" confirmed the subordination of local initiative to that of the centre and helped create an image of the UAW as "a combination of political machine and welfare bureaucracy" which "serviced the membership" and "policed the national contract" (Lichtenstein 1986: 126). It confirmed the trend to "workplace contractualism", which gave workers an impartial grievance procedure and seniority based on length of service and left managerial authority at the point of production if not entirely unchallenged at least conducted mainly on management's terms

(Slichter 1941: 1–3; Brody 1993: 224–5, 232–8). For the national economy, this was also a very effective politics of productivity, encouraging employers to accelerate labour-saving innovations to boost competitiveness and profits.

However, accelerated labour displacement touched a raw nerve. Memories of mass unemployment were still very sharp and the rapid pace of postwar technical change re-awakened fears of technological unemployment. Reutherism sought to treat these concerns through changes in social welfare and economic policy. Labour leaders persistently called for Keynesian policies as unemployment rose and blue-collar manufacturing jobs contracted in the later 1950s (Reuther 1955: 112; AFL-CIO 1962: 28). Most labour leaders were also keen to reduce the length of the working week, introduce early retirement and higher pensions, expand training and re-training, commit multi-plant companies to honour seniority rules across the entire organisation and raise the minimum wage (US Congress 1955: 126–38, 346; Weiss 1955; AFL-CIO 1962: 26–7). Reuther knew that these demands had little chance of success with the Eisenhower administrations of the 1950s, and typically pursued them through collective bargaining with the strongest automobile firms. The main goal during the 1950s was "the guaranteed annual wage" (GAW), which the historian of Reutherism archly notes was like the Holy Roman Empire, neither guaranteed nor annual nor a wage (Lichtenstein 1986: 129–30). It was rather a supplementary unemployment benefit, using payments by companies to temporarily laid-off key workers to raise welfare benefits closer to basic pay. The idea was developed first within government to deflect blue-collar unions from demanding the sort of guaranteed annual income customarily paid to white-collar staff.[4] It was taken up in 1952 by the steelworkers and other CIO unions. After five years of negotiations, the UAW and the Ford Motor Company reached agreement in 1955. Conservative industrialists were apoplectic, but there were also level-headed bureaucrats within the NAM, who saw that employee demands for security could not be brushed aside by management.[5]

In the event, the unions made limited headway with the GAW, but the pattern of management unilaterally adopting new technologies and compensating workers for dislocation spilled over into "automation agreements" (Clague 1961: 16–19). The Armour Meatpacking Company established a fund of $500,000 to ease problems arising from its modernisation programme. A similar arrangement was established by Kaiser Steel after lengthy discussions with the United Steel Workers, but the classic automation agreement was the 1960 deal between the

Pacific Maritime Association and the International Longshoremen's and Warehousemen's Union to provide a fund of $5 million per year for 5.5 years to guarantee minimum weekly earnings and an early retirement scheme, while giving the employers free hand to introduce containerisation (Snyder 1963: 8–9). On balance:

> From the business perspective, automation funds offered a relatively simple and affordable way to mute opposition to technological change, as well as providing a nice opportunity to demonstrate sympathy for workers. The shipping industry and Armour got significant public relations mileage out of their automation agreements. Labour had reason to accept the terms as the best possible option under existing circumstances, if companies seemed determined to mechanize and unions did not have much leverage or if automation appeared necessary to keep a company afloat (Bix 2000: 272).

In fact, union strength was ebbing from 1957–8. Cold War tensions remained strong and were manipulated to keep unions on the defensive. In October 1957 Sputnik emphasised the speed of Soviet technological catch-up amid reports of thousands of scientists and engineers in Soviet research institutes and Khrushchev identified automation as the source of Communist victory over capitalism. Senator Jacob Javits told New York unions to accept that the USA must automate or else "slip back to the position of a second class power" in the "life and death struggle of freedom" against Communism. Simultaneously, US industry began to lose home and export markets and unemployment, already high, rose rapidly in the "automation recession" of 1960–1 (Lissner 1960; 1961). Business used its influence with government to reinforce its power in the labour market with anti-union legislation (Soffer 2001: 781–6).

Thus, the 1950s saw the emergence of a corporate consensus; big business negotiated long-term deals with single industrial unions, which controlled the membership and enforced contract compliance, while allowing managers to drive productivity forward and restructure the labour process to maximise profits (Renshaw 1991: 125–51). This does not mean that shopfloor organisation disappeared and that management had a free run with production standards (Brody 1993: 238–45; Tolliday and Zeitlin 1986c: 107–12; Lichtenstein 1986: 129–39). Employers were constrained by seniority rules in laying off workers, and this could disrupt production and productivity (see Walker 1957: 138–9). There are also signs of industrialists being seduced by their own rhetoric of an automation race; many expensive automation projects failed to produce anything like the anticipated savings in labour costs (AMA 1956: 51–71). Nevertheless, profits rose across the board in US manufacturing industry during the Eisenhower years. Giant corporations managed to co-opt key union leaders into this vision, with high wages and business welfare as the bait. Unions happily traded jobs for the higher wages for those retaining their positions (NAM 1962: 8–9). Both business and unions moved inexorably to the right in this process.

The productivity-enhancing effects of this configuration waned more obviously in the 1960s. There is some force to the argument that, as markets became saturated, it was less easy to reap productivity gains by pushing the division of labour further in mass production industries (Piore and Sabel 1984: 133–220). It certainly became more difficult for firms to capture efficiency gains that exceeded the cost of living allowances in key collective bargains (Lazonick 1990: 280–1). Trade liberalisation brought US industry into competition with producers enjoying lower wage costs and equally advanced technology. The gradual rise of US inflation exacerbated these problems and simultaneously eroded the approval rating of the unions, already marginalised by their failure to mobilise minority workers, women and the radical young (Goldfield 1987: 3–54). The collective bargaining system came under increasing pressure from the late 1960s, when many employers stepped up their anti-union activities (with assistance from the Nixon administration) in the struggle to compete in tighter markets. The US politics of productivity that emerged in the first two postwar decades helped to create the world's most efficient industrial system, but its central features of heavy managerial costs and expensive manual labour became increasingly vulnerable and uncompetitive. Moreover, when the system soured in the 1970s, the response was necessarily fragmented and limited (Chapter 8).

Britain's politics of productivity and technical change

As already noted, Britain's politics of productivity and technical change had a much more active, if intermittent and reluctant, role for the state. At the end of the Second World War, British governments could hardly avoid massive new peacetime responsibilities. Shortages were rife, both at home and even more so in the countries in which Britain found itself as the postwar occupying power. Britain's external position was best described as a "financial Dunkirk", a very exposed position with extensive commitments from which Britain needed to withdraw.[6] There was general agreement within the wartime coalition that government controls should be continued until the worst shortages could be overcome, but precisely which controls needed to be retained and which could be jettisoned could not be agreed and had to be left to the results of the first postwar general election.[7] There was also agreement in principle during the lifetime of the wartime coalition to a programme of welfare reform, in effect raising the "social wage", which began to be implemented in 1944 (Addison 1975). Finally, it was widely assumed that the tripartite structures that had been created to inform wartime industrial policy would continue into peace. Thus, government had the need, the policy-making capacity and the bargaining chips with which to create a vigorous, state-centred politics of productivity and technical change (and the debate continues to rage about its decisions in this area).[8] The logical way to deal with this topic is by governments; accordingly we begin with the record of the Attlee governments.[9]

Under the Attlee government

The Attlee government came to power promising to restructure British economic and social life towards democratic socialism. It emphasised state ownership of industry as a necessary condition for efficiency, planning as vital to the maintenance of full employment and social welfare reform to extend the security of its citizens (Brooke 1992: 247–68; Tomlinson 1997b: 16–22). Moreover, it inherited from the wartime coalition not only tripartism but also much closer state control of industry, especially in the power and transport sectors; a workable system of short-term planning based upon the massive power of the state as purchaser and controls over the allocation, and to some extent the prices, of labour and materials; and wartime social welfare initiatives that were both national in scope and centrally planned.[10] However, the structures and practices of longer-term economic planning, which had thoroughly coloured the prewar debates on economic policy of the centre-left of British politics, were allowed to decline rapidly in the first months of the first Attlee government (Alford *et al.* 1992: 1–25; Brooke 1991; Durbin 1985: 160–95). This is not to suggest that "the state" was monolithic. There were differences within the cabinet, between ministers and civil servants and between the government and its more radical backbenchers on the details of policy and, in the early postwar years, considerable uncertainty as to the best administrative arrangements through which to drive economic "planning".[11]

These tensions were contained relatively easily; on the whole, the Attlee government handled Westminster and Whitehall with success, but it found producer politics much more difficult.

The trade unions emerged from war with their status greatly enhanced by their role in wartime economic policy-making and the ability of shopfloor radicals to present themselves as the voice of total commitment to the war effort.[12] Like government ministers, union leaders (and their radical critics) looked forward to full employment policies, a big programme of nationalisation and the creation of a peacetime planned economy in which trade unionists would have a decisive voice (Booth 1996: 46–8; Campbell *et al.* 1999b: 81–5; Panitch 1976: 7–14; Jones 1987: 15–36). The unions had played their part in delivering wage moderation in the face of extremely tight labour markets during wartime and many leading union leaders wanted to remain close to the centre of policy-making, and hinted at important concessions, notably on defensive workshop customs and practices.[13] On the other hand, TUC leaders wanted the state's involvement in collective bargaining to end with the defeat of Japan. Ministers were divided, but their decisions were coloured by growing signs that controls over the movement of labour had already begun to break down with the defeat of Germany. The government decided to retain some controls, which tended to be tightened during economic and financial crises, but the Attlee government's system of "manpower budgeting" was largely ineffective and attempts to develop wage planning as an alternative method of influencing the distribution of labour also foundered in the face of cabinet splits, official scepticism and the sheer impracticability of the scheme (Cairncross 1987: 385–99; Tomlinson 1997b: 174–84). With minimal direct control over labour allocations and continuing evidence of excess demand, the government had little option in managing the labour market but to rely upon exhortation, education and pleas for collective responsibility.[14]

There were similar problems in government relations with industry. The government's programme of nationalisation made private industry defensive and suspicious and ministers had few alternative plans to place before the private sector to address these concerns.[15] Given the national need for huge increases in output and exports, the government was extremely careful not to antagonise private industry. Business quickly found that it could dig in its heels against proposals by government to erode the right to manage and a number of relatively sensible, moderate policies were neutered. The Development Councils, a tripartite forum to modernise the old consumer goods industries with reasonable expectations in export markets (textiles, pottery and the like) foundered (Rogow and Shore 1955: 76–96; Henderson 1952: 460–2). Indeed, Dupree (1992: 158) notes of the biggest Development Council: "The experience of the cotton industry demonstrates that the Labour governments were able to work with a major, long-established industry once they gave up hopes of coercing it". As with labour policy, the government had to rely on exhortation and education.

Even controls over investment, which interwar radicals had seen as a potentially very effective tool of industrial control and modernisation, came too little. In practice, the control of investment was hampered by the shortages of materials and the Chancellor of the Exchequer's determination to encourage investment to avert another postwar deflationary slump, after the pattern of 1920–2 (Howson 1993: 92–3, 122). The government's influence over investment decisions was limited and after the 1947 dollar crisis everything was geared to short-run support for the balance of payments (Chick 1992: 74–5; 1998: 1–6; Cairncross 1987: 446–8, 454–62; Chester 1952b). In this context it made sense for firms to patch existing capital equipment and order machinery that could be supplied most quickly rather than focus on long-run modernisation schemes (Chick 1998).

In short, the Attlee governments faced immense postwar economic and industrial problems. The balance of payments was dire and industry had to be reconverted to peace and de-controlled as circumstances permitted. Government curbed domestic demand, rewarded exporters with allocations of scarce resources, and controlled imports, especially from the dollar area, as far as was politically and economically practical (Tomlinson 1997b: 23–67). It also borrowed heavily from the USA and then took its share of Marshall Aid, which made Britain's financial diplomacy with the USA a key element in recovery (Balogh 1952). Under intense scrutiny from the US Congress, the Attlee government had to ensure that competitiveness and efficiency were at the forefront of domestic politics. There were two important dimensions to this. Government was determined to ensure that excess demand for labour did not spill easily into wage and price inflation. Price controls were maintained well into the postwar period (Cairncross 1987: 335–6, 405–6) and pressure was put on (intensely loyal) trade union leaders to limit the wage demands from their members (Tomlinson 1991a; Hyman 1993; Howell 1999: 121–7; Panitch 1976: 20–9).

Ministers also stepped up pressure on both sides of industry to implement productivity improvements. Tomlinson (1994b) has noted that throughout the 1940s and 1950s, "productivity" invariably meant output per *worker* in the *industrial* sector, a definition that owed much to the peculiar circumstances of the labour-constrained economy after the war. This definition was underwritten in 1948 with the formation of the AACP, but this conception of productivity placed labour and the unions on the defensive. The TUC leadership was in no real mood to object. It constantly referred to the need for more investment (Booth 1996: 53) but its position was summed up in General Secretary Vincent Tewson's speech to a conference on productivity in late 1948 "Now, in the view of the General Council, there are three vital facts which dominate the [current economic] situation. First, if we have to pay our way, we must produce more. Secondly, we have no reserves of manpower which we can use for the production of more goods and, thirdly, cost is increasingly becoming an important factor in determining our ability to sell the goods which we produce" (TUC 1948a: 3). The General Council went much further, supporting a wide range of initiatives including prominent US labour management techniques such as work study.[16] Loyalty to the wider labour movement left the TUC with no alternative: "The living standards of *our* members, the social welfare policy of *our* government and the emergence from *our* present difficulties are at stake" (TUC 1948b: 10).

On the other hand, shopfloor radicals moved in the opposite direction. Having campaigned ferociously for higher production from 1941 until "the international earthquake of the Cold War" (Hinton 1994), they changed tack in 1948 and began to lead the opposition to the TUC's wage and productivity policies (Stevens 1999: 169). The TUC's rejection of continued wage restraint in June 1950 owed much to the ability of the shopfloor radicals to fan popular discontent as government tried to hold back wages when prices and profits were rising.[17] Like their American counterparts, British labour leaders intensified their anti-Communism, both from Congress House and within individual unions.[18] Ministers turned the screw still further by threatening statutory wage controls if the unions did not toe the line on wage restraint (Booth 1996: 54–61).

Ministers had much less leverage over the employers, who began to improve their own tarnished political profile after 1945 (Melling 1996: 9–16). The continuing shortages and the need for production, especially of exports, at all costs gave business a powerful argument with which to resist unwanted state intervention in industrial affairs during the later 1940s. In addition to obstructing the modernisation of the old, export-oriented consumer industries (see above) they stymied a range of sensible, moderate reforms in the later 1940s (Tiratsoo and Tomlinson 1993: 64–152). It is scarcely surprising that Labour ministers' principal policy weapon, constant encouragement and exhortation, fell on increasingly deaf ears.

Under the Conservatives

The election of the Conservative government in 1951 brought only limited changes to industrial politics. The new government relaxed the controls that remained from its predecessor, once the Korean emergency had passed, rhetorically setting industry free (Henderson 1962: 327–31; Kelly 2002: 95–110). Churchill's rather colourful past in dealings with trade unions encouraged him to appoint as Minister of Labour the relatively unknown Sir Walter Monckton, a man with no real political experience but a real talent for conciliation. Monckton was told to avoid strikes and his colleague, Geoffrey Lloyd, the Minister of Fuel and Power, was under orders to do nothing to antagonise the miners (Seldon 1981: 196, 246). To some extent this hands-off policy regime worked, and the economy performed well, with low, relatively stable inflation, low unemployment and a balance of payments on current account that was generally in surplus.[19] The conciliatory policy of Churchill and Monckton outlasted the former's resignation in 1955, but not by much. Ministers became increasingly aware of both the faster economic growth in continental Europe and the difficulties in restoring sterling as a currency for international trade and reserves. Ministers slowly assembled a Conservative ideology of decline in which the negative role of trade unions has had an especially prominent position (Tomlinson 2001: 51–8).

Treasury officials had already begun to identify Britain's comparatively low investment rate as a likely culprit for slow growth.[20] However, higher investment invariably meant a tighter labour market, rising inflation and pressure on sterling. Thus, the Chancellor of the Exchequer, R.A. Butler, devised an expansionist policy with incentives for investment and the promise of doubling incomes in the next 20 years in return for wage restraint and faster modernisation of work practices.[21] The trade unions agreed with much of this analysis, but at this stage they declined to enter a compact for faster growth.[22] As noted in Chapter 1, Butler's (pre-election) expansion overcooked amid a balance of payments crisis, leap-frogging wage claims and rising levels of unofficial strikes. Its electoral popularity falling, the cabinet saw an attack on the unions as a route to political recovery.

The Conservative Research Department pressed for legislation against unofficial strikes but cabinet rejected a British version of the US Taft-Hartley legislation.[23] Macmillan, the new Chancellor of the Exchequer, published a much-delayed white paper, which outlined the responsibilities of price-setters under continuing full employment and hinted that full employment might have to be abandoned in the quest for price stability and export competitiveness.[24] The cabinet also began a tough policy on public sector pay to give a lead to private employers.[25] The aim was a short term "price plateau" in the public sector leading to a long-term commitment to wage restraint across the whole economy.[26] There are also good grounds for believing that Macmillan led government into a secret bargain with the Engineering Employers' Federation (EEF) to co-ordinate resistance to union pay demands.[27] The EEF stood firm and had effective government support until ministers took fright in the face of a post-Suez sterling crisis. After this Cabinet then settled the outstanding public sector pay claims at levels that left the EEF with no choice but to back down (Wigham 1973: 180–2; Tolliday 1985: 123–31; Clegg and Adams 1957: 48–156). There were also longer-term problems for the authority of employers in engineering that will be discussed in Chapter 4. Following this failure of behind the scenes manipulation, the government used unemployment as a regulator to curb wage rises, with very rapid increases in 1957–9 and again in 1961–3 (Booth 2000). Ministers still hectored both sides of industry on the need for wage and price restraint and portrayed inflation as a result of union greed and aggression, but against a background of rising unpopularity.[28]

These measures on competitiveness were designed to nudge industry towards faster productivity growth. The turn towards Europe from the sterling area had similar goals; a number of key economic ministers saw Britain's effort to join the EEC as an opportunity to "shake up" British industry in a dynamic, competitive market (Tiratsoo and Tomlinson 1998b: 109–16). The weakening and then abolition of resale price maintenance was also designed to intensify competition and boost growth (Mercer 1995: 149–69). More directly, ministers modernised and expanded technical and higher education and encouraged improvement of management training (Tiratsoo and Tomlinson 1998b: 66–82, 126–40). However, in contrast to the Attlee government, the Conservatives followed Eisenhower and developed a politics of consumption, affluence and choice, most obviously encapsulated in Macmillan's (apocryphal) slogan, "You've never had it so good!" (Sampson 1967: 155–67; Horne 1989: 64–5; Ramsden 1977: 450, 455).

The limitations of this approach were however becoming very obvious in the early 1960s, when the use of unemployment to discipline the labour market left the government deeply unpopular. Tiratsoo and Tomlinson (1998b: 32) cite a Conservative Research Department memorandum of 1961 that accepted the limitations of the "competition plus" politics of production: "We have virtually exhausted the neo-liberal seam in economic policy. The existing armoury of economic weapons ... is admittedly deficient ... Yet ... we have done nothing visibly to examine the problems and search for new ones". Macmillan's government's emphasis on competition to sharpen industrial performance had failed, and the rhetoric of affluence and choice left a bitter taste when in July 1961 a "wage freeze" and a battery of tax rises, expenditure cuts and credit restrictions were imposed to curb a second blatant pre-election expansion (for the 1959 general election). Government opinion ratings tumbled (Whybrow 1989: 63) and, to sweeten the pill, Macmillan and his Chancellor, Selwyn Lloyd, looked to forge a partnership between government, employers and unions to devise policies for faster growth while working out the details for a long-term incomes policy (Blackaby 1978b: 17–22; Thorpe 1989: 326–30; Horne 1989: 249–50; Lamb 1995: 77–86).

Ringe and Rollings (2000) have shown that the parties to these discussions on wage restraint and faster growth had different goals and expectations. Within Whitehall, the Treasury wanted to strengthen the economy in order to make its task of managing public expenditure less difficult. Treasury officials hoped to use the new-found interest in growth almost as a mask to push through a range of measures that might improve competitiveness and efficiency in the longer run. However, they interpreted strengthening the economy in "Paishite" terms, with a higher average margin of unemployment and concentrating on the external rather than the domestic agenda.[29] Among leaders of large-scale industry, there was immense frustration that stop-go was damaging their ability to plan for the medium term. They displayed their anger publicly at the November 1960 conference of the Federation of British Industries, organised on the theme of "The Next Five Years" (Leruez 1975: 85–7; Brittan 1971: 233–5, 238–45; Blank 1973: 152–74). Following the conference, the FBI established a committee to examine the suggestion that: "Government and industry might see if it might be possible to agree on an assessment of expectations and intentions to be placed before the country as a framework for economic effort during the next five years. If, for example, the national aim was to achieve an annual growth rate of 3% ... the necessary implications and consequences could be assessed and the practical choices facing industry and Government determined".[30] This was very much the French system of indicative planning and the FBI's document alluded to the French belief that, by bringing business and government together, obstacles to growth might be identified and bottlenecks broken. The unions, on the other hand, were indignant about the wage freeze and the rapidly rising unemployment after Selwyn Lloyd's July measures. The TUC was, however, now led by George Woodcock, an intellectually able man who recognised the need for union reform, modernisation and wage restraint in the era of full employment and creeping inflation.[31] The TUC's Economic Committee had been pressing for a government commitment to planning for faster growth for some time before Lloyd's emergency measures but remained opposed to any commitments to wage moderation.[32] Many TUC leaders also knew that faster growth implied a policy for incomes.[33] From the time of Selwyn Lloyd's first request to the TUC to join the discussions, they tried to balance the dangers of entering into the policy-making process (primarily the expectation that they would have to talk about wages) against the dangers of remaining outside (above all, that wage restraint would be imposed on them).[34] They were assured that the link between pay and productivity was accepted, and faster growth would enable pay to rise more rapidly.[35] Woodcock finally prevailed and the TUC joined what became the National Economic Development Council in January 1962.[36]

NEDC restored the idea of a *national*, tripartite politics of productivity and fostered the growing tendency to link improvements in pay to improvements in productivity. A key personality in this development of "productivity bargaining" was Allan Flanders, an early and convinced advocate of a permanent state incomes policy and, like Woodcock, a supporter of modernising industrial relations to give workers a less oppositional, more co-operative role in the working of industry (Kelly 1999). His study (Flanders 1964) of the pioneering productivity agreements at Esso's Fawley refinery quickly became a classic in British industrial relations. Unfortunately, neither the NEDC nor the Fawley agreements delivered, but tripartism and productivity bargaining remained at the centre of Britain's politics of productivity until the advent of Thatcherism.[37]

Productivity politics and reform by consensus and conflict, 1964–79

Labour came to power in 1964 with a distinctive, and risky, programme to improve the underlying rate of productivity growth. At the core were two elements. The government would try to withstand external pressure without either devaluation or the sort of disinflationary "stop" in macroeconomic policy that had characterised Conservative policy. At the same time, it would pursue medium-term reforms in industrial relations and industrial structure that had preoccupied the NEDC, but in a more forceful manner (Beckerman 1972). Much rested on the ability of ministers to persuade both sides of industry to agree quickly on structural reforms to pay bargaining. Jittery financial markets left ministers needing quick and binding commitments from both employers and unions.[38]

George Brown, the minister in charge of the medium-term strategy, secured from both sides of industry a "Joint Statement of Intent on Productivity, Prices and Incomes" in December 1964 (text in TUC 1965). It established that the government's "economic objective is to achieve and maintain a rapid increase in output and real incomes combined with full employment. Their social objective is to ensure that the benefits of faster growth are distributed in a way that satisfies the claims of social need and justice". Both employers and trade unions recognised the need to "raise productivity throughout industry and commerce, to keep increases in line with increases in real national output and to maintain a stable general price level". The joint statement also promised the creation of a body to investigate proposals to increase wages, salaries or other money incomes in excess of a target to be agreed with both sides of industry. The unions bargained resolutely over the details of the new policy but finally committed at the end of April 1965, albeit with expectations that there would be sufficient scope for many "special cases" to be made to exceed the target rate of growth of incomes.[39] "Productivity bargaining" was seen by the unions, and was to some extent encouraged by the government's National Board for Prices and Incomes (NBPI), as the best method of making a special case for pay increases above the norm, but increasingly doubts were raised about the employers' ability to monitor and enforce these deals. The reports of the NBPI (1969a: 21) were increasingly critical of management: "Our general experience is that the crucial factor in raising productivity is almost always the quality of management and management control". Among the major criticisms were: the weakness of management information systems, the poor quality of costing techniques and budgetary controls, and the poor control of labour costs (a criticism that was directed regularly towards the retail banks, as will be seen in Chapter 7).

However, it was the extent of opposition within organised labour to the prices and incomes policy that attracted most attention. The TUC's endorsement of prices and incomes policy at the outset was grudging and ebbed away as government progressively tightened the policy to calm nerves in the currency markets.[40] Thus, the government stiffened the policy incrementally until it introduced a statutory six-month wage freeze in July 1966 and followed it with a year of "severe restraint", both of which were imposed on the unions with the threat of worse to come if they did not fall into line.[41] The Prime Minister became increasingly convinced that the practices and strategies of British trade unions were damaging the economy, citing restrictive practices, restrictions on training and apprenticeship and union opposition to productivity improvements.[42] This was a cathartic period for British trade unionism; McIlroy and Campbell (1999) have identified an expansion and deepening of workplace organisation, especially in manufacturing, subtle shifts in the politics of the TUC's General Council with limited gains for the left but a resilient centre right loyalism and radicalisation of the membership over wages. The signs of rank and file discontent were obvious in the surge of plant-level bargaining, the flattening of pay differentials and the upward trend in the number and intensity of strikes (Durcan *et al.* 1983: 132–71, 400–24; Cronin 1979: 142–6).

These disturbances merely confirmed to governments that reform of trade unions and the systems of industrial relations was long overdue. In part there were continuities with the strategies of 1945–64, especially in the resort to tripartism to bring union leaders into policy-making. The Heath government's attempts to involve union leaders in dialogue after 1972 and the post-1974 Wilson-Callaghan Social Contract are clearly of this type. There were two new features of policy after 1964. The first is the willingness to use legislation to re-shape the role of unions in industry. Again this was shared by both main parties, being characteristic of both the Wilson government's programme set out in *In Place of Strife* and the Heath government's Industrial Relations Act of 1971. The other new feature was the more intense and extended effort to re-shape the structures of British industrial relations by education, influence and persuasion. The combined impact of all these initiatives was to create a more viable and lasting politics of productivity in the British workplace.

The Royal Commission on Trade Unions and Employers' Associations was established in the early months of the Labour government and seems to have been conceived as a genuine attempt to investigate the problems emerging in British industrial relations rather than a quick political fix.[43] Indeed the royal commission took three years to produce its report, and even then was divided.[44] The most frequently-quoted passages of the report pointed to structural conflicts within British pay bargaining, identifying two systems of industrial relations. One was the formal system embodied in the official institutions of national agreements between employers associations and national trade unions. The other was the informal system created by the actual behaviour of trade unions and employers' associations, of managers, shop stewards and workers (Donovan 1968: 36).

> The formal and informal systems are in conflict. The informal system undermines the regulative effect of industry-wide agreements. The gap between industry-wide agreements and actual earnings [wage drift] continues to grow. Procedure agreements fail to cope adequately with disputes arising within factories. Nevertheless the assumptions of the formal system still exert a powerful influence over men's minds and prevent the informal system from developing into an effective and orderly method of regulation.

This was less an assessment of the state of Britain's industrial relations in general than an insight into the problems of the engineering industry. It had little relevance for workers in the public sector, the continuous flow industries or much of the service sector. But the main recommendations did have wider resonance and were intended to create less confusing structures. The report proposed that bargaining be formalised at the plant or company level to force employers to take responsibility for formulating personnel policies. The commission looked to comprehensive and authoritative agreements within the firm, including the establishment of effective negotiating and disputes procedures, written agreements, and new wage systems and structures (Donovan 1968: 41–5). Many have argued that the reforms proposed by the Donovan Commission were designed to make incomes policy more successful but they were certainly geared to make productivity bargaining easier and more widespread. Donovan's proposals to make management more aware, better informed and in greater control of personnel policies echoed the criticisms of British management from the NBPI. In this, Donovan advocated changes that the more progressive British employers had already begun to introduce (Gospel 1992: 140). The report emphasised the mutual confidence of managers and shop stewards where plant-level bargaining was institutionalised and implied that if bargaining were formalised at this level managers would have to address efficiency and productivity issues (McCarthy and Parker 1968: Table 12; Donovan 1968:28, 42–3; see also Brown 1973). The Donovan analysis underpinned a major expansion of plant-level bargaining; the number of shop stewards almost trebled between 1961 and 1978 (c. 90,000 in the early 1960s, 175,000 in 1968 and 250,000 by 1978) and number of full-time shop stewards rose five-fold between 1968 and 1980 (Terry 1983: 67–71). At the same time, managements introduced a wide range of procedures for negotiations, handling grievances, consultation, discipline and dismissal and for health and safety, while work study and job evaluation techniques spread very rapidly (Purcell and Sisson 1983: 103–6; Gospel 1992: 140–6). Thus, bargaining over pay and effort changed quite dramatically between the mid-1960s and early 1980s, giving the UK a soundly based system of relating pay and productivity and simultaneously providing a much more solid framework for negotiating over new technology. These changes were, however, scarcely noted outside industry as popular attention became fixated with control of trade unions.

It will be recalled that in the mid-1950s the Conservatives briefly considered legislation to curb the right to strike (a "British Taft-Hartley"). That challenge encountered opposition from employers, unions and the Ministry of Labour's resolve to preserve voluntary bargaining. However, the pressure to bring the law into industrial relations continued in the emerging debate on the "decline of Britain". Both Shanks (1961) and Shonfield (1958) produced highly influential best-sellers on endemic British economic weaknesses that focused on the restrictions imposed by "craftist" unions led by unrepresentative shopfloor militants (Tomlinson 2001: 22–3; Taylor 1993: 116–18). Eric Wigham (1961), labour editor of *The Times*, and a supporter of trade unionism, floated the idea of legal curbs on the right to strike and legal protection only for those unions that operated openly democratic processes. The issue of a legal framework for industrial relations was considered in depth by the Donovan Commission but its (majority) recommendation for piecemeal change was widely regarded as pusillanimous, not least by the Conservative press. This, in part, was the stimulus to Labour's attempt to use the law to reform trade unions and collective bargaining.

In 1968 the Prime Minister appointed a new minister, Barbara Castle, renamed the Ministry of Labour as the Department of Employment and Productivity and encouraged her to push beyond the Donovan prescriptions and make trade union behaviour more responsive to the national economic need, a position that the Ministry of Labour (1965: 2) had already reached in its submission to Donovan.

However, as is well-known, Castle's proposals in the white paper, *In Place of Strife* (DEP 1969), for relatively supportive reform of labour law, found a bleak rejection from the trade unions, albeit after a passive initial reaction (see Panitch 1976: 165–203; Wrigley 1997: 65–77; Taylor 2000: 150–5; Pimlott 1992: 527–46; Castle 1974: 84–6, 574–5). The internal splits and humiliating retreats that the Wilson government had to make to achieve any sort of compromise with the TUC led the Conservatives to put union reform at the centre of their programme. Their initial ideas were available before the publication of the Donovan report (Conservative Party 1968) and, on taking office, the Industrial Relations Bill headed the government's first legislative programme.[45] It was both libertarian (outlawing the closed shop and creating the right not to join a union) and corporatist in tone (by creating a strong and independent Registrar of Trade Unions to ensure that union rules were just and democratic with the goal of giving union leaders stronger control of their members); it had strong pro-union measures (legal provisions to ensure that employers recognised unions and the right to legal action for unfair dismissal, *inter alia*) and other provisions that unions would find objectionable, notably on the right to strike (Taylor 1997: 164–9). The bill moved quickly through its Parliamentary stages but against a backdrop of worsening industrial unrest as inflation accelerated. The rapid progress of a bill that many trade unionists instinctively saw as vindictive class legislation exacerbated the deteriorating climate of industrial relations and allowed the whole union movement to unite behind extra-Parliamentary action to neuter the Act. United working class opposition forced the Heath government and its Labour successors into tripartite crisis avoidance to enable voluntary pay bargaining cope with the roller-coaster movements in prices during the mid-1970s.

This demonstration of organised labour's ability to resist the modernising force of Labour and Conservative governments encouraged a massive growth in the literature on responsibility of trade unions for economic and industrial under-performance. It ranged from the academic to the popular and the downright polemical but all implied, often on the basis of dubious evidence, that the unions were culpable for slow productivity growth and inflationary pressures.[46] However, when the Thatcher onslaught on trade union powers brought precious little change in the performance of the British labour market (Blanchflower and Freeman 1994) a major reassessment was necessary. Both unions and managers had shown extraordinary flexibility in devising and operating new bargaining structures and embracing new bargaining agenda. If, as has been argued elsewhere (Booth 2003), the extent of the "failure" of British manufacturing during the long boom has been greatly exaggerated, these signs of flexibility and responsible bargaining deserve more attention and credit than they have hitherto received.

Conclusion

Despite the differences between the decentralised American system of bargaining and the pattern of increasing, but reluctant and frustrated, state involvement in the UK, there was one important common principle. The core proposition on both sides of the Atlantic was that management insisted on its sole right to decide the technical conditions of production. This was established quickly, if not always painlessly or totally, in the USA in company-level bargaining and was underwritten by the contractual requirements of national unions to control their members. It would be very wrong to imply that US managers enjoyed *carte blanche* to select technologies, decide work loads and vary work speeds; in the case study chapters there is ample evidence to the contrary.[47] But the focus of US bargaining was on pay and supplementary welfare benefits, over the distribution of profit, even if this meant accelerating the introduction of labour-displacing technologies. The possibilities for transplanting this approach to the UK were always remote. British workers did not find it easy to identify a common interest with their employers, even when managers tried hard to build worker commitment (Chapter 8); "craftist" sentiments remained strong, as so many critics of British trade unionism pointed out. On the other hand, many employers, particularly in private sector manufacturing, showed little real interest in developing a shared high-wage/high-productivity vision. Some firms created internal labour markets, social welfare schemes and even profit sharing, but they were the exception rather than the rule and tended to be concentrated on white collar rather than manual workers (Gospel 1992: 148–67). But for the majority, there was always the external labour market and the perception of labour as a variable cost, rather than an asset to be developed. Thus, for many British managers technical choices were made while fire-fighting on other fronts of the industrial relations system.

It took a long time for postwar governments to realise that they would have to intervene to force managers to negotiate more effectively with their workers over productivity. British policy-makers were aware of how these issues were tackled in the USA, as the backwoods Conservative calls for a "British Taft-Hartley" illustrate. Equally, the Oxford school's advocacy of a Scandinavian-style centralised incomes policy was loud and clear from 1950 onwards (Kelly 1999: 205–6). Neither alternative was, however, politically attractive. Conservative politicians were acutely aware of the political costs of pursuing what would be construed as class legislation. The Attlee government's difficulties made Labour politicians conscious of the enormous problems in creating a "national interest" on incomes, effort and technical progress in industry. It is scarcely surprising that British governments should fall back on a middle way of free collective bargaining plus "crisis concertation", which had been effective during wartime.[48] Indeed, "crisis concertation" was well-suited to the shape and scale of the problems faced by the British economy during the long boom. It is too little realised that Britain's industrial problem was neither galloping inflation, nor was it deteriorating price competitiveness; on both measures the British economy performed reasonably well during the long postwar boom.[49] The problem for policy-makers was the tendency of the foreign exchange market to suffer recurrent bouts of concern about the value of sterling, as the previous chapter made clear. British incomes policy was, therefore, primarily concerned with managing foreign confidence in sterling. Unfortunately, as confidence became more fragile in the 1960s, crisis concertation worked less effectively and governments were forced into more direct intervention, albeit through the establishment of a royal commission. The Donovan reforms pointed both to Continental centralised incomes policy, as might have been anticipated from the views of the Oxford school, and to decentralised plant bargaining (1968: 40–6, 52–3). In the event, decentralisation was a much more powerful force and laid the foundations for major increases in the number of workers covered by agreements in which pay was in some part dependent on productivity or performance, accompanied by a major replacement of rather loose rate-fixing by much more rigorous work study techniques (Sisson and Brown 1983: 141–3). Thus, the post-Donovan reforms slowly equipped Britain with a more effective, decentralised politics of productivity, but without the rigidities imposed by the contractualism of decentralisation in the USA. Paradoxically, these positive developments in the UK occurred as the US system began to run out of steam. With large parts of US manufacturing coming under increasing pressure from Japanese and European imports and domestic markets for major consumer goods becoming saturated, US industry needed a more flexible and vigorous response than could be achieved under the cumbersome and bloated postwar system (see Katz 1984). The "annual improvement factor" and the COLA had initially provided stability when industrial relations were disturbed and continuity in bargaining thereafter, but by the early 1970s they simply imparted inflexibility when profound changes in product markets were evident. The search for new systems only really began, however, when the full force of Japanisation was appreciated, an issue to be considered in Chapter 8.

4
Automation in Engineering

Engineering has been the key manufacturing industry of the mid-twentieth century. It is conventionally divided into vehicles, mechanical engineering (such as the making of machine tools, civil engineering plant), electrical and electronic engineering and instrument-making. There are, however, different national conventions about where these divisions fall, making international comparison very difficult (Saunders 1978: 11–13). Methods of production are extremely varied, and are conventionally divided into "mass" and "flexible" production, though each can be sub-divided and the boundaries between them are uncertain.[1] Some parts of engineering were profoundly changed by automation in the 1950s, with the introduction of automatic transfer machines (ATMs) in "volume" branches and N/C machine tools in "specialty" production. From the early 1970s production engineers began to see the potential of N/C tools and "robotics" in volume production, though this change is frequently associated with "Japanisation" (Chapter 8 below).

Comparative performance of British and American engineering

Despite the difficulties associated with international comparisons, we have Broadberry's estimates of relative labour productivity in British and American engineering in Table 4.1. The data are patchy but show clearly that from 1950 until the later 1960s the average US engineering worker produced about three times as much as the UK counterpart. The engineering productivity gap was wider than for manufacturing as a whole, though it narrowed appreciably by the mid-1970s (Table 2.2). Before 1970, the better sectors include machine tools, agricultural machinery and shipbuilding (though its relative labour productivity deteriorated over the long boom). Cans and metal boxes were the worst case and vehicles the most enigmatic.[2] The motor industry was the largest branch of engineering, with almost 11 percent of industrial output and a higher share of industrial investment (Armstrong 1967).

British engineering has been accused of technological incompetence in the postwar years. Both Owen (1999: 172–207) and Broadberry (1997a: 316–45) have suggested that disaster awaited those British engineering firms that attempted to apply "Fordist" mass production methods, whilst those companies producing customised products for niche markets prospered in relative terms. Tiratsoo (1995; 1999) and collaborators (Tiratsoo and Gourvish 1996; Tiratsoo and Tomlinson 1997; 1998a) have laid the blame for these problems at the door of managers, arguing that they undervalued technical competence and professional training. By contrast, Broadberry and Crafts have claimed

Table 4.1   US/UK comparative labour productivity in engineering, 1929/30 to 1967/68
(UK = 100 in each year)

	1929/30	1935/37	1947/48	1950	1967/68
Mechanical engineering	292	268			
Agricultural machinery (exc. tractors)				429	
Agricultural machinery (incl. tractors)					146
Machine tools				221	162
Electrical machinery				239	255
Radio/electronic components					193
Electronic tubes				355	
Broadcast receiving equipment					288
Radios		347	336	400	
Household appliances				412	239
Electric lamps	446	543		356	
Shipbuilding	154			111	185
Motor vehicles			365	466	438
Motor cars	725	294	284		
Motorcycles	135				
Bicycles	176		180		
Aircraft	315				381
Railway rolling stock	173				
Cans and metal boxes		577	496	561	466
Engineering	333	289		337	294
All manufacturing	263	218		273	276

Source: Broadberry 1997a: Table A2.1.

that the weak competitive environment of pre-Thatcherite economic policy allowed restrictive practices by management and labour to flourish (Broadberry 1997a; Broadberry and Crafts 1996; 2001). Alternatively, the unions have been seen as a substantial constraint on faster productivity growth, especially in the largest factories (Davies and Caves 1987; Prais 1981: 59–83; Pratten 1976; CPRS 1975). This analysis has been echoed in the ethnographic studies of British engineering labour, which has emphasised the power of the workgroup, its "craftist" culture and its power to erode managerial control (Lupton 1963; Beynon 1973; Thornett 1998). However, these positions have been questioned (see, for example, Nichols 1986; Booth 2003) and it has been argued that, in general, the perceptions of failure have been exaggerated and distorted (Supple 1994; Tomlinson 1996).

These debates on the postwar performance of British engineering can be illuminated by automation. The two automation technologies most obviously associated with engineering were, as noted above, ATMs and N/C machine tools. Both technologies were sophisticated, demanding and probed managerial expertise, with ATMs of most significance to the volume producers and "Fordist" methods. N/C tools had a more restricted use, at least before 1970, but were linked with attempts by US managers to wrest control of production from highly skilled machinists, especially in defence-related industries. Together, these two automation techniques can cast light on the recurrent criticisms of British engineering.

Automatic transfer machines in the automobile industry

The production process in engineering is dominated by the movement of parts and materials around the factory. Tiratsoo (2003: 52) notes that in any manufacturing process approximately 90 percent of the total time taken is spent in moving and handling materials in temporary storage; for each ton of finished product, almost 50 tons of materials are handled. He argues that, although the materials handling branch of engineering grew rapidly after 1945, British firms were slow to substitute cheap mechanical devices for labour in this area. The ATM was at the expensive, ultra-sophisticated end of materials handling because it combined handling, positioning and cutting devices in a single machine, but even ATMs came in different shapes and sizes. Much automation publicity in the 1950s focused on huge, multi-station ATMs. More common, however, were much smaller, rotary machines that performed three or four operations on a much less complex part (Griffith 1955; Bezier 1955).

As noted briefly in Chapter 2, the ATM with automatic work transfer and self-acting clamping mechanisms was pioneered by Morris Motors engines branch in 1923, but proved unreliable and was abandoned (Woollard 1956: 32–3). In the mid-1930s US automobile producers linked functionally specialised machine tools by transfer mechanisms that automatically moved cylinder blocks from one operation to the next and were controlled by cams, timers and limit switches (Bright 1958: 60–1). The industrial unrest of the later 1930s and then the shift to military production during wartime stifled further development but interest in ATMs revived in the Ford Motor Company's postwar modernisation plans for the River Rouge plant (Nevins and Hill 1962: 324–88; Hounshell 1995: 54–8). The principal architects of Ford's automation were Charles H. Patterson, head of motor production at the River Rouge, and Delmer S. Harder, vice-president for manufacturing in FMC, one of the executives brought from General Motors by Henry Ford II and his lieutenant, Ernest Breech. Harder's group began work on introducing automatic machinery into the machining of valves, pistons, coils, wheels, frames and rear axles, initially at River Rouge, which was already regarded as cramped and inadequate (Hounshell 1995: 64). In 1949, however, work began on the first factories designed for extensive use of automation; the Buffalo Stamping Plant, which made sheet metal parts such as doors and floors, and the new Cleveland engine plant and foundry. The whole enterprise was in part an attempt to move production away from the skilled, militant workers at the core River Rouge plant, and in part an effort to become more vertically integrated and self-sufficient (Hounshell 1995: 57–60).

"Detroit automation" involved massive ATMs and, as noted in Chapter 1, in its fiftieth anniversary celebrations, FMC made much of these machines at the Cleveland engine plant.[3] However, the Buffalo stamping plant should not be forgotten. Much of the early work on automation within FMC was concerned with loading and unloading stamping presses and when the new Buffalo plant opened it contained "hundreds of automation devices for loading and removing work from the huge presses and machinery to carry work pieces from one press operation to the next" (Hounshell 1995: 63). The new methods helped to speed work flows, squeeze labour costs and almost eliminate accidents to press operators (Woollard 1956: 43–5; Graves 1955: 32–5; Davis 1955: 54–5).

The intended scale of production and capital costs were huge by any standards. The initial budget for the Buffalo stamping plant was $35 million, with a further $80 million for Cleveland (including a new foundry) but actual tooling costs alone far dwarfed this amount. The annual production target of Cleveland was 400,000 engines per annum (which in 1951–2 was roughly equivalent to total UK output) and was designed to match Chevrolet's volume (Bright 1958: 59). The FMC philosophy was standardised production on specialised equipment produced by machine tool makers to Ford specifications. However, FMC's giant ATMs, and especially the much-publicised cylinder block line, had weaknesses. First, they were very expensive, costing 25 percent more than the conventional machine tools they replaced. Second, they experienced significant teething problems and the system was fully "de-bugged" only after a couple of years. Third, Ford engineers learned that they could not achieve production surges and productivity gains in their automated plant as they could elsewhere in their operations. A cylinder block line could produce 140 units an hour at 80 percent efficiency, but if the company introduced a new model and demand increased rapidly by an estimated 30 percent, it would be impossible to produce 182 units per hour on that equipment; new production lines would have to be laid down (Davis 1955; Bright 1958: 63–4; Hounshell 1995: 76–7). These problems were well-known in US auto engineering circles. Bright, whose study was based on interviews with senior Ford managers, including Harder, reported (1958: 60) that, during 1950–2, "Ford engineers were on the defensive in technical society meetings and informal get-togethers with other engineers in the automotive industry over some of the mechanisation innovations. ...[N]egative opinions on automation were multiplied by the great difficulties encountered in [the Cleveland engine] plant, and rumours further exaggerated those difficulties". Ford's competitors exploited these rigidities in the "horsepower race" that involved frequent changes in engine design causing Ford to scrap some machinery prematurely. Ford was forced to look to Europe and the flexible automation systems developed in France and the UK and which were well-known to FMC's production engineers (Davis 1955: 66).

Steps towards a European flexible automation had begun in Vichy France with a proposal from the motor industry for fewer models, greater standardisation of parts and greater volumes of production (Vinen 1991: ch. 10; Kuisel 1981: chs. 5–6; Kipping 2000: 220–6). However, it was only in 1945–6 that Renault, with other European car firms, arranged a long-term programme of visits by managers and engineers to see US technology (Zeitlin 2000a: 34). Renault engineers saw the experimental transfer machines of the 1930s and heard FMC's plans for Buffalo and Cleveland. However, shortage of both foreign exchange and domestic machine tool capacity and its lower, more fragmented demand led Renault to develop their own ATMs, which were lighter, much more flexible and designed to be reconfigured to meet changes in product specification (Zeitlin 2000c: 23–4; Bezier 1954; 1955). The chief production engineer, Paul Bezier, outlined the philosophy and practice to an influential meeting of the Institute of Production Engineers at Margate in 1955. For the machining of smaller parts, such as bushes and unions, Renault developed rotary and drum transfer machines that fed and positioned the workpiece, undertook a complete machining cycle, and ejected the finished item. For more complex operations, such as the machining of a cylinder head or a camshaft, Renault unitised and standardised as far as possible. Component parts of ATMs were standardised but had in-built flexibility, notably in the platens which could hold workpieces of very different size. The parts for Renault's ATMs were made in bulk and were fully interchangeable between all modules, which gave major advantages for maintenance, repair and reconfiguration. They were designed with inspection points to check the effectiveness of the most fragile cutting tools, strict replacement schedules for all cutting tools and sophisticated lubricating systems, all of which made maintenance downtime as short as possible.

When Austin engineers planned to overhaul their production system after the war, they turned to Renault rather than to Detroit, in part because, like Renault, they knew that they faced tax regimes and driving conditions that discouraged large cars with powerful engines, and needed a lower volume, more flexible strategy than contemplated by FMC. Like Renault, Austin was relatively short of capital, though this did not prevent Leonard Lord, chairman and managing director of Austin (and a brilliant production engineer) from beginning an investment programme in 1945 to turn Longbridge into a world-class factory (Turner 1971a: 92).[4] However, Austin and its successor, BMC, remained relatively short of investment funds thanks to Lord's rapid expansion and the nature of the European car market, where small cars invariably yielded small profits (Williams *et al.* 1983: 219–25).

Lord needed to rationalise the design and expand output of those units that could be produced in large quantities. In part, this was achieved by the merger of Morris and Austin in 1952 and the introduction in 1954 of a rationalised range of engines (from nine to three, of which two – the "A" and "B" series formed the core of the model range), gearboxes (two types only) and axles. Although the merger between Austin and Morris is usually described as a "missed opportunity" the rationalisation of these major components allowed the new company to produce well above minimum efficient scale.[5] By 1954, the company was producing on the new ATM machining lines more than 400,000 engines per year to power redesigned new models planned before the merger. High-powered variants of the A and B series engines were also tweaked, at low cost, for sports cars that met the twin requirements of limited development costs and strong performance in niche markets (Whisler 1995: 90–8).

Capital constraints obviously shaped this expansion strategy. Like Renault engineers before them, BMC needed cheap, unitised ATMs with trouble-free operation (Maxcy and Silberston 1959: 92–3; Williams *et al.* 1994: 134–65; Woollard 1954: 142–51; Zeitlin 2000c: 19–28). As at Renault, Longbridge ATMs were capital-saving, in that they cost less than and were at least as flexible as the machines that they replaced (Griffith 1955: 110–11; 1961). Williams and colleagues (1983: 220) estimate that *total* investment by BMC between 1954/55 and 1961/62 (including the development costs of five new models and one pioneering front-wheel drive power train) was just under £80 million, approximately equal to what FMC spent on tooling for its new engine in 1950–3 (Hounshell 1995: 70–1). With that modest sum, BMC doubled its production capacity. Equally importantly, this investment was space-saving; cutting overhead costs per car. As in FMC, expansion of automated production meant duplicating assembly and machining lines. BMC's ATMs, like those of Renault, were designed to economise on downtime, with detailed inspection regimes, automatic fault recognition, low cutting speeds to conserve tools and other innovations to speed and cheapen repairs (Woollard 1956: 36–9; Maxcy and Silberston 1959: 60; Griffith 1955: 109). Whereas FMC was embarrassed by the cost of re-tooling to meet the "horsepower race", at Longbridge, changes in engine design were accommodated far more easily with comparatively little cost in re-tooling (Davis 1955: 53, 62; Woollard 1956: 38–41). The production engineering at Longbridge reached "world class", and extended to the delivery of parts to sub-assembly and thence final assembly lines in ways that produced tightly controlled production programmes and impressively quick product changes.[6] Finally, Austin worked with suppliers to deliver parts to its construction schedule – "just-in-time" production and low stock ratios long before their discovery by Japanese engineers.

The company was much less successful, however, in rationalising body designs. BMC managers believed that the British market was fragmented, with significant brand loyalty among customers and, to capture market share, they needed a range of body shells.[7] This strategy clearly implied low volumes in body pressings, a problem that was only partly addressed in the mid-1950s by the introduction of a common floor plan, the most costly body-shell pressing (Whisler 1999: 49). To achieve scale economies in this area, firms needed more than one million identical pressings per annum, far beyond the sales of any individual model in the UK (Maxcy and Silberston 1959: 85). Contemporary surveys of BMC's production engineering in the 1950s tend to contrast heavy use of transfer machines in engine production with lower levels of "automation" in the press shop (Graves 1955: 33–6). Similarly, the variety of body shells made investment in automated body-painting plant uneconomic but electrostatic painting booths were introduced for smaller, standardised parts, such as wheels. BMC exacerbated its problems by extending the product life of strong-selling models like the Morris Minor and saddling itself with an ever-expanding product range (Whisler 1999: 49–50).[8] From 1959, BMC tried to limit the number of body shell pressings through "badge engineering", minor differentiation in style and trim, but lacked the discipline to limit body variations for up-market saloons and rarely covered the additional tooling costs of these low-volume marques (Williams *et al.* 1994: 143; Whisler 1999: 50–2). In Europe, only Volkswagen achieved real scale economies in pressings.[9] When a delegation from the British motor industry visited Wolfsburg they were astonished at the scale and sophistication of the conveyor feeds and hydraulic handling on the Volkswagen press shop line.[10]

The competitiveness of the British market also handicapped BMC. It was rare for a single model to sell more than 250,000 units per year (Williams *et al.* 1983: 230–5; Foreman-Peck *et al.* 1995: 140–4). The small car segment (up to 1100cc to the mid-1960s and to 1300cc thereafter) accounted for about half of new British car registrations and was strongly competitive. BMC's best-sellers were in this class, but Ford did well with the Anglia/Popular and the early Cortina and Vauxhall's introduction of the Viva in 1963 added a further respectable competitor. The next biggest share of the market was for medium cars, of 1500–1600cc, which accounted for approximately one-fifth of total demand in the long boom. Initially, this segment was divided with BMC, Ford, Rootes and Vauxhall having good models, but in 1960s and 1970s was dominated by the Cortina, which became the best-selling car on the British market in the early 1970s. The loss of market share in this part of the market hit BMC's automation strategy, as weak demand for BMC's mid-range saloons created excess capacity on the

"B" series engine line, while strong sales of small cars created shortages of smaller engines.

Ford, on the other hand, coped with fragmentation and competition with greater success (Whisler 1999: 181–242; Tolliday 1991: 86–94). Unlike BMC, it did not have to defend market leadership and Dagenham could always call upon the resources of its American parent at a multitude of points in the design production and marketing processes (Foreman-Peck *et al.* 1995: 137–9; Tolliday 2000: 107–17). It adopted a conservative strategy, producing high volumes of a much more limited model range, using more capital-intensive methods and achieving substantial scale economies, while at the same time catering for the fragmented domestic market by a wide range of expensive optional extras (Tolliday 1991: 86–8; Zeitlin 2000c: 32–5; Rhys 1972: 30–4). Ford's stock of fixed capital overtook that of BMC in mid-1956, even though Ford had a significantly lower market share (Church 1994: 55).

Equally interesting was the automation strategy pursued by Vauxhall, the foundations of which had been laid in the late 1930s. Under loose control from General Motors Corporation (GMC), which had acquired Vauxhall in 1925, it was as much a maker of commercial vehicles as cars. From 1937, GMC engineers began interesting experiments with car design in both its European satellites, Vauxhall and Opel of Germany, designing and producing a unit-body car (where a single structure creates both the chassis and the body). Vauxhall built its own body plant, containing impressive and expensive arrays of metal stamping and welding equipment. After the war, Vauxhall was the first British producer to invest in ATMs, with 12 transfer stations in its cylinder block line, but its need to switch easily between car and truck engines limited investment in "automation" at this stage. Vauxhall continued to produce cars in relatively low volumes, but concentrated on a single body shell. Buoyant revenues from commercial vehicles funded this re-tooling of engine building and a further crash investment programme between 1956 and 1959, when Vauxhall extended automation in both engine production and automatic handling in the body plant (Maxcy and Silberston 1959: Tables 3 and 19; Rhys 1972: 23–4; Tolliday 2000: 85–7, 107–9).

For the other auto producers, the smaller the levels of output, the less progress was made in automating machining and body pressing operations. Rootes and Standard-Triumph, with lower volumes than BMC and Ford, could not take automation as far as in Longbridge and Dagenham, and the quality producers, such as Rover and Jaguar, had even less reason to change over to transfer machining and transfer presses. The heads of Rootes and Standard-Triumph knew, however, that the minimum efficient scale of production in the industry was rising as automation advanced and both launched ambitious, and ultimately frustrated, plans for expansion, usually by means of a strategic alliance with another producer. Neither company realised its ambitions because neither had attractive, popular cars to generate profits for investment on the scale required (Thoms and Donnelly 1985: 161–73; Tiratsoo 1995: 88–108; Whisler 1999: 58–75). But Standards is more famous for its alleged inability to blend automated mass production with "British" systems of labour control, and it is this issue to which we now turn.

Controlling engineering labour

The postwar priority for Standard-Triumph's managers was to increase the scale of production and in 1945 Standards began a major investment programme that more than quadrupled fixed assets per worker in three years. At the same time it looked for new structures of industrial relations to overcome the deterioration that had occurred during wartime. The solution devised by the managing director, John Black, was to organise the workforce into gangs, controlled by shop stewards rather than foremen, pay high wages with generous bonuses (paid to the whole gang) for hitting production targets and reduce the working week. He believed that stewards were best placed to co-ordinate work, ensuring that the expensive capital equipment was fully utilised and cutting the cost of front-line supervision (Melman 1958; Lewchuk 1986: 195–202; Tolliday 1986: 208–12). This system worked effectively in the short run but encountered problems when Standards' cars failed to meet sales targets. With deteriorating cash-flow, management cut the cost of production labour, leading to the "automation strike" of 1956 described in Chapter 1.

Lewchuk (1987: 195–202) sees Standards as an indicator of deep problems in motor vehicles and the wider engineering industry. In very schematic terms, he argues that interwar incentive payment systems (piecework or production bonuses) allowed British engineering firms to drive workers to higher production and productivity and economise on management. The employers' victory in the 1922 lockout and the threat of redundancy at a time of mass unemployment ensured managerial control of the effort bargain. However, in the postwar full employment, shopfloor workers forced up piecework rates, reduced their effort yet still gained higher wages. Faced by a strong sellers' market, managers implicitly conspired in this inefficient production, over-manning and low productivity. The explosion of shopfloor bargaining created anarchy at the engineering workplace. There is much support for this analysis, which in its most elemental form has been described as "the British disease" (Allen 1979; Barnett 1986).

On the other hand, Nichols (1986: xi (quote) and 53–93) has described a "familiar jingle" in which the words "British workers" were invariably coupled with: "don't work hard enough", "laziness", "restrictive practices" and "too much power". He has demonstrated very clearly that the idea that British workers frustrated the pace of technological change and productivity growth sits on very uncertain statistical foundations. Simultaneously, labour historians have qualified Lewchuk's dynamics of shopfloor control. After the war, the engineering employers were determined to reassert their right to unilateral control of work processes and payment systems (Melling 2007). However, their control strategy of using the engineering industry's elaborate disputes procedure was too remote and cumbersome and informal, personalised, deals between local managers and union representatives were done at the workplace to maintain the flow of production in the face of strong consumer demand. The engineering employers, and indeed national trade union officials, opposed this informal workplace bargaining.[11] Workplace bargaining was not the same as labour control of the effort bargain, as Lewchuk has implied. Tolliday and Zeitlin (1986c: 103; see also Lyddon 1983) have suggested that strong shopfloor control applied in the 1950s only to Standard Motors and the smaller Coventry motor companies which together accounted for a small part of vehicle output. "By 1956 Morris Motors was only 25 percent unionised; Vauxhall was well below 50 percent; Ford was in the same range and notorious for its limitations on shop stewards; Austin fluctuated between 60–90 percent unionisation during most of the 1950s, but there too the shop-floor organisation had made only limited incursions on managerial authority during this period. In all of these firms, the consolidation of strong shop-floor organisation occurs only in the late 1950s and early 1960s – and at Vauxhall it is arguable whether there has ever been a powerful shop-floor organisation" (on Vauxhall, see Lyddon 1996: 196–8).

Senior managers in engineering were particularly unhappy with the "wage drift" that flowed from workplace bargaining and prepared a counter-attack through tough stances in national pay negotiations.

The desire to crush the unions in pay bargaining led to the compact with government in 1957 and the demoralising defeat in the engineering pay dispute discussed in Chapter 3. Defeat for the EEF caused a collapse of morale and a long period of introspection (Wigham 1973: 189–211). By contrast, shopfloor confidence soared (Fishman 1999: 259–60); McKinlay and Melling (1999: 236–7) suggest that the authority of foremen was systematically undermined by ordinary workers and shop stewards aggressively expanded their range of activities. Thus, the expansion of shopfloor organisation in vehicles and engineering more generally during the late 1950s flowed directly from the strike of 1957.

This picture of expanding shop steward power and declining managerial authority sits uneasily however with the general satisfaction expressed by managers in engineering with the way that shop stewards represented the wishes of workers (McCarthy and Parker 1968: Tables 12 and 13). Even Dick Etheridge, a radical BMC shop steward, conceded that his role was to settle disputes on the shopfloor for management.[12] The forensic examination of BMC's accounts and production data by Williams and colleagues reveal a complex position, with the company able to raise production and productivity of its major volume models during upswings of the demand cycle and control costs in the downswing (Table 4.2) notwithstanding the increasingly turbulent industrial relations. During upswings the management laid down more assembly lines, speeded up existing lines, worked extensive overtime, introduced nightshifts and altered incentive payments and achieved high levels of capacity utilisation to exploit its more automated production processes. During downswings the company remained above break-even, primarily by laying off workers, often by brutal methods. The major redundancies in 1956, for example, were called at extremely short notice with no offer of compensation, earning a rebuke from the Minister of Labour.[13] For the motor industry, "working-days-lost" through strikes moved contra-cyclically, provoking Turner to conclude that redundancy strikes "represented the industry's substitute for an agreed means of dealing with recurrent labour surplus" (Turner *et al.* 1967: 332). Conversely, the number of strikes moved pro-cyclically, suggesting that during upswings managers settled disputes quickly to minimise disturbance to production schedules (Turner et al. 1967: 109–11). The emerging consensus indicates that the chaotic bargaining of the 1960s did not produce sharp rises in labour costs and that the strike pattern did not inhibit adjustments of supply to meet the often abrupt changes in demand (Durcan *et al.* 1983: ch. 10; Marsden *et al.* 1985: ch. 6; Tolliday 1991: 94–5). On the

Table 4.2 Austin, Morris and BMC output surges, 1947–67

Trough year	Peak year	BMC total vehicles produced in year	Longbridge volume line output	Longbridge and Cowley output	Longbridge and Cowley's share of BMC total output	BMC combine employment	BMC percent above break-even point
1947–8			33,000	121,000			
	1949–50		102,000	231,000			
Trough to peak increase			209%	91%			
1952–3		279,000	114,000	220,000	79%		
	1955–6	440,000	242,000	366,000	83%	60,000	30.3
Trough to peak increase			112%	66%			
1956–7		363,000	111,000	281,000	77%	60,000	15.4
	1959–60	669,000	243,000	530,000	79%	76,000	29.7
Trough to peak increase			118%	89%		27%	
1961–2		600,000	259,000	443,000	74%	80,000	4.6
	1964–5	886,000	353,000	680,000	77%	93,000	15.4
Trough to peak increase			36%	53%		16%	

Notes: Longbridge volume lines are those producing recently introduced volume cars which were important in product planning terms and whose best annual sales exceed 70,000 units. The models are: 1947–50, A40 Devon/Somerset; 1952–6, A40, A30 & A50; 1956–60, A55, A35, A40 Farina and Mini; 1961–5, Mini, 1100, 1800. All listed models meet the criteria except (i) the carry-over A40 of the early 1950s which remained fresh because it was a postwar design in a world of car shortage and (ii) the 1800 which never sold much above 50,000. Percent above break-even indicates the margin by which sales revenue (or physical units produced) exceeds labour and depreciation costs incurred within the firm.
Sources: Williams *et al.* 1983: 222; Williams *et al.* 1994: 149.

whole, therefore, there is no solid evidence to suggest that shopfloor control prevented British firms from achieving the production runs that guaranteed the profitability of their automated processes.

Chapter 1 sketched an enterprise-level model of diffusion, which combined the basic microeconomics of the firm with the idea of the business as a "learning organisation". The evidence above suggests that the economics of ATMs depended ultimately on the scale of production of standard engines, axles, gearboxes and bodies, and that British automobile producers were by no means slow to adopt the technology, with the exception of the transfer press. There is no real evidence that workers captured rents by extending the frontier of control and compromising managements' ability to vary the pace of production to suit changes in market demand. British automobile producers (and Renault) revealed themselves to be very effective organisational learners, taking (back) the idea of transfer machine technology and adapting it to European market conditions. The resulting "flexible automation" was sufficiently impressive to demand attention from the production engineers at FMC. The idea that British motor producers could not manage mass production because of technological incompetence and/or labour obstruction has no real foundation. The failure of BMC to match its modern machining lines with equally impressive body pressing and painting shops reflected two judgements that were not ratified in practice. Managers believed both that they needed a full model range to achieve scale economies in engines, axles and gearboxes and that the cost of different marques would be covered by higher sales. Ford and Vauxhall, on the other hand, followed a more classic Fordist strategy, albeit a more flexible path than followed by their US parents, by investing heavily in automated production facilities for very limited body and engine types. The heavy investment by Ford and Vauxhall gave them obvious economies of scale; the increasing productivity gained by BMC in its volume lines was snuffed out by its labour-intensive methods for assembling niche products and defending its market share.

Numerically-controlled machine tools

The simplest N/C machine tools coupled an electric control system to a standard machine tool, but such methods were invariably disappointing as conventional machine tools could not tolerate the stresses involved (Stokes 1955: 197). It did not take long before machine tools were designed specifically for electronic control systems. The simpler systems positioned the cutting head (usually for drilling or punching machines) or cut in straight lines (usually milling machines or lathes). For these operations, the computer program defined the co-ordinates at which the cutting operations would take place and translated these co-ordinates into movements of servo-mechanisms that moved the table holding the workpiece into the required position. The more complex operations, such as contour milling, required far more pre-production planning because of the huge increase in the scale of information required to machine a workpiece with curvatures in two and three dimensions (PERA 1963: 7–8; Gebhardt and Hatzold 1974: 23–4). There was a separate category of automatic welding machines under development for aerospace in the 1950s, but which made maximum impact in automotive engineering in the 1970s.[14]

Early American propagandists for automation foresaw enormous advantages if machine tools could be programmed and re-programmed for a wide variety of operations, making the technology potentially suitable for every machine shop (Diebold 1952: 59–67; Buckingham 1961: 19–20). The sheer scale of the potential for N/C tools should not be underestimated. Merchant (1973: 357) estimated that three-quarters of US metalworking manufacture consisted of lots numbering less than 50 pieces at a time when metalworking was the largest single component of manufacturing.[15] Furthermore, Carter's (1971) study of work flow in batch production metalworking shops revealed that the average workpiece spent only 5 percent of its time on production machines and, of that 5 percent, only about 30 percent was actually spent as productive time in shaping the part. N/C machine tools had a revolutionary potential to cut machining and idle time, radically reduce stocks of work-in-progress and improve the economics of small- and medium-size manufacturing plants. The real optimists predicted that by the 1960s, 75 percent of the machine tools sold in the USA would be N/C; in fact the figure was less than 1 percent (De Barr 1973: 371). This is a story of the relative failure of automation, especially in the USA, where expectations were highest.

Chapter 2 referred extensively to Noble's (1984) study of the evolution of N/C machine tools in the USA, and his view of the extent to which Cold War tensions were allowed to push technological innovation. The involvement of the military-industrial-educational complex pushed the trajectory of development towards machines with multiple capabilities suitable for the most complex work on military aircraft and aero-engines. These machines were so intricate and expensive that they were not commercially viable in ordinary machine shops, and the

USAF had to devise a very elaborate system of contracting and subsidies to ensure their use in military aerospace contracts. Most controversially, Noble also argues that more commercially promising approaches, notably the General Electric [GE] system of "record-playback", were in effect neutered by high ranking officers and industrialists because they ultimately depended on skilled machinists.[16] At a time of intense Cold War hostility, the radical leanings of the skilled machinists in the United Electrical, Radio and Machine Workers [UE] caused policy-makers to search for production methods that eliminated any threat of labour control of the production process. However, this "Bravermanian" (see Chapter 1) attempt to de-skill work failed because the skills, experience and awareness of the workforce could not be displaced by the computer control system. In Noble's (1984: 269) words:

> The cost-effectiveness of N/C, then, was dependent upon optimum utilisation of the equipment, and this could only occur with effective maintenance of the machinery, careful co-ordination of the production process as a whole, and efficient machine operation. All of these factors, however, were dependent in the final analysis, not only upon greater management supervision, planning, or the use of computers, but on the initiative, skill, judgement and co-operation of the workforce. Here, then, lay the central contradiction of N/C use; in its effort to extend control over production, management set out to de-skill, discipline and displace the very people upon whose knowledge and goodwill the optimum utilisation, and thus the cost-effectiveness, ultimately depended.

We shall return to the control of the highly skilled labour force later in this chapter.

British experience helps put some of Noble's more contentious points into context. In general terms, the British machine tool industry was regarded as a weak performer. Postwar academic studies focused on the familiar themes of craft skills, export performance and long-run decline (AACP 1953; Beesley and Troup 1961; Prais 1981: 165–88). There were numerous proposals to restructure the industry during the 1950s and 1960s, but change was slow and limited (Bufton 2004: 154–5). Nevertheless, N/C machines were developed independently in the UK and without massive state support.[17] The earliest postwar experiments in computer controls of machine tools began with analogue computers (DSIR 1956: 20–2), but three firms, Ferranti, Electrical and

Musical Industries (EMI) and British Thomson-Houston (BTH) developed N/C machine tools in the 1950s. Ferranti's work began in 1950 at their Edinburgh factory, supervised by (Sir) John Toothill and Theo Williamson, to overcome the delays and expense of machining complex parts to tight tolerances for the gyro gun sight and radar equipment. They had no close US contacts, but Williamson heard about the work at MIT and both visited the Servomechanisms Laboratory in 1951. Significantly, Williamson "did not learn anything that subsequently proved useful. He considered that the MIT work was pedestrian and it misled the American machine tool industry" (Feilden 1995: 522). Ferranti turned instead to work on computing at the National Research and Development Corporation (NRDC) and on optical measurement at the National Physical Laboratory (NPL). When Ferranti's optical measurement system was combined with US improvements in machine tool design, very high precision N/C tools became a possibility.[18] A working prototype was available in mid-1955 and demonstrated at the Olympia Machine Tool Exhibition in 1956. Ferranti claimed that their system cut machining time from 300 hours to less than five. Initially, they hoped to undertake the data processing on a Ferranti computer, but costs were prohibitive and they opted instead for a digital differential analyser programmed (hardwired) to undertake specific tasks (Feilden 1995: 524). Ferranti believed that their system was cheaper and more accurate than the MIT approach, a claim that was validated in tests run by the USAF in 1957.[19] Like Ferranti, EMI developed a sophisticated system of continuous control, which was less flexible but cheaper than the Ferranti method. Still less sophisticated was BTH's point-to-point machine, which used punched cards rather than tape, and claimed to halve machining time. The final initiative was a record-playback system developed by the established machine tool company Alfred Herbert, but this was primitive and did not lead to a production model.

British N/C machine tool makers were also very bullish in the mid-1950s. The Board of Trade's (1957: Appendices II & X) survey noted low levels of current demand, confined mainly to the airframe and aero-engine producers, but confidence among machine tool makers that the technology would spread; they expected demand to increase tenfold in the next five years. However, these hopes were largely unfulfilled. The post-Suez credit squeeze did not help. Early models frequently broke down in the heat, dirt and noise of the average machine shop, an alien environment for complex electric circuits (PERA 1963: 11). The development process was expensive and took the pioneers away from mass applications. The most successful was EMI, which worked with a number of companies in machine tools and the automotive industry to design a control system for a drilling machine. Ferranti collaborated with Fairey Aviation to develop a technically outstanding milling machine to mill aircraft wing spars. The "success" in the USAF trials brought Ferranti a contract with the Bendix Corporation to supply a numerical control system and digital measuring machine for application to US machine tools. But commercial difficulties took the British N/C machine tool developers along the same path of high-precision/high-cost applications as in the USA. The Board of Trade (1957) automation survey quoted a price of £2,000 for a standard 28 inch milling machine, and £18,000 for the computer-controlled model, with an extra £50,000 for the computer (able to control a number of machines) and delivery times of three to four years. These were expensive machines.

The price of control units fell significantly during the 1960s, and accelerated the pace of diffusion. The figures in Table 4.3 indicate a spurt of sales from 1966, which was accompanied by a surge of export demand in the same year (Board of Trade 1967). However, the limited flexibility of control units remained a problem: "the logic of these first numerically controlled machine tools was made of hardwired circuitry and, if new functions were to be performed, a change in the hardwire had to be made" (Jacobsson 1986: 9). Cheap and reliable minicomputers became available from the early 1960s (Hamilton 1995: 85–6), but the minicomputer producers did not apply this technology to the control of machine tools until the early 1970s. Only when the Japanese introduced microchips, even before the computer industry

Table 4.3 National stocks and diffusion levels of N/C machine tools, 1966–70

	Austria	FRG	Italy	Sweden	UK	USA
Stocks						
1966	4	450	110	109	1,000	...
1967	...	730	150	220	1,500	12,000
1968	...	1,030	400	269	2,100	...
1969	75	1,450	500	330	2,700	18,000
1970	115	1,930	...	400	3,200	20,000
Diffusion levels, end 1969						
NC machines per 000 employees	0.1	0.2	0.1	0.4	0.3	0.9

Source: Gebhardt and Hatzold 1974: Tables 3.3 and 3.4.

had recognised the value of this technology, into numerical control units for machine tools could the technology diffuse more widely in manufacturing (Jacobsson 1986: 10; Yonekura 1997: 255).[20]

These factors are evident in the diffusion statistics assembled during 1969 by Gebhardt and Hatzold (1974) from questionnaires and interviews with managers in firms that were likely to utilise the technology.[21] Table 4.3 shows that during the 1960s Britain had the second highest stock of N/C machine tools, well behind the USA, but scored less well when the stock was related to the size of the workforce. However, even in this sample of firms most likely to use N/C technology, production was dominated by "standard" machine tools. From their sample of 142 firms in six countries, Gebhardt and Hatzold (1974: Table 3.5) found that in three-quarters of the firms N/C machines comprised less than 5 percent of all machine tools used. This confirms the disappointing production and diffusion data given at the start of this section.[22] The task, then, is to explain extensive diffusion in a limited number of branches of engineering and very limited penetration elsewhere.

The enterprise-level model of Chapter 1 suggested that diffusion should be examined in two perspectives: the microeconomics of the firm, and the business as a "learning organisation". There was certainly general pressure on engineering firms from the labour market to find skilled-labour-saving technologies, with general shortages of skilled labour and extremely severe competition for the most highly skilled.[23] Equally clearly, the high cost of N/C tools did not justify investment until the mid-1960s at the earliest for the vast majority of engineering firms. It is also clear, albeit from fragmentary evidence, that the displacement of skilled workers was more difficult than imagined. Jones (1985: 238) notes that "craftist" traditions in British engineering had resulted in workers raising the theoretical minimum manning levels and precluding the use of cheaper, semi-skilled labour in aerospace during the 1970s. Similarly, the introduction of the first N/C machine tool into BMC's Longbridge factory in 1967 led to protracted negotiations over pay and grading, which resulted in the payment of the full skilled rate to the operator and the creation of a new post of programmer.[24] This problem was by no means confined to Britain; after examining several industrial processes in US industry, Piore (1968) suggested that jobs were seldom "de-graded" when new work techniques or equipment were introduced. Indeed, the confrontations over the "de-skilling" aspect of N/C tools in the USA were far more severe than in the UK. One of the major users of this technology, GE's Aero

Engines Group, faced resistance for more than a decade from its machinists, as it sought to downgrade and speed-up work (Noble 1984: 263–323). GE managers could achieve neither the machine utilisation rates nor the quality standards they desired without the tacit knowledge of their skilled machinists. For their part, after early defeats by managers in bargaining, the machinists learned guerrilla tactics to disrupt production, despite the underlying contractualism of US bargaining and the strategy of GE management to limit bargaining with the unions.

Why, then, would any firm introduce N/C tools? Aerospace users were among the heaviest in the UK, USA and Sweden, as illustrated in Table 4.4. In all three countries, the predominance of aerospace is almost certainly under-stated in Table 4.4, since a significant part of the use in mechanical engineering surely represented subcontractors for aerospace work.[25] Despite different government-industry relationships in the three countries, there is a strong suspicion that states were slow to enforce cost reduction on aerospace suppliers (Jones 1985: 226–36). In Britain at least, there was a very strong view that the aerospace industry had been featherbedded in the postwar boom (Hartley 1996: 213–14). Military procurement protocols anyway allowed purchasing to be based on quality rather than cost criteria. However, lax competitive pressures can be only a very partial explanation since it was the complexity of work in airframe and aero-engine production that was the critical factor.[26] Continuous path N/C tools, capable of machining in three dimensions, were at the upper end of the price range for British N/C equipment and were almost invariably designed for the aerospace industry or supplier firms (PERA 1963: 39–43).

Table 4.4   Distribution of N/C machine tools among industries in five market economies (1969)

	Austria	FRG	Sweden	UK	USA
Percentage Distribution					
Mechanical engineering	70.0	65.4	17.1	56.0	49.1
Electrical engineering	} 30.0 {	7.5	40.9	12.0	12.0
Motor vehicles		10.7	...	3.0	1.3
Aerospace	...	1.8	18.1	25.0	18.2
Others	...	14.6	23.9	4.0	19.4
Total	100.0	100.0	100.0	100.0	100.0
Estimated quantity	75	1,450	330	2,700	18,000

Source: Gebhardt and Hatzold 1974: Tables 3.3 and 3.10.

For less exacting work, the economics of N/C machines depended on batch size and the amount of machining to be done. The greater the amount, the more time would a skilled machinist need to read technical drawings, measure the workpiece and make adjustments to cutting tools and the more attractive it might be to machine automatically without this "downtime" (Board of Trade 1957: Appendix II; Puckle 1957: 42). The question of batch size was much less clear cut. The leading N/C machine tool makers produced sample costings to show that N/C technology was more efficient over a range of batch sizes and machining types, but these were accounts that costed planning, set-up and machining at notional rates with no allowance for breakdown, maintenance and other vital functions (PERA 1963). Moreover, the efficiency of N/C tools depended less on individual batches but on the ability to keep the machines running more or less continuously with a succession of jobs, and this involved significant staffing in technical and planning support (Thayer 1963; Knopf 1963; Johnson 1963). Gebhardt and Hazold (1974: 46) considered that N/C techniques were most appropriate for batch sizes in the range five to 50 pieces, which were complicated to machine and for which repeat orders were relatively frequent.

Not surprisingly given the size of Britain's stock of N/C tools, there is no real evidence that British firms were unaware of this technology. British entrepreneurs were extremely well-networked; they heard about N/C tools much earlier than their European counterparts. Gebhardt and Hatzold (1974: 42–3) identified a "decision gap" (between the first information becoming available to the firm on N/C machines and the decision to purchase), which was longer in the UK than elsewhere in Europe but this almost certainly reflects the very high cost of the early machines rather than entrepreneurial conservatism.[27] British N/C tool users were, on the contrary, very enterprising, looking to source from both the USA and Switzerland when order books for domestic suppliers were overfull.[28]

There is, however, a problem for both British and American engineering in relation to this branch of automation. Why did automobile manufacturers not match German car-makers' use of N/C technology (Table 4.4)? Gebhardt and Hatzold (1974: 54–7) suggested that opposition from trade unions, albeit less severe in the UK than in the USA, was the main impediment. However, this may be exaggerated. In general, British unions were well-disposed towards automation, anticipating higher wages and shorter working hours provided they were consulted about the pace of introduction (TUC 1956). Within the TUC, there was more concern that automation would come too slowly to preserve jobs in increasingly competitive markets, rather too fast to create unemployment (TUC 1957: 461–2). Union leaders saw weaknesses in Britain's machine tool industry as a danger.[29] The AEU was committed to nationalisation of the engineering industry for more than a decade (in the "Plan for Engineering"), but its debates on automation were concerned with short-term issues rather than longer-term panaceas.[30] At both national and local levels, trade unionists were more concerned with preserving jobs than with opposing change (Booth and Melling 2007). The Longbridge AEU wanted to ensure that *its* members were recognised to operate the first N/C tool in the factory and that tool room staffing was not cut.[31] There was no British equivalent to the war between GE and the UE.

Labour opposition clearly will not explain the failure to push N/C into automobiles and similar branches of British and American engineering. An answer may lie in the literature recognising that different sectors might have differing "technological regimes" that govern the pace of innovation (Nelson and Winter 1982; Malerba 2005). If the UK did not possess a military/educational/complex, there was an informal network linking the NPL, the NRDC, the Telecommunications Research Establishment and innovative electronics firms (Burns and Stalker 1994: 40–51). State aid was available after the war to extend these links to new firms in electronic engineering and revitalise less ambitious companies (Burns and Stalker 1994; Freeman *et al.* 1965: 41–2). As noted above, machine tool and aerospace firms were drawn into the network in the early 1950s to solve complex machining problems in the aircraft and electronics industries. The Ferranti Applications Laboratory in Edinburgh became the focal point of these activities in Scotland and Toothill played a critical role in modernising Scotland's postwar industrial structure from heavy industry to "Silicon Glen" (Burns and Stalker 1994: 53–6). However, the links to automobiles were weak, notwithstanding the role of Rootes in developing EMI's N/C systems.[32]

The automobile firms tended to work closely with trusted machine tool suppliers (Asquith, Archdale, BSA Tools and the UK subsidiary of Cincinnati Milling are frequently mentioned) or created their own machines from within (Zeitlin 2000b: 148–9). Their contacts with firms developing control systems for N/C tools, such as Ferranti, EMI, Mullard and Plessey, were very limited. Above all, early N/C machine tools were deemed unsuitable for large volume production.[33] Finally, there were no prods from US automobile producers towards N/C machines. GMC installed an N/C drilling machine in 1960, but met employee resistance and withdrew (Noble 1984: 253–5). Both British and American car producers were taken by surprise by the N/C systems and robotics developed by German and Japanese producers. The robotics revolution caught the British volume car industry at the all-time low in its financial performance and new investment had to be negotiated with a government that was sceptical by a management that did not really understand the business (Williams *et al.* 1987a: 35–66).

If American producers and management consultants were unable to act as "change agents" as defined in Chapter 2, pressure for reform had to come from within the UK. From the discussion above, Ferranti was clearly well-placed for such a role. However, Tweedale (1992) has underlined the company's lack of resources for the technical and commercial development of its computer businesses. Instead, it concentrated on a profitable niche in the defence market. Ferranti's Automation Systems Division, which used the same defence computers, experienced rapid growth but, like other British minicomputer-makers, its margins were threatened when US producers invaded the British market (House of Commons 1969–70a: 75–7; Hamilton 1995: 91). Thus margins were low, marketing and after-sales contacts were limited and British minicomputer-makers did not develop software for their machines. They targeted niche markets, almost invariably those firms that could recognise the potential of cheap computing power and already had a corps of experienced programmers to develop software. Aerospace producers were in this loop, but the mass producers of cars and other consumer goods were at best peripherally and sporadically involved. The activities of potential change agents were extremely narrow and limited.

Conclusion

Britain's record of innovation in engineering is rather better than the traditional "declinist" literature allows.

The British motor car industry, far from being caught between "Fordism" and "flexible specialisation" (Broadberry 1997a: 320–3; Tolliday and Zeitlin 1986b), managed to innovate a capital- and space-saving, high volume system of production that was widely copied elsewhere in Europe. Similarly, the postwar travails Britain's machine tool *producers* should not divert attention from the creditable record of N/C *users* among high technology and precision engineering firms and their principal suppliers. British firms were aware of US research in machining technologies and were capable of adapting the main principles to the different conditions in British product and labour markets. The narrowing productivity gap between British and American engineering after the mid-1960s (noted in Table 2.2) can be only marginally explained by automation, but it is enough to question the traditional story of failure.

Moreover, there are some signs that the British tended to handle labour and automation rather better than their American counterparts. Managers in both Britain and America insisted on restoring managerial rights after 1945, but the more extreme culture of control in the USA led to questionable commercial decisions.[34] FMC's "bug-prone" Cleveland engine plant owed a part of its inflexibility to management's determination to outflank labour and GE's inability to recognise that even N/C machine tools needed skilled operators flew in the face of repeated problems in production (Noble 1984: 263–323).[35] British managers chose to confront labour relations problems by adapting established procedures and managerial practices to new labour market conditions rather than follow the siren voices promising technological solutions to shopfloor militancy, at least until the 1980s.[36] Perhaps as a result, British workers' resistance to automation was muted.[37] In the USA, where blue collar manufacturing employment contracted steadily from the early 1950s, diffusion became more problematic after the 1960–1 "automation recession" (USNCTAEP 1966: 22). There were national and state-level strikes over technological redundancy in 1963, and the issues of automation and unemployment again became a major issue for US public opinion (Bix 2000: 259–73). American union leader George Meany, who had welcomed automation in 1959, opened the 1963 AFL-CIO convention by denouncing automation as a curse for society because he (probably correctly) believed that automation was being used to undermine union strength at the workplace. No British union leader made such an equivalent declaration. But in general, the similarities rather than the differences between British and American patterns are most evident. The weakest aspect of British performance was the failure of the British-owned car firms to invest as heavily in transfer pressing as in transfer machining, but this ultimately was based on perceptions of market segmentation that had some justification.

5
The Continuous Flow Industries: Feedback Control and Computerisation

Continuous flow industries process bulk raw materials into finished or intermediate products by physical or chemical means to produce a finished product with the desired attributes (Laspe 1957: 420). Although many process industries operate around the clock, others produce in very large batches or in near-continuous systems. It is a very diverse group. The classic examples are oil refining, the petrochemicals industry, and parts of the iron and steel industry, but branches of the building materials and food processing industries had been making the transition to continuous processing from the late nineteenth century; the dividing lines between very large batch and continuous operation were often indistinct. Production processes in these industries were transformed during the twentieth century by two major developments. First, these industries tended to become more scientifically-based, with attempts to understand more clearly the basic science of the reactions upon which production depended. Secondly, as scientists understood the chemical and physical processes of production, they needed increasingly sophisticated and robust measuring devices to monitor changes in an increasing array of chemical and physical properties and intricate servomechanisms to move controls by precise amounts. By these means closed loop feedback controls allowed the chemical reactions to be monitored and controlled much more closely, often with dramatic consequences for the industry concerned.[1] The business histories of these industries and of the giant businesses that dominated them have done much to explain the scientific research and development work but it is essential to turn to the automation literature of the 1950s for insights into the development of instrumentation, control mechanisms and the rapid expansion of automatic control.

The AIEE's definition of feedback control was given in Chapter 1 (note 35) and the closed loop aspect simply meant that the control system worked independently of human intervention (Wiener 1947b). The commonplace example of a closed loop feedback control is the standard room thermometer which regulates the domestic central heating system, but when scaled up to industrial processes control problems increase substantially. There was a tendency for the more complex systems to oscillate between extreme states rather than stabilise in the desired ranges. By the end of the 1930s, fundamental understanding had advanced significantly in electronics in phase control (the basis of all automatic control systems), pulse code modulation (the basis of control systems, as well as of radar and digital computers) and information theory (for mathematical analysis of the behaviour of complex switching circuits) in the work of Harry Nyquist, R.H. Reaves and Claude Shannon (Chestnut 1957). During the war the theory and practice of control systems was developed further in the rush to develop radar-controlled gunfire systems. The foundations for the postwar transformation of continuous flow industries had been laid. As Noble (1984: 48–9) has noted:

> ... there was now a mature technology of automatic control, which included precision servomotors, for the careful control of motion; pulse generators, to convey precisely electrical information; transducers, for converting information about distance, heat, speed and the like into electrical signals; and a whole range of associated actuating, control and sensing devices. Finally, the wartime projects [in the USA] had created a cadre of scientists and engineers knowledgeable in the new theory of servomechanisms, experienced in the practical applications of such systems, and eager to spread the word and put their new expertise to use.

This work provided the intellectual foundation for the practical and popular literature on the "automatic factory" in American business and news magazines in the later 1940s (discussed at the beginning of Chapter 1 above). This literature continued into the 1950s, concentrating on feedback controls; *Scientific American* (1952) devoted a whole issue to "feedback", whilst *Mechanical Engineering* carried numerous articles on the subject in 1952–3.[2]

The application of these techniques was *essentially* an American development, and this chapter begins by examining US control engineering, interpreted in its widest sense to include instrumentation, switchgear and the development of electronic control systems. Thereafter, the chapter assesses British performance in three main sectors: oil refining, petrochemicals and iron and steel. This is followed by a brief conclusion.

American control engineering

Not surprisingly, the US military provided the main user of electronic control devices in the first postwar decade (Diebold 1959: 13–14), but capacity of the electronics and control engineering sector grew rapidly, with the creation of new entrepreneurial firms like Fairchild, Texas Instruments and Hewlett-Packard to compete with the industry giants such as GE, RCA, Westinghouse, AT&T, Bell Laboratories and Western Electric (Noble 1984: 48). Although some commentators believed that civilian industry was too slow to adopt these innovations (Jones 1956: 39) take-up of the simplest, most reliable devices surged ahead in the mid-1950s as prices began to fall.[3] The main users of automatic control devices were petroleum and chemicals, and both experienced major investment surges in the early postwar years. Chemicals was responsible for almost one-tenth of the investment in plant and equipment in US manufacturing in the first postwar decade, reaching stocks of capital equipment per worker well above the manufacturing average.[4] It was estimated that approximately one-fifth of this investment went on automatic control devices (US Congress 1955: 152–3). Productivity *per operative* was rising rapidly, with output up 50 per cent between 1947 and 1954 and the number of production workers roughly stable, but over the same period the number of non-production workers (in professional, supervisory, clerical and sales work) doubled and in 1954 there were two operatives for each non-production worker (US Congress 1955: 153–4).

Very similar trends were evident in oil refining, with the average size of refinery increasing from 8,000 barrels per day in 1946 to 25,000 in 1954, and in the latter year seven refineries were under construction, with an average capacity of 58,000 barrels per day (US Congress 1955: 474–5). A leading industry analyst claimed that the average refinery employed approximately 700 workers regardless of its size, and employment patterns were shifting towards technical and managerial staff, just as in chemicals.[5] Here, too, levels of capital per worker were very high and increasing rapidly, giving output per operative well above the average for manufacturing as a whole. At this stage, both chemicals and oil refining were using a mixture of pneumatic and electronic control systems and a mixture of open and closed loop methods.[6] But the trend was undoubtedly towards electronics and closed loop systems, as Thomas Walsh made clear (US Congress 1955: 484–5):

> Acetylene would be an excellent new material for making many new chemicals ... To make acetylene from natural gas we would have to crack it in the order of 1.3 seconds. Right now we cannot control the process. It gets away, and we wind up with carbon black and hydrogen, and they might be desirable but they are not as valuable as acetylene. A high-speed computer that can figure out in a thousandth of a second what was going to happen under these conditions would have a jump on a process that takes 1.3 seconds. A man just does not think that fast. We cannot learn that much about it, and I believe that this is one case, one situation, where automatic plants in the future, with high-speed computers, deciding what the operating conditions should be, are going to become a possibility.

In the mid-1950s computerisation seemed imminent because of the growing complexity of operations at chemicals plant and oil refineries. The desire to extract or produce increasingly complex, valuable products required careful control of temperature, pressure and chemical composition of the process. In the mid-1950s, the instruments to analyse the chemical composition of liquids and gases were becoming available in the USA (Laspe 1957: 447–53) but were somewhat slower to appear in the UK.[7] Closed loop systems provided close control of individual processes but not of interaction between them, and chemical engineers of the mid-1950s looked to computerisation to simplify the calculation of the optimum mix of inputs and outputs, and also interaction between processes to achieve even more control of production systems (McCallum 1955: 114).[8]

Early computers were ill-suited to this task. Even into the late 1950s, valve technology was insufficiently reliable, flexible and consistent in operation over long periods to fulfil the role of master controller of a production system (Young 1955), but the invention of the transistor by Bell Laboratories in 1947 offered a potential solution to the problem. It took time to resolve limitations in both performance and production technologies but the development 11 years later by Fairchild Semiconductor of the planar process offered cheap and reliable transistors and supply expanded rapidly. Established valve manufacturers, large consumer products firms such as Motorola and a large number of new start-ups began to shift into transistor production. These newer companies began to dominate the industry and push aggressively for new applications against what they perceived as the conservatism of US manufacturing industry (Braun and MacDonald 1982: 58–62; Jones 1956: 39–40). However, the automatic control industry had its own problems. Its rapid growth had left in its wake confusing terminology and uncertain perceptions of the potential of electronic control systems. The sheer speed of industrial automation had also encouraged the introduction of under-developed products and systems, leaving some users with severe and lasting problems (Ziebolz 1957: 99). The major institutions in electrical and radio engineering began to address these problems from the later 1940s, and in the first half of the 1950s terminology was standardised in a number of major industrial countries, institutions began to produce bibliographies of works in English and foreign languages and in September 1957 an International Federation of Automatic Control was established in Paris (Bennett 1976: 116–18). At the same time, product reliability slowly improved, especially for the more complex electronic components, as new production methods were developed.

The final element of US technological lead in the continuous flow industries came with the evolution of the minicomputer for the control of industrial processes. The development of computer control of continuous flow operations is very similar to that of numerically controlled machine tools considered in the previous chapter. In the 1950s, US firms, such as General Automation and Foxboro, created special-purpose controllers for specific industrial process applications using electro-mechanical technologies (Hamilton 1995: 83). During the later 1950s and early 1960s, demand for these systems increased with the massive expansion of interest in industrial automation and demands from users for increasingly complex controllers, and the control engineering industry developed general-purpose systems that could be programmed, using inexpensive read-only memory, in the anticipation that these instruction sets would be changed rarely. However, electronics firms on both sides of the Atlantic were working to create fully-fledged electronic computers, initially from electronic command and control for aircraft and missile guidance.[9] In 1959, a two-year-old US company, Digital Equipment Corporation (DEC), produced the first commercial minicomputer, the PDP (Programmed Data Processor)-1, which was a commercial extension of the early interactive solid-state TX-0 computer developed at MIT and on which DEC's founders, Ken Olsen and Harlan Anderson had worked (Langlois

1992: 7). Even cheaper computers, the PDP-4 and the PDP-5, followed and were targeted at instrumentation and control applications (Flamm 1988: 127). Similar machines were produced by other new start-ups, SDS (again originating from missile guidance computers) and Data General, formed by three former DEC engineers in 1968 (Flamm 1988: 129–31). DEC dominated the market for minicomputers, much as IBM dominated the market for mainframes, and with a similar marketing strategy based on a proprietary family of machines (the PDP series followed by the VAX family) with allied peripherals and software (Langlois 1992: 7). The sheer size and diversity of the US market meant that product and software development were well in advance of that in other countries and in turn funded the investment in miniaturisation and printed circuits that enabled the minicomputer industry to provide increasingly complex machines at falling prices. The rapid development of ever more complex integrated circuits certainly helped miniaturisation and falling prices, even if the military was the principal consumer of integrated circuits until the mid-1960s (Braun and MacDonald 1982: 88–104).

US firms enjoyed a substantial productivity lead in the continuous flow industries after the war. The maturity of American control engineering, instrumentation and electronics combined with the affluence and growth of the domestic consumer market helped to make American firms world leaders. The comparative labour productivity figures, again taken from Broadberry, are given in Table 5.1. Insofar as we have data, they appear to show that the productivity gap in these industries was

Table 5.1   Comparative labour productivity in selected large batch and continuous flow industries, 1947–67/68
(US/UK labour productivity differential; in each industry and year, UK = 100)

	1947/48	1950	1967/68
Mineral oil refining	302		224
General chemicals		372	258
Iron and steel (general)			259
Blast furnaces	417	408	
Iron and steel smelting and rolling		269	
Bricks	166		169
Glass			218
Cement	115	116	191
Manufacturing		273	276

Source: Broadberry 1997a: Table A2.1.

wider than the manufacturing average in the immediate postwar period but closed more rapidly than for manufacturing as a whole by the later 1960s. However, a very important note of caution needs to be added. The figures are fragmentary and these industries were subject to very large variations in output across the business cycle. No comparative productivity figures control for cyclical variations, and we must expect some of the productivity differences to be caused by the different phases in the cycle in the two countries.[10] These figures are therefore very broad indicators of comparative productivity, and no more than that. The addition of Anglo-German comparisons can help a little, but not much as the same cyclical problems arise. Broadberry's (1997a: Table A2.2) benchmark estimates for 1967/68, show a bigger Anglo-German productivity gap in the continuous flow industries than in manufacturing as a whole, with the exception of general chemicals, where the labour productivity gap was almost exactly the same as the manufacturing average. However, by 1973 Britain's general chemical industry had closed the gap and oil refining industry had a large productivity lead over its German equivalent, and general chemicals had roughly the same level of labour productivity as the German industry (Broadberry 1997a: Table 12.3). But the cyclical nature and capital intensity of production in many of the continuous flow industries gave variations in capacity utilisation and thus efficiency levels. Thus any comparative measures are invariably unstable and subject to significant fluctuation. All we can say with confidence is that in the continuous flow industries both Britain and Germany were rather slow to exploit the opportunities offered by the increasing scale of production and the growing ability to monitor and control complex scientific processes.

British oil refining and petrochemicals

American technical and productivity leadership in oil refining led to the formation of firms that offered a combination of civil and design engineering services, designing and building refineries for an international market (Freeman *et al.* 1968: 30–1). As the chemicals industry became an ever more intense user of petroleum products, similar developments occurred also in this branch. During the third quarter of the twentieth century, technology became truly internationalised. In the terminology of Chapter 2, design engineering firms acted as the most prominent "change agents" in the oil-using industries. For oil refining, this was already an established practice in the interwar years and BP, for example, made much use of the US design engineering firm

M.W. Kellogg and Company, to negotiate the acquisition of patented processes and supervise the construction of new plant, in both the UK and its major Iranian refinery at Abadan (Bamberg 1994: 193, 202). BP turned to Kellogg to design and build an isomerisation plant at Abadan from technical data supplied by Standard Oil, New Jersey, and BP's own technical research centre at Sunbury, making it the first full-scale isomerisation plant in the world (Bamberg 1994: 245).[11] If not exactly a "reverse flow" in the terminology of Chapter 2, this technological development certainly illustrates the complexity of technical change in twentieth century oil refining. Although much of the capacity in design engineering was concentrated in the USA, and US firms were most prominent in export markets (Freeman *et al.* 1968: 32–44), R&D was international in scope and collaborative as other countries established their own civil and design engineers.

There was an enormous expansion of domestic refinery capacity in the early 1950s, as can be seen in Table 5.2. The new refineries also contained enhanced facilities to capture a wider range of refinery products.[12] Williams (1984: 321–2) has illustrated the pressure from government on the oil companies to create domestic refining capacity to reduce the import of refined products that were priced in dollars and on the chemical industry to switch to (domestically refined) oil from coal feedstocks. This big domestic expansion of oil refining capacity in the 1950s also relied heavily on the expertise of American design engineers.[13]

The new refineries contained the most modern control equipment (and there were already in 1956 trends towards standardisation and unitisation of instrumentation for the industry),[14] and moved quickly into the use of computers at the refineries to undertake technical work. Esso installed its first refinery computers for technical work in 1957 and

Table 5.2   Imports of oil into the UK, 1934–56
(annual averages in millions of tons)

	Crude	Refined
1934–9	2.1	8.9
1948	4.6	13.2
1950	9.2	9.9
1953	25.6	6.1
1956	28.6	9.4

Source: Burn 1961c: Table 8.

chose IBM for compatibility with the international division of its head-quarters at Standard Oil (New Jersey) (House of Commons 1969–70b: 222, 227). Headquarters found it much more difficult than anticipated to develop common software packages, but a series of materials inventory control programs developed at Fawley were adapted for use throughout the wider group. Fawley was relatively slow to use process control computers, with the first (a DEC PDP-8) installed only in 1968 (House of Commons 1969–70b: 227). Shell International also used IBM for its business machines for compatibility reasons, but selected process control computers from a wider range of suppliers and appears to have used them more extensively than Standard Oil (House of Commons 1969–70b: 237–9). In purely technical terms, therefore, there appears to have been no great gap between British and American refineries in terms of instrumentation and control systems.

However, it was impossible for British oil refiners to achieve the levels of labour productivity recorded in the USA. There appears to have been little difference in refinery design; the same design engineers were equally prominent in the USA and the UK. The largest British refineries of that time were comparable in size to the best of the USA, but Britain had a number of tiny refineries that remained in production because of the very rapid growth of demand.[15] In the mid-1950s, the US labour productivity lead resulted from larger refineries on average, and fewer workers per refinery. This issue of manning levels came to the fore in 1955 at Fawley when the parent company introduced new statistical comparisons of manpower utilisation in which Fawley made a comparatively poor showing (Flanders 1964: 65). The British problem was high levels of overtime working and relatively inflexible work practices.[16] The Fawley management called in US industrial consultants who proposed a low-overtime/high-wage system and a series of measures to improve the flexibility and utilisation of labour (Flanders 1964: 257–64). The productivity bargaining between management and unions at Fawley had mixed results. According to Flanders, the better results occurred in reducing the number of workers in the maintenance and construction department, though achieving only half the target reductions. Overtime was much reduced, and Flanders (1964: 193) estimated the labour productivity increase for this group of workers at 50 percent between 1960 and 1962. Little progress was made on more flexible craft working arrangements, however, despite very protracted negotiations with the unions (Flanders 1964: 175–90).

In his study of Fawley in 1983, Ahlstrand (1990) concluded that progress on labour flexibility continued to be very limited, but that the culture of extensive overtime soon returned and Fawley continued to have low labour productivity compared with the parent company's other refineries. Ahlstrand argued that Fawley's management lacked commitment to the low-overtime/high-wage strategy because they doubted their ability to extract the required level of effort from the workforce. Furthermore, the bureaucratisation and detailed specification of work rules that had been the central thrust of the company's attempt to deal with its unions had a similar impact in Fawley as did "workplace contractualism" (see Chapter 3) in the USA. Workers learned to manipulate formal managerial rules, in this case the conventions surrounding job demarcation. Ahlstrand's conclusions may however be unduly harsh, as he appears to have uncovered a "European condition" rather than undeniable symptoms of "the British disease". Labour productivity in German oil refining continued to oscillate around British levels without taking a decisive and lasting lead, but there is a sense in which these productivity comparisons are academic when studying an industry as globalised and integrated as oil refining. The oil giants are able to absorb extra costs at any one stage in the production process by recovering elsewhere (for example, in production or distribution) without great concern (Lynk 1986: 123–4). Their global refining capacity means that cuts in production can be concentrated on any refinery or refineries, and we know both that working below capacity was the critical element in efficiency at this stage of the production process and that demand for oil fell after 1973.[17] Furthermore, the opportunities for transfer pricing make the concept of "value added", upon which labour productivity calculations depend, equally problematic.

The chemicals industry switched to the same system of "design engineers" in the postwar years, with Kellogg equally prominent in this industry (Freeman *et al.* 1968: 30). As is well-known, the main US chemicals producers (apart from Du Pont) shifted from coal to oil feedstocks during the 1930s, giving US design engineering firms a competitive advantage. ICI had been considering its own production methods, and before the war was contemplating different feedstocks (coal via calcium carbide and acetylene; molasses via alcohol; or oil, using the distillation and cracking processes)[18] but were diverted by rearmament and the implications of its technology-sharing agreement with Du Pont (Reader 1975: 318–28).[19] In the 1940s it decided to switch into oil, and designed a new plant at Wilton on Teesside to be the main focus for oil-based production systems (Reader 1975: 391–408). Wilton's most significant feature was a cracking plant to produce chemical raw materials from light oil (naphtha) supplied from the Abadan refinery of the Anglo-Iranian Oil Company (BP). The very strong growth of demand for plastics, detergents and other products of the chemicals industry made the Wilton plant an apparent success, as the quote from Milward and Brennan (1996: 245) note:

> During the 1950s output of petroleum-based organic chemical expanded at a phenomenal speed to meet the demand for goods like detergents, nylon hosiery, synthetic rubber tyres, plastic upholstery and car parts, insecticides and fertilisers. Between 1950 and 1962 the contribution of petroleum as a source of organic chemicals in the United Kingdom grew at an average annual rate of 30 percent as against a 7 percent growth rate for chemicals as a whole. At the end of the 1950s, ICI's Teesside plant was the biggest petrochemical producer in Europe. From its beginnings with the manufacture at the Shell Stanlow refinery of a synthetic detergent the industry expanded into a range of organic chemicals.

ICI's Teesside plant (Wilton) embraced the feedback controls, instrumentation systems and continuous flow production that so excited the automation enthusiasts (McCallum 1955).

But the growth of the industry strained ICI's finances and left it struggling to compete in the aggressive postwar markets as new entrants poured into petrochemicals (Owen 1999: 341–2). ICI responded by investing heavily in the development of Wilton. In 1947 the ICI Board agreed an investment of £25 million at the site, by 1957 the sum sanctioned had risen to £114 million, and it continued to mount as the board tried to ensure that capacity increased evenly across the range of its petrochemical operations (Roeber 1975: 120; Young 1955). But in the 1958 recession ICI discovered that too many of its production plants were small and too many were still dependent on coal feedstocks (Turner 1971b: 148–9). In this difficult market environment, new investment at Wilton virtually dried up, but ICI's new chairman, Sir Paul Chambers, began to accumulate comparisons with equivalent American firms revealing that for a selected group of similar activities, ICI employed approximately three times as many people per unit of sales and more than twice as many people per unit of assets (Owen 1999: 343). Chambers unleashed a major investment programme after 1963, much of it at Wilton to raise the scale of production, when the organic chemicals industry again moved into vigorous expansion. Measuring in 1972 pounds, £330 million had been invested at Wilton by 1965 and by 1972, the figure was £560 million, representing a quarter of the company's total assets (Roeber 1975: 120). The first naphtha crackers had an annual capacity of 30,000 tons per annum, but by 1966 three new naphtha crackers had been built with a combined annual capacity of 600,000 tons and two further crackers built in the late 1960s had a combined annual capacity of 650,000 tons (Pettigrew 1985: 216). During this process of development, ICI developed the first all-electronic control system for chemical processes,[20] and was among the world leaders in computerising key stages in the production process. Programming a computer to control the cracking of the more volatile hydrocarbons was far more difficult than Thomas Walsh (see above) had imagined. It took two years to devise a programme to control the cracking of ethylene (described as "a characteristically erratic process"), but ICI was one of the first companies to introduce the system in its Wilton plant.[21] These capacity increases were undertaken at considerable risk.[22] ICI managed to push sales in Western Europe and North America, but found lower margins there than in the UK and continued to experience great difficulties in the downswing of the cycle for many of its bulk chemicals (Pettigrew 1985: 76–8).

Prompted by the Fawley productivity deals, Chambers also attempted to raise the productivity of ICI's workforce through its own productivity programme, the Manpower Utilisation and Payment Structure. The company concluded an agreement with the manual workers in 1965 and extended it to staff workers in the Weekly Staff Agreement in 1969 (Roeber 1975). In some of the smaller plants of the ICI empire, the programme was very success-ful,[23] but was especially difficult at Wilton because of the fragmenta-tion of management authority at such a complex site. These difficulties were slowly and directly addressed after John Harvey-Jones took overall responsibility for Wilton (Pettigrew 1985: 231–3). In many ways, the outcome of productivity bargaining at Wilton was similar to that at Fawley. Unions of the semiskilled were relatively enthusiastic but craft workers resisted job flexibility and managers avoided engagement (Pettigrew 1985: 229–33; Roeber 1975: 133). Like ESSO, ICI concluded a productivity bargain of sorts, but failed to convince the craftsmen. Indeed, this was a very long-established problem.[24] Once again, however, we may be seeing aspects of the European condition rather than of the British disease. As in oil refining, German productivity levels in general chemicals, one of the undoubted successes of German manufacturing, oscillated around those in the UK without taking a decisive lead (Broadberry 1997a:

Tables A2.2 and 12.3). Labour difficulties over multi-skilling clearly had only the most marginal impact on the pace and scale of automation in general chemicals.

ICI's main problem was size. It proved difficult to change the structure and culture of the organisation when markets became more liberalised and international in the 1970s and 1980s. In these new, more volatile market conditions, with uncertain prices for the main raw materials, there were great advantages in retreating from the continuous processing of bulk chemicals that had so captured the imagination of commentators on automation in the 1950s and 1960s. However, organisational change in major chemicals producers was difficult. ICI brought in American social scientists to invigorate the process, but with mixed results (Pettigrew 1985). The key to success in this new phase of the international chemical industry was to shift resources into the production of specialty chemicals, with higher added value, lower capital intensity and greater innovation in growth areas. In short, the chemical industry in the rich capitalist nations became "more market- or user-oriented and less technology- and output-oriented" (Pettigrew 1985: 61). In this phase ICI started relatively slowly, but caught up in the 1980s and 1990s (Owen 1999: 346–57).

British iron and steel

The established steel-making processes of the early postwar years might better be described as continuous batch processing. Molten steel would be produced and poured into an ingot mould. When it had solidified, the mould would be stripped off, the ingot placed in a soaking pit, reheated and taken to a blooming mill to be rolled into a semi-finished state. At this time, the USA was seen as the technological leader in iron and steel and, as in oil refining and petrochemicals, design engineering firms (often linked to innovative steel-makers) were active in technology transfer.[25] However, technical and cost conditions in the long boom tended to revitalise smaller-scale production, while simultaneously favouring very large, integrated plant. The two main developments were the falling price of scrap and the development of the basic oxygen process.

The falling price of scrap favoured the development of the electric arc furnace because it could operate efficiently with a charge made entirely of scrap. Before 1950, electric furnaces had been used for small batches of steel whose composition need to be controlled very precisely, but the long run fall in scrap prices enabled bigger electric furnaces to be built. The capital cost of this technology was much lower than the open hearth system as producers did not need blast furnaces, coke ovens and ore supplies (Haller 1966: II–186–7). Pulling in the opposite direction was basic oxygen steel-making, developed initially in Austria, which blew oxygen through the molten metal, raised the temperature quickly and burned off the impurities more rapidly and economically than the open hearth process.[26] Because oxygen steel-making depended upon the heat from the original molten charge, it could use only a relatively small proportion of scrap (30 percent in the 1960s) and needed blast furnaces on the same site (Meyer and Herregat 1974: 149–52). This technology favoured very large-scale production by integrated firms and needed very precise heat control to avoid expensive damage to the oxygen converter.

At the same time, new casting processes were developed to eliminate the need for ingot moulds, soaking pits and blooming mills, making possible considerable savings in capital cost, fuel and space. Continuous casting employed a mould, open at both ends, into which the molten steel was poured. As it passed through the mould, it cooled and emerged as a continuous strand of the required cross section. The strand was cut to suitable lengths to go to the hot rolling mill. Pressure casting saw molten steel poured into a covered ladle. Air or gas under pressure forced it through a tube into a mould, from which it also could be hot-rolled (Haller 1966: II–189). This made (parts of) steel-making into a truly continuous process industry, but all the technical changes of the postwar years depended upon better instrumentation, much closer control of processes and a more scientific approach to production.

From the late 1940s, British steel-makers were steered towards larger scale production and Americanisation. The iron and steel productivity team that visited the USA under the AACP concluded simply enough: "In all sections of the British iron and steel industry the greatest limitation on productivity today is the size of the unit of plant" (AACP 1952: 17). American steel workers produced between two and three times more output than their British counterparts thanks to a range of scale-related leads, but British steel-makers had considerable cost advantages, not least in labour, and their steel was comparatively cheap (AACP 1952: 14, 16). The British also had areas of technical excellence, notably in the design, instrumentation and control technology of blast and open hearth furnaces (AACP 1952: 18).[27] The AACP's assessment was similar to that reached by "independent" British visitors who were keen to catch up with US technological developments.[28] The steel-founding team thought that the spirit of competition and competitiveness was a key to the US technological lead (AACP 1949), and this has resonated with later analysts.[29] However, in 1947 the US Federal Trade Commission had charged the American Iron and Steel Institute with price-fixing and conspiring to kill competition, citing Bethlehem Steel and United States Steel among other giant firms (Carew 1987: 141). Whatever the impact of the Commission, the situation had not changed much by the early 1960s, with surprising price stability and continued dominance by the same largest firms as at the start of the decade.[30]

The actual progress of the industry after the war was not quite as had been anticipated by the AACP productivity teams and the architects of the early postwar plans for the industry. The most positive sign was the technological progressiveness fostered by the broadly based research activities within the industry. While the industry remained in private ownership, each firm had its own research laboratories, which undertook basic R&D work to meet its specific production and process needs, and the British Iron and Steel Research Association undertook a central organising role to avoid duplication of effort within the UK and ensure that ideas from overseas were assessed and circulated quickly within the industry.[31] The British Iron and Steel Federation's return to the Board of Trade (1957: Appendix II) automation inquiry mentioned increased deployment of conveyors to handle raw materials and of automatic control equipment to monitor and adjust variables such as temperature, air flow and pressure and air/fuel ratios. Interestingly, the industry was also experimenting with automatic quality control and regarded itself as on the technological frontier in this aspect of production. For example, the Joint Iron Council noted:[32]

Since about 1950, foundry engineers have thought seriously of automation in a fuller sense (e.g. non-human control of individual machines or of processes) but the use of this and of electronic data processing equipment for control purposes is still extremely limited and largely experimental.

As in petrochemicals, it took much more time than imagined in the mid-1950s to develop the potential of computers for controlling these industrial processes, but the creation of reliable minicomputers in the early 1960s gave a huge boost to innovation in this area. By the middle 1960s the steel companies had already installed computers to control parts of the production process and/or produce management data from processes.[33] In 1970, the nationalised British Steel Corporation listed 36 such machines, of which five were concerned solely with data logging and one was dual purpose (House of Commons 1969–70a: 147). They were spread around the corporation's many plants, but Ravenscraig and Port Talbot had four each. Throughout the organisation they had three broad areas of activity: control of furnaces, dimension control of rolling mills and optimisation of cutting operations and developed software on the process control side (especially for controlling electric arc furnaces – where it considered itself a world leader) that was exported in the design engineering work undertaken by Davy-United (House of Commons 1969–70a: 156). The British industry's sophistication in the new technologies of the 1960s can be seen also in the leading role of the British design-construction-engineering firm, Babcock-Wilcox, in the building of continuous casting plant and equipment in the USA, including the prestigious project for Republic (the third largest US steel producer at the time) at Canton, Ohio (Haller 1966: II–190–1). The AACP (1952: 116–18) steel productivity team had patriotically applauded the research excellence of the British steel industry and its collaborative research organisation with good cause. The British steel industry was by no means technologically backward.

However, its productivity performance was much less impressive. Despite committing to larger scale plant in the early postwar years, progress was disappointing. Chick (1992: 83–9) has pointed to the patch and repair investment policy in the context of postwar shortages of steel, lengthening completion times for the construction of new plant and a crisis of authority within the industry. Burn (1961d: 290) berated the industry in characteristically uncompromising terms for its lack of central authority and fragmented decision-taking. Rationalisation continued to be delayed by the strong demand for steel and was subsequently avoided because of the highly "political" nature of decision-making within the industry. Ranieri (1993) has shown that the British steel-masters wanted to retain the protective devices and cartel mentalities that had been assembled between the wars rather than engage with the rationalising potential of the European Coal and Steel Community, with ministers and civil servants unable to shake these convictions despite the clear attractions of the European initiative. Politicians could be equally mistaken, as when the Macmillan cabinet decided in 1958 to build two under-resourced strip mills (at Ravenscraig and Newport) rather than the one giant facility favoured by Richard Thomas and Baldwins (the company proposing the investment) and the industry's central authority (Vaizey 1974: 169–76).

Under a system of five year planning, capacity continued to increase (from approximately 14 million tons in 1945 to 32 million in 1965) but pressures on the least efficient to improve their performance were limited (Vaizey 1974: 148, 162). The central authority fixed prices and attempted to equalise costs to ensure stability and under this system British steel prices were low and extremely competitive into the later 1950s (Burn 1961d: 292) but the determination to provide a stable planning framework meant that too many obsolete plant were retained and the manning levels of even the industry's largest installations were generous. The return of a Labour government in 1964 and its re-election in 1966 with a more substantial majority raised the spectre of nationalisation and stimulated the industry to plan concentration of bulk steel production in the five biggest and most modern works (Port Talbot, Llanwern, Scunthorpe, Lackenby and Ravenscraig) (Benson 1966). The Wilson government was not persuaded and nationalised the industry, launching its own modernisation plan based on the same five plants.[34] This vision lasted until the deputy chairman of the nationalised British Steel, Sir Monty Finniston, visited Japan, saw the very large-scale, modern Japanese plants, where labour productivity was three or four times higher than in the UK (and almost twice as high as America's best).

Rather like ICI, British Steel embarked upon a huge investment programme, a major increase in annual output and a surge in productivity growth. However, British steel was destined to contract rather than expand despite regaining competitiveness after the devaluations of 1967 and 1971. The sharp appreciation of sterling in 1977–82 however undermined competitiveness and forced British Steel into major financial losses (Cockerill 1988: 86). The incoming Conservative government of 1979 balked at the rapidly worsening finances and the closure programme was accelerated, provoking a major confrontation with the steel unions in 1979–80. Sterling's appreciation created huge competitive problems of British manufacturing more generally, with inevitable consequences for British Steel's market share. The rationalisation of the industry was taken further and pushed faster, with impressive results in terms of productivity and competitiveness, though fundamental changes were taking place in the international structure of the industry. As in chemicals, the production of bulk products was becoming much more globalised, in part evidence of the maturing of automated measurement and control systems, and production was shifting to lower-wage developing economies.

The postwar history of the British iron and steel industry appears to be a story of technical competence married to commercial ineptitude until the "Thatcher effect" (the interpretation favoured by Owen), but we need to recognise that the record of the American industry was almost as dire in the 1970s (Crandall 1981). Even in France and Germany, rationalisation of capacity was painful and impossible to achieve through what might be termed "normal management practices" (Owen 1999: 146–50). The steel industries of all developed western countries have required a cultural revolution to cope with the emerging processes of globalisation.

Conclusions

There are similar patterns in these industries. They were at the leading edge of automation; they made extensive use of closed loop feedback controls in the 1950s and were at the forefront of computer-controlled processes as instrumentation became more complex and reliable in the 1960s. The key development was the creation of instruments to measure product quality under the harsh conditions of continuous industrial production. The steel industry was less completely automated than petrochemicals and oil refining, reflecting the multitude of shapes and sizes supplied by the bulk steel producers. The main reference point for British producers, at least until the early 1970s, was North America, thanks to the large productivity lead developed by US steel, oil and chemicals during the 1930s. Many British firms had excellent channels of communication to US technological leaders thanks to the cartel systems of the 1930s and the collaborative industrial research associations in sifting and disseminating promising innovations. The AACP only strengthened and broadened the contacts in steel and chemicals, and the growth of design engineering consultancies accelerated the international transmission of new technologies.

However, the major firms in these industries were also resistant to change. In steel, rationalisation was delayed until the industry was overtaken by fast-changing economic and financial events. The postwar business history of ICI is marked by persistent attempts by reform-minded managers, often from unconventional backgrounds, to re-shape the firm. In oil refining, similar issues faced BP. BP's commercial strategy before 1973 had been based on selling unrefined Iranian crude oil, which could be produced more cheaply than any other crude in the world. Bamberg (2000: 496–8) describes the culture shock in BP when OPEC nationalised oil production; it needed to refocus the whole business on downstream refining operations which had hitherto been peripheral to the company's activities and had operated at a substantial loss. The company needed a fundamental strategic reappraisal.

The most popular answers to the question why these changes in organisation did not come earlier identify culprits among the stakeholders within the firm; the unions insisted on over-manning and slowed the pace of change; managers were inadequately trained and could not manage the technological demands of continuous production; or the market framework was insufficiently rigorous to force the firms to address their problems. There are elements of truth in each of these popular explanations, but individually they cannot be very convincing. It is undoubtedly true that staffing levels in the oil refiners, ICI and British Steel were generous, particularly where skilled manual grades were concerned. However, labour costs comprised a small part of total costs in these industries, and the firms were compensated for low labour productivity by relatively low wage levels. As has been pointed out above, the British steel industry was a low cost producer into the late 1950s and its labour costs per tonne of output were pretty comparable in the 1970s and 1980s with the much more efficient West German industry, except when exchange rate movements were particularly unhelpful. There is evidence from these industries that skilled maintenance craftsmen were very keen to resist job flexibility and work extensive overtime, but this was a strategy by employees to maintain earnings differentials and by managers to retain workers whose skills were highly transferable to other firms and sectors (Marsden 1983: 287). It should not be interpreted as sabotage of technical change. Both ICI and the steel industry enjoyed solid labour relations for most of the postwar period; steel was selected by the DSIR (1957) as a shining example of consensual methods of dealing with the labour consequences of technical change.

The case against management in these sectors is also less strong than commonly assumed. There was a culture of technical proficiency in steel, ICI and the major oil refiners. ICI had "the most educated management in British industry" and in the postwar boom "provided a perfect bridge into industry for the young science [or engineering] graduate" (Turner 1971b: 139–42). BP and Shell were also heavy recruiters of graduates with technical backgrounds, blending Oxbridge arts with provincial science and engineering backgrounds (Bamberg 2000: 70–1; Turner 1971b: 139). Shell, ICI and BP were among the world's top 200 companies for R&D spending in the 1990s (Jeremy 1998: 430). The steel industry, more pragmatic and more empirically-minded (see Tweedale 1987), had a strong co-operative research culture. However, in all three sectors technological proficiency too easily translated into productionist mentalities. ICI managers of the early 1970s recognised that their culture had to shift from prime concerns with conservatism, rationality and technology towards greater market focus, commercialism and accountability.[35] The expansion plans of the re-nationalised British Steel Corporation have been described in very similar terms as "a technocratic, production-led vision which paid insufficient regard to the customer" (Owen 1999: 138). Managers did not foresee the fundamental problems they encountered in the 1970s because they had been conditioned by the continuous economic growth of the 1950s and 1960s. Both ICI and the British steel industry had seen cyclical downturns, but the underlying expansion was powerful and shortages of capacity consistently emerged. In such conditions, it is scarcely surprising that firms built new, larger-scale production units and retained outmoded capacity longer than advisable. Shortages were not simply a British phenomenon, but were endemic in the upswing in the cycles of steel, oil and petrochemicals.

Might the government have been more active at promoting competition rather earlier in the postwar boom? Broadberry and Crafts have suggested that British industries subjected to stronger competitive pressures tended to have smaller productivity gaps with their counterparts in the USA. For these continuous-flow industries, however, this analysis seems misplaced for two reasons. First, it is very unlikely that one can produce a key, summary measure of competitive pressure from which robust statistical conclusions can be drawn. In these industries, the strongly cyclical pattern of demand and the high level of fixed costs made price cutting especially prevalent during recessions. The summary measures of competition (the levels of tariff protection and/or the proportion of industry output generated by the three biggest firms) cannot capture this dynamic position. Secondly, the competitive structure of these industries tended to be set by their cost structures rather than by government. Cockerill's (1988: 82) assessment of steel would apply equally to most capital-intensive, continuous-flow industries:

> Severe fluctuations in prices and the likelihood of losses at times of poor demand have at various times encouraged steel producers in most industrialised markets to control the market either by means

of a formal cartel or through more formal arrangements. The intention in this way is to regulate the outputs of the participants so that supply and demand are broadly matched and prices are maintained at levels that permit profitable operations. Agreements that achieve these aims are however very difficult to devise and maintain in operation.

As noted above, the American steel industry colluded in the later 1940s and almost certainly attempted price leadership thereafter. In chemicals, the main producers concentrated on their own national markets during upswings of the cycle and fought against dumping during downswings (Pettigrew 1985: 53–60). It is by no means certain that these industries would have been helped by exposing the domestic market to foreign competition at a time when minimum efficient scale was rising so rapidly and capital development programmes were so huge.[36]

Finally, we must note how little pressure came from shareholders for changes in the strategic direction of these industries. In steel, the role of shareholders as providers of new finance was somewhat muted, not least because the threat of nationalisation and re-nationalisation made it difficult and expensive to raise finance in the ordinary capital market. The industry relied heavily on the Finance Corporation for Industry for developmental finance, but neither it nor shareholders pressed for rationalisation of capacity. It was only the threat of nationalisation in the mid-1960s that prompted the industry to propose its own scheme. Similarly, the shareholders of ICI and the main oil refiners created little friction for senior managers, though the government as majority shareholder of BP exerted a profound influence over senior board appointments (Bamberg 2000: 48–58).[37]

During the long boom, the main companies in steel, chemicals and oil refining epitomised the Keynesian public corporation, privately owned but directed towards national economic goals as much as private profit. From its creation, the board of ICI was conscious that "in all their major measures they would have to take the public interest into account, even, if necessary, ahead of the shareholders. They were frequently not free, as Du Pont's management usually were, to consider the return on capital employed or the purely commercial aspects of a situation" (Reader 1975: 473). Equally, BP had to take very careful account of the wishes of its majority shareholder, the British government, in framing its investment and dividend policies (Bamberg 2000: 130–40). When not in public ownership, the steel industry was closely regulated up to privatisation in 1988, and regulators paid particular attention to pricing policy. The Attlee government wanted cheap steel to facilitate postwar reconstruction and modernisation. When the Conservatives privatised the industry for the first time in 1953, its Iron and Steel Board imposed maximum prices, based initially on average historic costs and increasingly in the mid-1950s on new plant costs (plus an allowance for the considerable capital costs of new capacity), and continued subsidies, as noted above, to keep down input prices and prolong the regime of low prices. These major companies thus had a vision of the national interest that embraced technological sophistication, a commitment to import substitution across the widest range of products and the pursuit of scale economies. This vision became increasingly difficult to sustain as trade liberalisation gathered momentum and developments in automation allowed production of bulk commodities in countries with much cheaper labour. But these firms had developed their research and technological resources since the war, and it was their technical competence that enabled them to engineer these changes with some medium-term success.

6
Office Automation: Computers, Clerical Work and Management Systems

The explosion of interest in automation in 1955–6 was as much concerned with office work as with manufacturing. The Office Management Association held its conference on office automation a month before the Institute of Production Engineers' conference on the automatic factory in June 1955. Leading US commentators had already suggested that automation would have far more impact on the office than the factory (Fairbanks 1952; Diebold 1952: 94). This chapter examines why office work was automated, how it was automated and the impact for management of the new ways of producing, storing and analysing information. Office work has been comparatively neglected by business and economic historians, though there have been some recent signs of interest.[1] This has been a surprising omission, given business historians' interest in "the rise of the corporate economy" and "the managerial revolution". Other social scientists have produced most of the detailed and authoritative work on clerks and the evolution of office work.

Sociologists came to office work via social stratification and the apparently anomalous position of clerical workers – modestly paid workers involved in management (Klingender 1935; Parkin 1971; Stewart *et al.* 1980; Lockwood 1989). These debates have been sharpened by feminist perspectives, since in virtually all advanced societies clerical work has been transformed from a predominantly male to a female dominated occupation since 1900 (Crompton and Jones 1984; Dex 1985; Lockwood 1986; Lowe 1987; Crompton and Sanderson 1990). No recent study of clerical work can ignore the strategies and discourses that sustain segmentation by gender in the market for clerical labour (for a summary see Crompton 1997: 6–24). Twentieth century social and cultural historians have explored occupational segregation by gender (Glucksmann 1990; Morgan 2001), but rarely in the context of office work (but see Silverstone 1976). But the most challenging sociological analysis of office work comes from industrial sociology and Braverman's work on the labour process.

In Braverman's view, the logic of capitalist production is to "de-skill" the production process by rationalising, routinising and mechanising the flow of work, at first on the factory floor and then in the office. Workers have lost control of the pace and content of work and merely execute the plans of management and their lieutenants, the work study engineers. He believes that in the first decades of the twentieth century Taylorite ideas were extended into blueprints for office reorganisation. Braverman concludes that the clerical worker has become fully "proletarianised". In a much-quoted passage, he describes how clerical workers have become a "giant mass of workers who are relatively homogeneous as to lack of developed skill, low pay and interchangeability of person and function (although heterogeneous in such particulars as the site and nature of the work they perform)" (Braverman 1974: 308–9, quote 359). Braverman's answers to the how, why and impact of office automation are that it occurred *when* employers found it impossible to push the division of clerical labour further, they *used* automation to strengthen their control over the pace and content of work, *leaving* managers in a much stronger position over the production of clerical work. This thesis is however controversial when applied to the UK.

First, it implies that there was a pre-mechanisation "golden age" of the clerk, when clerical employment ensured high earnings, easy access to promotion and security of tenure but this notion has been undermined by historical research on the British case (Anderson 1976; 1977; Klingender 1935; Crompton and Jones 1984: 16–34). Clerical work became increasingly differentiated from 1850 and those clerks undertaking more routine work were increasingly subject to job insecurity and squeezes on pay. Braverman also implies that office work was increasingly organised on Fordist lines, with large-scale production, involving clearly differentiated and repetitive tasks, but in twentieth century Britain the great majority of clerical work occurred in small offices, except in financial services, public administration and the public sector more generally (Lockwood 1989: 74–80, 235–8, 246–52). Finally, the idea that white collar work has been "de-skilled" is undermined by surveys of clerical workers in the 1970s, who welcomed the introduction of word processors and computers into the office and registered an increase in job satisfaction, arising in part from the acquisition of new skills (Daniel 1987: 198–209; Lane 1988: 77–8). Above all,

Braverman has been criticised for exaggerating the coercive power of employers.

Since Braverman, sociologists have explored the range of strategies by which employers, and indeed employees, manufacture rather than enforce consent to managerial control (See Thompson 1989: chs. 5 and 6). Historical reconstructions of the labour process have tended to concentrate on the power of organised workers to resist managerial controls through collective bargaining over effort, reward and the frontier of control (see, for example, McKinlay and Melling 1999) but these studies are of limited value in understanding the behaviour of office workers (Thompson 1989: 180–209, 246–50). They do, however, point to Hirschman's (1970: chs. 2, 3 and 7) distinction between "voice" and "exit" as channels of communication between managers and workers. White-collar workers certainly became more tightly organised and bargained aggressively but the strong underlying demand for clerical labour offered unrivalled opportunities to register dissatisfaction by "exit" for work elsewhere, and was available equally to males and females (Bain 1970; Prandy *et al.* 1983; Price 1983; Crompton and Jones 1984: 167–208; Lockwood 1989: 135–98, 253–62). However, "exit", especially when measured by crude turnover rates (i.e. the proportion of employees leaving each year), holds a number of pitfalls as a measure of dissatisfaction among female clerks. Females were expected to leave paid employment on marriage or at the birth of the first child. Employers became concerned when high turnover forced up the costs of recruitment and training and when vacancy levels left them short-staffed.[2] Employers needed to pay attention as never before to the pay and conditions of clerical workers.

Thus, office automation in the mid-twentieth century has to be seen in the context of managerial efforts to control costs and the pace of work of a labour force with opportunities to resist by moving to another employer. The post-Braverman literature cautions against assuming both that automation was the only method of exerting tighter managerial control and that it was appropriate for all offices. The feminist critique of the labour process literature underlines the importance of sensitivity to the sexual division of the market for clerical labour. Furthermore, the professionalisation and specialisation of management in the twentieth century imply the potential for divisions within management on how best to control the enterprise. Office automation created a new group of specialists (systems analysts, programmers, data processing managers) who needed to create a role for themselves within management structures.[3] These themes are taken up in the chapter as follows. The next two sections examine the growth of the market for clerical labour and the signs of tension from the mid-1950s as turnover rates increased. The third section examines the postwar period from the perspective of the office machine suppliers and notes the extension of mechanisation and the rapid expansion of computerisation from the late 1950s. Next the focus shifts to the internal politics of management and the efforts in the larger, more bureaucratic firms to create management information systems that would allow instant access to and appraisal of huge "data banks" of information about the firm's performance. Discussion of the failure of this innovative use of computers by large firms is a stepping stone to consideration of the fragmentary material on the impact of office automation on costs and productivity.

Growth in the market for clerical labour

The third quarter of the twentieth century saw huge and consistent growth in clerical employment. Figure 6.1 shows that the number of clerical workers increased roughly fourfold between 1911 and 1971, from 0.9 to 3.5 million workers.[4] Clerks formed approximately 5 percent of the total workforce in 1911, 7 percent in 1931, 11 percent in 1951 and 14 percent in 1971. There was an administrative revolution in the twentieth century (Lowe 1987: ch. 2). In manufacturing, it reflected the increasing scale of production, the professionalisation of management with the rise of the corporate economy and the internalisation of decision-making within the enterprise. In the service sector, the growth of education, the health services and public administration were accompanied by bureaucratic management systems and lavish use of clerical labour. But beyond the boundaries of an administrative revolution, the postwar years have also seen considerable growth in demand for finance and business services, which resulted in rapid growth of demand for clerks (and shop-workers) (Millward 2004: 240–7).

More fundamentally, these shifts reflect changes in expenditure patterns and labour markets that have unfolded since the late-Victorian years. On the demand side, the expansion of clerical jobs resulted from increasing personal real income and changing patterns of expenditure, the growth of government and the increasing sophistication of production and marketing as real incomes rose. On the supply side, falling family size and changing ideas on the participation of married women in the market for paid labour allowed increasing numbers of mothers to combine their family responsibilities with (often low-) paid employment. At the same time, the steady expansion of secondary and higher education and the trend to improved examination performance provided a growing stream of candidates qualified for better-paid service sector employment, especially from the early 1960s when the "baby boom" generation began to appear on the labour market. The apparent difficulty of securing labour productivity growth at the same pace as in manufacturing has also been a feature in the rapid growth of employment (Baumol 1967; Mayes and Soteri 1994).

These deep-rooted changes help explain the pace and extent of expansion, but not the obvious changes in the gender division of labour evident in Figure 6.1. In 1861, clerical work had been a male preserve, but the number of females grew rapidly, especially after 1900 (Anderson 1976: 56–66; 1977: 113, 126–9). The huge expansion of clerical work created a large number of routine jobs, notably in taking shorthand, typewriting and operating telephones and telegraphs, and especially in London and other major commercial centres. These jobs did not lend themselves to career development into management and were regarded as unsuitable for males (Anderson 1976: 14–16; Lockwood 1989: 21–7, 122–32, 224–30). There are debates within the literature about how jobs become gendered but there is no doubt that, once labelled as "women's work", occupations became low-paid and

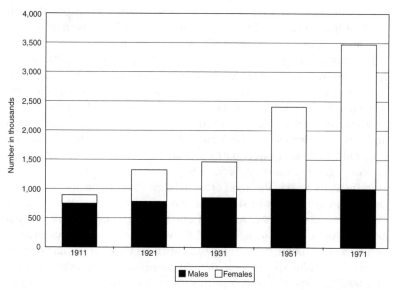

Figure 6.1 Number of clerical workers in Great Britain by gender, 1911–71

gender-typed in various ways.[5] It is also evident that women's clerical work has been closely associated with the introduction of machinery, though there are disagreements, mostly at the theoretical level, whether categories of work have been mechanised and "de-skilled" to facilitate the employment of women or whether women have entered mechanised, routine, clerical work (see Thompson 1989: 199–200). Most historical accounts suggest that, since the late-Victorian period, women clerks have formed a separate segment of the labour market, competing less with men than with themselves (Anderson 1976: 60–1; Silverstone 1976).

Although clerical work undoubtedly became "feminised" in the twentieth century, the number of male clerks actually rose slightly between 1911 and 1971, but at a much slower rate than the number of females. By 1951 females comprised almost 60 percent of the clerical workforce and female clerks 20 percent of the female workforce (Routh 1980: Table 1.1). Female clerical work continued to grow and by 1971, the females constituted just over 70 percent of the clerical workforce and more than a quarter of female employees were in clerical work. Lockwood (1989: 75–7, 235–7) estimates that in 1950 half the clerks in manufacturing were in establishments of 26 or less and two-thirds were employed in establishments employing 80 or fewer. Little had changed by 1982. Data for the average number of clerks per establishment in the public sector and private services is simply not available, though the best indications are that in private sector services it is smaller than in manufacturing but in the public sector larger on average.

To measure the success of employers in filling these posts, salary data (collected by Routh) are given in Tables 6.1 and 6.2. Table 6.1 shows average annual clerical salaries by gender indexed on 1955–6 and clerical salaries relative to average annual earnings. Pay for females has grown more rapidly than those for males, both since the early 1920s and postwar. However, these figures must be treated with care because they reflect different career paths of males and females. Male clerks can expect regular promotion and rising salaries throughout their full working careers. Female clerks are much less likely to be promoted and often fall significantly in status and pay when returning to work after family responsibilities (Crompton and Jones 1984: 129–66). Annual earnings *standardised for age* would show female salaries before age 25 in a more favourable light. Table 6.2 illustrates the differential between clerical and industrial workers, defining the latter as semi-skilled males and females respectively. It confirms the well-known point that the difference in pay between male clerks and male manual workers disap-

Table 6.1 Average annual clerical salaries by gender and as a percentage of national average salaries, 1922–78

	1922–4	1935–6	1955–6	1960	1970	1978
Male clerical workers						
Average annual salary (£ current)	182	192	523	682	1,337	3,701
Index (1955–6 = 100)	35	37	100	130	256	708
Percentage of average annual earnings for year (m and f)	116	119	98	97	97	93
Female clerical workers						
Average annual salary (£ current)	106	99	317	427	839	2,730
Index (1955–6 = 100)	33	31	100	135	265	861
Percentage of average annual earnings for year (m and f)	68	61	60	61	61	69

Source: Routh 1980: Tables 2.27 and 2.29.

Table 6.2 Differentials between annual average clerical and semi-skilled manual earnings by gender, GB, 1922–78

	1922–4	1935–6	1955–6	1960	1970	1978
Male clerical workers						
Ratio of male clerical to male semi-skilled manual earnings	144	143	112	117	104	97
Index (1955–6 = 100)	130	129	100	105	93	87
Female clerical workers						
Ratio of female clerical to female semi-skilled manual earnings	108	99	118	126	130	116
Index (1955–6 = 100)	92	84	100	107	110	98

Source: Routh 1980: Table 2.27.

peared in the postwar years. Female clerical workers opened an earnings differential in the "transwar" period and improved it during the long boom but this was more the result of falling relative pay for female factory workers than gains by white collar grades.[6]

The figures considered so far are national averages, but more anecdotal material from the late 1960s and early 1970s indicates that female secretarial staff in London could command far in excess of the figure given in Table 6.1. Well before 1970, clerical staff employment agencies regularly reported salaries of over £1,000 p.a. for secretaries in London, with large differentials over other cities.[7] The concentration of head offices in London also fostered the growth of the executive secretary, with a salary in the late 1960s up to and beyond £2,000 p.a. and generous fringe benefits.[8] The particular problems of the London market for clerical labour were acknowledged by the Wilson government's Prices and Incomes Board, which was closely concerned with pay for clerical workers (NBPI 1968a; 1968b).

On the whole, however, the clerical labour market appears to have been very orderly. Both rapid growth of numbers and gender transformation were managed with minimal disturbance to relative salaries, at least nationally. Problems were more apparent in London, but this was true for all classes of worker. And yet, employers of clerical labour regularly complained about their inability to control costs.

Tension in the market for clerical labour from the 1950s

From the mid-1950s, employers complained ever more loudly about rising costs, staff shortages and other malfunctions in the labour market. The Board of Trade's survey on automation in 1955–6 received forthright views. One of the major petroleum refiners, for example, was considering computers "to provide management with better and more up to date facts for decision making and to halt the tremendous growth of clerical staff".[9] One member of the Excavator Makers' Association calculated that the cost of a computer and auxiliary equipment would be paid for within four years by anticipated reductions in clerical staff. The Multiple Shops Federation reported on the "current shortage of clerical staff and the need to reduce clerical costs" and Lloyds of London, though admitting that its members were unlikely to incur the expense of installing a computer, nevertheless complained of the excessive costs of "unskilled and unsettled" junior clerical staff. Significantly, the larger employers in banking, insurance and local government hoped to curb the growth of clerical costs while improving the quality and accuracy of work. By the early 1960s, the banks in particular were alarmed and angry (*The Banker* 1961: 522):

The turnover in young girls [aged 18, 19 and 20] is alarmingly rapid, and youngsters who leave their banks after less, than, say, a year's service have given the banks little or no return for the money (in training as well as salary) invested in them. In each successive summer, as the banks wait impatiently for the new school leavers, the staff problem in the larger centres becomes increasingly difficult. Other employers, of course, have similar troubles, but few have them in so acute form as the banks, where rapidly increasing business presses on a staff still working unpopularly irregular hours in a five-and-a-half day week.

Among the most frequent reasons given by young women for "premature" quits were boredom, job monotony and lack of promotion (McNally 1979: 164–70).[10] In such circumstances, "Bravermanian" control strategies had little chance of success.

Nevertheless, efforts to tighten control were commonplace in the 1960s. Standard Telegraph and Cables introduced a clerical work improvement (CWI) scheme from 1964 because of difficulties in recruiting and retaining adequate clerical staff (Bayhylle 1968: Appendix A, quote p. 5, emphasis added). Management was urged to exert greater control over the flow of clerical work, by measuring the time taken to complete standard tasks and establishing work targets. CWI was but one of a number of schemes proposed to contain the growth of clerical costs. In all, "the real heart of the matter ... is *control* of the [clerical] work force necessary to do the job within stated requirements" and involved measurement, reporting and enforcement. Within the public sector, the pressures to cut costs became evident in both central and local government from the early 1950s and resulted in the spread of organisation and methods departments in the larger local authorities and public corporations (*Public Administration* 1951; 1954; Nottage 1954; 1955; Agar 2003: 252–9, 293–305).

But for every employer that tried to tackle the problem of high turnover, many more accommodated to it. They worked with the growing number of clerical and secretarial employment agencies.[11] The Alfred Marks Bureau, established in 1919 as an employment agency for catering staff, moved into the secretarial field in 1955.[12] The growth of employment agencies into the early 1970s reflected the sellers' market for labour (McNally 1979: 106–7). In the 1960s, employers began to use "office temps" in the face of pervasive difficulties in recruiting permanent clerical staff.[13] Despite their relatively small numbers, "office temps" helped foster the image of a highly volatile labour market.

On balance, it appears likely that employers were more concerned about their inability to *control* clerical staff than about costs. Given the ease with which clerical staff could evade tightening of managerial control systems by relatively costless quits, many employers continued to seek technical solutions to these problems. As before, technical methods of controlling labour implied pushing mechanisation further, and mechanisation remained the only real option for the average employer of clerical labour. But for the larger, more bureaucratic office systems, automation became a viable alternative in the later 1950s and early 1960s.

Clerical work and office machinery

The telephone, typewriter, adding machine and tabulator began to transform US office work at the turn of the century, but in Britain (where clerical labour was relatively much cheaper), the growth of the office machinery market took off only during the First World War, when shortages of clerical workers combined with the growth of larger-scale business to mechanise clerical work.[14] Wardley's (2000: 83–4) inventory of the office equipment of the typical large-scale commercial office of the early twentieth century includes the telephone, typewriters, steel filing cabinets and adding machines, with accounting machines following in the later 1920s.[15] However, British offices were a long way behind American levels of mechanisation, and remained so into the 1960s, by which time they were also a long way behind both Germany and Sweden.[16]

Demand for office machinery in the UK grew strongly after 1945 and much was supplied from heavily protected (by tariffs in the 1930s and quotas in the 1940s and 1950s) British firms (Prais 1981: 228–32; Campbell-Kelly 1989: 72–152; Milward and Brennan 1996: 258–60). Typewriters, simple accounting machines and cash registers were readily available; the supply and sophistication of duplicating equipment expanded consistently. Significantly, although the first document copiers were installed in 1946, supply did not grow rapidly until the mid-1950s (Hays *et al.* 1967: 54–7). Dictaphones, duplicators and copiers enabled economies in the use of copy- and shorthand-typists. Punch card tabulators and accounting machines allowed large-scale routine clerical tasks (such as payroll calculations and stock control) to be mechanised but were subject to long delivery delays for the newer and more attractive equipment (Campbell-Kelly 1989: 172). Thus, many employers responded to labour market pressures further mechanisation. But for others, British and US trends pointed to automation.

After 1945, employers of clerical labour, like their manufacturing counterparts, regularly visited the USA to observe new technologies at work. As noted in Chapter 2, among the first were two management accountants from the catering firm J. Lyons and Co., which had long been a leader in office management systems.[17] The road from this visit to the production by the catering firm of business computers, office software and clerical work systems is now well known.[18] In addition to work for the parent company, the first LEO computer undertook payroll work for Ford, Stewarts and Lloyds steelworks, Kodak, Every Ready batteries, Tate and Lyle sugar and RAF officers' salaries for the Glyn Mills Bank (Hendry 1987: 88; Caminer *et al.* 1998: 54–6, 64, 229–48). Some of this agency work led directly to sales of the next generation of LEO computer and, in the later 1950s, LEO machines were in use for data processing at Stewarts and Lloyds, Ford and Imperial Tobacco.[19] LEO Computers received a constant flow of managers keen to see at first hand the potential of office automation. The newly formed British Computer Society also acted as a powerful propagandist for business applications and many firms relied on the well-established method of learning about new technologies from visits to the USA.[20]

Table 6.3 gives reliable estimates of the quickening pace of computer installation in the 1950s.[21] As well as the LEOs noted in the previous paragraph, in 1958 Elliott 405s were in data processing applications at ICI, Unilever, Legal and General Assurance, Reed paper-producers, Reckitt and Sons and the North West Gas Board. EMI machines were used by the British Motor Corporation, Boots and Glaxo. IBMs were used by AEC, Bristol Aeroplane, Goodyear, Shell, Rolls Royce and General Electric, Tube Investments and the National Coal Board. The Ferranti Pegasus II was used by A.V. Roe, Armstrong Siddeley, British

Table 6.3   Computer orders and deliveries for commercial work in the UK to June 1959

	Storage medium		Total
	Punch-cards or paper tape	Magnetic tape	
Firm orders received at June 1959	67	42	109
Number delivered by			
June 1955	1		1
June 1956	2		2
June 1957	7	3	10
June 1958	30	12	42
June 1959	49	27	76

Source: Goldsmith 1959–60: 97.

Table 6.4   Uses for computers ordered or installed by June 1959, UK

	Storage medium		Total
	Paper, cards	Magnetic	
Firm orders received by June 1959	67	42	109
Number of applications running or planned			
Payroll	36	16	52
Stock control	16	18	34
Costs	21	6	27
Sales invoicing	8	9	17
Sales statistics	8	9	17
Production control	9	5	14
HP, insurance or government	10	5	15
Other	6	4	10

Source: Goldsmith 1959–60: 98.

Thomson Houston and Babcock and Wilcox. The oil companies used computers for data processing and the Central Electricity Authority also reported the use of a computer in routine accountancy and scientific calculations involved in loading generating plant in day-to-day operations. The main uses at this time are set out in Table 6.4, which shows that routine but relatively large clerical tasks predominated. However, even at this stage the range of applications was impressive. The aircraft manufacturers needed computers to undertake the technical calculations needed for aircraft design and specification. The oil companies, the Metal Box Company, Unilever and Pilkingtons developed linear programming to optimise inputs and outputs for continuous process operations. British Rail used its Elliott 405 solely for research calculations. Within government, nine installations had been delivered, all from British suppliers, for central government by June 1959, where the Treasury O&M department had identified a long list of computerisation projects. There are indications that local government was even further advanced.[22]

In 1956, LEO Computers Ltd judged that its automatic office would suit any firm with a clerical staff of over 400, provided that the clerical routines were repetitive, involved a significant amount of computational work and managers needed statistical information to monitor details of the business (Board of Trade 1957: Appendix IV). There were only around 100 offices with clerical complements in excess of 400 in private manufacturing at the time, but undoubtedly more in the public sector, which, in combination with the data in the previous paragraph, suggests that the public sector was rather slow to embrace office automation. By the end of the following decade, however, the economics of office automation had changed dramatically.

In the 1960s, the computer began to mature as an office machine. Technological progress had been rapid; transistors replaced the inherently unreliable vacuum valves in the late-1950s and in turn were replaced by integrated circuits in the mid-1960s. These transformations are often used to differentiate first (valve), second (transistor) and third (integrated circuit, or "chip") generations of computers. For users and applications it is more useful to distinguish scientific calculation, batch processing and real-time, on-line computing into three generations. The early scientific computers had a small stored memory, fast processing speeds and undertook long, complex calculations. When more sophisticated input-output equipment was added computers could undertake the many simple calculations and produce the complex outputs required for commercial applications. The first commercial computers processed work in batches, using the full power of the computer for each task successively. The real limitation of this generation was stored memory, but between 1960 and 1965, "the memory size and speed of computers both increased by a factor of ten – giving an effective performance improvement of a hundred" (Campbell-Kelly and Aspray 1996: 196). This leap forward enabled programmers to develop "real-time" applications, those that could respond to external messages within seconds. This potential developed from military applications, but was quickly diffused after the enormous success of American Airlines' SABRE seat reservation system.

SABRE developed from a partially automated system, the "Reservisor", which was heavily publicised by the first "automation experts".[23] However, the Reservisor had obvious limitations and American Airlines soon began to plan with IBM for a computerised real-time operation that could undertake more tasks, provide the airline with a huge "data bank" of customer information and integrate more of the airlines management systems (McKenney *et al.* 1995: 100–14; Gallagher 1961: 161–74). SABRE took and developed innovations that IBM had introduced into the US Department of Defense's SAGE air defence system (see Chapter 2 above), but ten years and $40 million (approximately the cost of six Boeing 707s) were needed to pass from plan to implementation (Gallagher 1961: 168–70; Flamm 1988: 78–9, 88–95, 116–17). SABRE gave American Airlines 10 percent better load factors for its airliners than the industry average (McKenney *et al.* 1995: Fig. 4.2) and appeared to be the foundation of a lasting competitive advantage. Its real-time potential was known even to British audiences from 1961 (Hope 1961–2). SABRE became fully operational by December 1964, shortly after IBM had announced its System/360.[24] IBM promised real-time operations and multi-programming, which helped boost computer sales into the second half of the 1960s. At the time, the best way to carve out a competitive lead seemed to be in real-time computing and restructured management systems, though management strategists now doubt whether companies can protect a technological lead for any length of time (Kay 1993: 101–12).

The use of computers for commercial work certainly grew very rapidly in the UK in the 1960s. Ten years after the figures given in Table 6.3, there were 4,013 computers in use in Britain, of which 42 percent were in manufacturing industry and a further 33 percent in services (House of Commons 1969–70b: 12, 20–1). The pattern of specialisation emerging in 1959 was now more pronounced. First, the continuous flow process industries used small computers to control production processes or logging data on continuous process, as considered above in Chapter 5. At the other end of the scale, the aircraft manufacturers, atomic energy authority, oil and chemicals companies used powerful "super-computers" to undertake complex calculations involved in product design or the increasingly elaborate linear programming developed by the oil industry and others to optimise production.[25] However, the bread-and-butter work of computers remained clerical-labour-replacing routine commercial work on payroll, stock control, invoicing and accounting (House of Commons 1969–70b: 11).

It is easy to understand why computers were used more extensively in basic clerical and accounting work in the 1960s; costs were falling rapidly. IBM quoted the cost of doing 100,000 additions on its most advanced machine; in the mid-1950s the cost was approximately 10s. (50p.), in 1965 the cost had fallen to 2s. 3d. (11p.), and in 1970 to 4d. (1.67p.). The estimate for 1980 was 0.01d. (0.004p.) (House of Commons 1969–70a: 86). At these levels computerisation became attractive to smaller firms, especially in standard areas like payroll and stock control. The National Computing Centre estimated that there were 20,000 users of computer service bureaux and that 60 percent of British firms would use computers in some way (House of Commons 1969–70b: 10). The Wilson government established the National Data Processing Service using Post Office computers to provide both data processing for large consortia of users and bureau services for smaller firms (House of Commons 1969–70a: 321–2). It was now possible for medium-sized firms to automate their more mundane, labour-absorbing clerical tasks.

The Post Office provides classic examples of office automation from the 1960s. On 16 December, 1964, it ordered five LEO 326 computers as the first instalment of computerising the clerical and accounting side of the telephone service – at the time the largest order for general purpose commercial computing anywhere in Europe and only part of a huge project to extend computerisation of clerical work throughout the GPO and Department for National Savings.[26] Of the latter project, the senior consultant for LEO computers described this commission as bringing the Premium Bonds Office at Lytham St Annes "straight from quill pen to high tech ... [The Office] was housed in wartime Nissen huts, each bearing the letters of the accounts for which it was responsible, such as 'Ta to Tg'. There were clerks whose entire life was encompassed by a single letter of the alphabet". Even allowing for hyperbole, this was a very sharp technological transformation that vividly illustrated the potential of computers in transforming routine clerical work.

Paradoxically, this explosion in office automation was accompanied by growing sense of frustration and dismay among the user community.[27] ICI, for example, noted its new IBM 360 had consistently performed below initial expectations despite the best efforts of IBM and its own staff (House of Commons 1969–70a: 167–8). Late deliveries were common, but the dominant problem lay in the operating systems of third generation machines. The earlier generations had been relatively easy to program and operate. However, as memory expanded and processing speeds increased, more complex programming was feasible and the industry discovered that software had developed with much less speed and sophistication than hardware. The introduction of third generation machines was swiftly followed by a software crisis that engulfed the entire industry. IBM was at the centre of this storm. As the manager of software development for System/360 acknowledged: "The effort cannot be considered wholly successful ... The flaws in design and execution pervade especially the control program ... Furthermore the product was late, it took more memory than planned, the costs were several times the estimate, and it did not perform very well until several releases after the first" (Brooks 1995: xi). Despite increasing the number of programmers working on the software (which did more harm than good), the "bugs" in the system proved intractable, especially in the multi-programming version which was badly delayed. IBM eventually spent more on software development than on any other aspect of System/360 (Pugh *et al.* 1991: 331–45; Brooks 1995: 14–25; Mobley and McKeown 1989: 36–7). Its competitors were in at least as much trouble.[28] No third generation machine had a reliable operating system in the mid-1960s (Campbell-Kelly and Aspray 1996: 196–200; Sobel 1981: 221–30).

The most obvious consequence of the software crisis was to tighten the market for computer specialists as hardware manufacturers, software developers, commercial users and bureau operations competed for programmers and systems analysts.[29] The software crisis made an already difficult situation simply unmanageable. Salaries rose and attracted teachers away from colleges into industry.[30] What remained of the training system simply did a poor job; three quarters of employers complained about the low quality of their systems analysts and, as will be seen from the banks in Chapter 7 below, the standard of those hired from agencies was probably worse. Rapidly rising salaries discouraged employers from investing in training for fear of poaching, and they preferred to poach from rivals, driving up salaries still further. Only those organisations with scientific culture and a long commitment to computing (ICI and UKAEA, for example) were able to cope, but even they had to pursue conservative technological choices to economise on scarce programming skills.[31] These strains in the labour market had most impact on those attempting an "American Airlines" strategy – innovative, real-time, multi-programming initiatives, as will be seen in the next chapter. For those wishing simply to automate routine clerical work, the shortage of specialists was irritating rather threatening. Computer bureau services could always provide an interim safety net.

Office automation and management systems

Firms investing in office automation in the 1960s were seeking many objectives – less disruption from high labour turnover, closer control of the quality and volume of work and lower (or less rapidly rising) costs. It is possible to identify a hierarchy of "office automaters", with bureau users at the bottom, above them the computer owner/leaser driven mainly by cost reduction and above them the larger firms, with more ambitions to use the computer to its maximum potential in managerial decision-making. It was commonplace almost from the introduction of office automation that using computers in routine clerical tasks was unimaginative and short-sighted (Diebold 1958; Caminer 1958–9). In the 1960s and 1970s a series of studies bemoaned the uninspired uses of computers in British industry (Coopey 1999: 65). More recently, the debates on the "IT paradox" (see below) have suggested that computers will produce significant efficiency gains only in those firms that restructure management as part of an automation strategy (David 1990; Mowery 2003). Finally, the most cited article in the *Harvard Business Review* suggested that firms should reengineer to concentrate on their core competencies, making managerial transformation almost a *sine qua non* of corporate success (Prahalad and Hamel 1990; see also Hamel and Prahalad 1996: chs. 4–6).

However, there is more to be said for those at the bottom of the ladder of ambition than was believed at the time. Computer bureaux offered cheap processing power.[32] In both the USA and UK computer users found it difficult to load their machines fully, encouraging them to sell computer time cheaply and thus keeping bureau prices low.[33] The bureau market grew very quickly, at approximately 30 percent per annum in the 1960s, and was dominated by the services provided by both ICL and IBM as a shop window for their hardware. Bureau users were primarily medium-sized firms without the resources to invest in computer methods, but also included larger firms wanting complex systems and a number (Marks and Spencer and Wedgwood, for example) that questioned the economics of running a computer but wanted to reduce the cost of routine clerical work. Given the availability of cheap processing, the febrile market for computer specialists and the uncertainty surrounding software for third generation computers, cost saving via a computer bureau looks a sensible business choice.

On the next rung were those with their own computer, but with relatively mundane and modest operational uses. Commentators complained that third generation hardware was commonly used to support second generation systems in the private sector, and both McKinsey and Booz-Allen suggested that between two-thirds and three-quarters of British commercial computer installations were uneconomic in 1970.[34] The public sector invariably reported that computers were justified by cash savings, but the arcane systems of public accounting invites scepticism about the impact on total costs.[35] It is not difficult to see how the critics concluded that most computer installations were commercial failures. This does not imply that all firms undertaking routine clerical work employed inappropriate hardware nor even that all users of third generation computers placed a cost burden on their firms by carrying out simple programs. The logic of the mass market strategy of IBM System/360 (one-size-fits-all) was that the hardware and software architecture could deliver solutions to common business problems. There clearly were customers whose computing needs could be met very successfully by prefabricated solutions.[36] However, both theory and contemporary empirical observation suggest that the really successful computer users would be those who could harness the potential of the new hardware and software to the mass of commercial information generated within the firm to transform managerial decision-taking and in the process restructure management and the firm itself. Such was the potential of computers and the "management information system".

The idea was born in the USA during the Second World War as "planning" techniques spread throughout the economic system as mobilisation gathered pace. Thomas Haigh (2001) has described the efforts of "systems men" to take the lessons of successful integrated planning into the peacetime era. They believed that wartime planning had demonstrated the value of the systems approach to management, bringing together all the technical and management information and skills together in a single administrative services department which should be the locus of planning in the enterprise. They claimed the right to design, shape and control the flow of information within the firm and establish themselves as pre-eminent generalists among fragmented groups of management specialists. This vision was heavily promoted within the American Management Association, not least by members of the Systems and Procedures Association of America (SPA – formed in 1947), into which "systems men" were organised.[37] Although it was taken up by leading personnel in McKinsey and other management consultancies and was promoted in influential publications, the systems approach had limited success in the 1950s.[38] In the early 1960s, however, it alighted upon the potential of the computer and academic developments in information and organisation theory to proclaim the potential of the "integrated" management information system (Anshen 1960; Daniel 1961; Ewell 1961; Barab and Hutchins 1963). Systems men redefined the terminology of business computing – no longer "electronic data processing", the IBM formulation, but the creation of management information systems. A full management information system had three elements: computers to capture and manipulate data produced by the firm, communication links between computers within the firm and the use of this data to inform decision-making at all levels of management. This was primarily an American movement that was sustained and nurtured by national institutions of management education and information. But control of information flows within the firm, the scale and scope of computer installations and the basis of strategic planning were certainly politicised in a number of large British companies in the 1960s.

As noted above, British firms, especially those with large-scale bureaucratic administration and a scientific corporate culture, had been among the early users of computers and tended to purchase machines with scientific capabilities. As a result, they pioneered the use of mathematical techniques to illuminate business decisions. BP, for example, was a recognised leader in the application of operations research to business decisions.[39] With the advent of the raw computing power of third generation machines and the software to allow multiple, remote, real-time access, they were in the vanguard of consolidating their computing onto a small number of fast, powerful machines, which would store enormous quantities of commercial data (captured from automated office systems) and perform sophisticated business calculations.[40] Many were clients of McKinsey in the 1960s.[41] They went to McKinsey because they suffered a variety of management difficulties and received advice to decentralise and improve the quality of management information for strategic decision-makers.[42] It is hardly surprising that they should be seen as world leaders in creating management information systems.[43] In each, the interrelated questions of business structure, computerisation, control of management information and managerial responsibilities became highly politicised and critical to corporate success.

Shell, for example, had experienced rapid growth between 1900 and the mid-1950s, but its management system had grown haphazardly, leaving the company ill equipped to deal with the emergence of much tougher international competition. The board commissioned McKinsey to reappraise management structures and attempted, not altogether successfully, to shift directors from executive to strategic responsibilities. Information management also needed improvement and Shell became a major investor in computer systems, moving up quickly through the "generations" of computers, and adopting management information techniques, pioneered in the US operations.[44] Early in the process of automating clerical work in Shell, there were deep divisions between the "data processors" and the "mathematical modellers" over the choice of equipment and the place of computing within the company, but the board recognised the difficulties and placed a succession of young high-fliers in charge of the operation. At board level, the importance of management information was recognised by the appointment of a senior director with responsibilities for planning and co-ordination between the parts of a global company. In the late 1960s, satellite transmission made internationalisation of data communications networks possible and Shell interlinked large-scale Univac "super-computer" installations in France, Germany, the UK and the USA, providing large databases of commercial information and capacity for sophisticated modelling. In short, Shell was one of the more successful users of management information systems. Centralised data systems had helped a company, that in the 1950s had become dangerously divided between its two head offices and rival power structures in London and The Hague, "to overcome the nationality barrier" (Turner 1971b: 102).

As was evident in Chapter 5, in ICI change was more difficult. The same conjuncture of slowing markets and intensifying competition also led the chairman in 1960 to McKinsey's door for help to reform management structures. Sir Paul Chambers, the charismatic chairman from 1960 to 1968 tried to transform the company, but his agenda opened up divisions within the boardroom (Pettigrew 1985: 70–3, 449–50; Turner 1971b: 99–106, 139–63; Owen 1999: 339–52). Organisational change required robust central structures to allocate resources, establish priorities and create a durable, management information system among units that had a strong culture of independence. No such machinery was contemplated until the return of Richard Beeching to ICI in 1965 from his attempts to reorganise British Railways. He established a powerful corporate planning department, which became the focal point of those wanting stronger central control.[45] Unfortunately, there were operational and political difficulties in creating computer systems to support such a role, and Beeching's vision of a much more flexible, dynamic but smaller ICI was rejected by the board, causing his resignation.[46] The board preferred a more evolutionary approach to change.[47] In the 1980s, John Harvey-Jones was able to make more effective use of the available, and often discomforting, management information to persuade the board to foresee both competitive conditions and company strategy five years ahead, rather than wait until the market delivered its painful judgements (Pettigrew 1985: 395–410, 417–37; Owen 1999: 348–52). But even then, the processes were far from smooth and involved liberal use of external consultants, vigorous lobbying behind the scenes at board level and opportunistic exploitation of the mishaps and discomforts of opponents.

The public sector also came under the influence of arguments that the combination of computerised data processing and sophisticated modelling techniques could revolutionise management if sufficiently powerful computers were available. The technique most commonly adopted during the 1960s was PERT (Program Evaluation Review Technique), initially developed in the USA by Booz, Allen and Hamilton for the US

Navy's Special Projects Office to handle the development of the Polaris missile range. PERT was essentially a method of critical path analysis to allow sensible planning and scheduling for complex projects and was quickly taken up by US defence and aerospace suppliers (Miller 1962). Booz, Allen appointed Christopher Bland, an Englishman with excellent contacts in local government, as Managing Director of its London office and PERT was rapidly adopted in local government in the mid-1960s (Kipping 1999: 213; Agar 2003: 333–42). Within Whitehall, it was taken up first by the Ministry of Transport to help plan the complex land acquisitions and planning decisions needed in motorway building, and spread from there to the Ministries of Aviation and Technology in a vain effort to manage the costs of the Concorde project. In ways that exactly parallel developments in private industry, Agar concludes that groups within management structures of central and local government managed to persuade their superiors to acquire more computing power than was necessary for the job in hand, in part because the size of the computer should reflect the prestige of the organisation that purchased it. The choice of software was also politicised – PERT was useful not only to the Ministry of Transport, because it was used to centralise control of motorway building away from local authorities, but also to the experts who staffed the specialist groups who executed the technique. Just as with the business elite, "political power increasingly accommodated the application of computers and the expert movements that promoted them" (Agar 2003: 52).

Thus, the critics of British industry's use of computers in the 1960s were for the most part on secure ground. Many firms and organisations had bought more powerful hardware and software than they really needed. In the 1960s, the most successful British users of computers in clerical and managerial functions were those at either end of the size spectrum. Small- and medium-sized firms that relied heavily upon bureau services to meet their computing needs had chosen well. Some of the very large firms made successful uses of mathematical techniques to enlighten decision-making. In fact, there are many parallels with the USA. All the grandiose designs to use computers to build integrated information systems, giving executives new powers of control over their firms, came to nought. Haigh (2001: 52) reports that "Computer hardware, though powerful enough to inspire enormous confidence when compared to earlier machines, was hopelessly inadequate to the task of building a [management information system] ... MIS was ubiquitous in theory but unknown in practice". Even McKinsey turned against the idea in 1968. There were successful transformations of a company's competitive position by combining automation of clerical tasks with carefully tuned managerial structures, but they tended to depend upon special conditions: firms led by a technologically innovative chief executive who could rely on a "maestro of technology", a manager with a combination of business acumen and well-developed IT skills, and an innovative team to implement the new methods (McKenney *et al.* 1995: 4–6). For the great mass of US firms using computers in clerical and managerial roles, contemporary judgements echo the British complaint of second generation systems running on third generation machines. A leading writer in *Fortune* claimed, "Most companies – even the most advanced – seem to agree that computers have been oversold – or at least overbought. It turns out that computers have rarely reduced the cost of operation, even in routine clerical work" (Alexander 1969).[48] Just as in Britain, most US commercial computers were under-utilised (Schroeder 1971: 15). Contemporary judgements are by their very nature suspect, but they tend to confirm the "IT paradox" that has baffled later analysts.

According to the eminent US economist, Robert Solow, there is an "IT productivity paradox" in the late twentieth century – computers are everywhere except in the productivity statistics (cited by Morrison 1997: 471). The debates about the productivity of computer investment in both manufacturing and services have rumbled for more than a decade and have become bogged down by the highly intractable measurement problems (See Griliches 1994; Jorgenson and Stiroh 1995; Sichel 1997; Whelan 2001). Much of the discussion is tied to specific dynamics of aggregate US labour growth, with comparatively little research on the UK, none of it for the period under discussion here.[49] However, there is also growing agreement that firms which have also restructured have been the most successful in reaping productivity gains from computerisation (David 1990; Roach 1991; Loveman 1994).

Fortunately, neither elaborate econometric models nor sophisticated historical comparisons are needed to explain the limited impact of computers on economic performance in the 1960s and 1970s. The speed of computers increased rapidly during the long postwar boom and the cost of undertaking standard calculations plummeted. However, commercial users did not undertake standard calculations; they needed operating software to undertake a variety of tasks. For a critical period in the mid- and late-1960s operating systems were unable to match the potential of the hardware and productivity inevitably suffered.[50] But to make profitable and efficient choices of computer hardware and software, companies needed to have a clear vision from the boardroom of how clerical and management operations could be re-shaped by automation. This appears to have been as scarce a resource in the USA as in the UK. The average business executive did not understand computers and many resisted the reorganisation necessary to make best use of office automation and management information systems.[51] In the 1960s and 1970s, computers may even have retarded the rate of productivity growth.

Conclusion

The main reason for introducing office automation was the emergence in the 1950s of a severe problem in the production of clerical work. The volume and complexity of clerical work was rising and employers, especially in the major cities, were experiencing great difficulty in recruiting and retaining suitable staff. Job turnover could be especially high among the young, unmarried females that were drawn in ever increasing numbers into office work. The postwar boom and the growing confidence and independence of young females in the labour market eroded the control over costs and the clerical labour process that interwar employers had wrested by mechanising and re-drawing gender boundaries. Some employers reacted to the tighter postwar labour market in classic fashion by extending to clerical work the basic principles of Taylorist scientific management, but the environment was unfavourable. Clerical work was generally undertaken neither in large units nor with great specialisation of function, and labour market conditions allowed easy quits for those suspicious of "time and motion" in the office. The office machinery industry tried to cope by producing bigger, faster and ever more specialised machines for the comparatively few large-scale, specialised offices and an increasing range of more commonplace office machines – electric typewriters, duplicators, photocopiers – to enhance the productivity of the modal clerical worker, undertaking a range of tasks in a relatively small office.[52] But large-scale employers needed a more substantial technological solution to their problems, and the computer was developed initially as a superior tabulating machine – indeed, it probably used punch-cards and used many of the same types of peripheral equipment.[53]

In the 1960s, many firms appear to have been swayed more by fashion and internal politics than rational commercial calculation in their decision to computerise. Firms computerised before exploring the potential of "traditional" means of reducing costs and raising labour productivity in clerical work. In the USA, informed observers believed that firms were capable of raising the level of clerical labour productivity by work simplification, form re-design and related systems-and-procedures techniques (Gallagher 1961: 33; Bayhylle 1968). There was also much still to be gained on both sides of the Atlantic from work study, especially when accompanied by job enrichment and similar initiatives. If employers thought that they could side-step these mundane and politically sensitive initiatives by using a computer, they were probably mistaken – unless, of course, they simply bought in data processing services from a bureau.

Where office automation *promised* (or, perhaps, threatened) to break new ground was to automate management. The idea of a huge array of instantly available information on the company, its operating units, the wider industry and international conditions seemed to offer chief executives unrivalled power over their organisations. Computer suppliers undoubtedly encouraged customers to believe that their machines, especially of the third generation, could store, locate and probe huge quantities of data, allowing senior executives to grapple instantly and directly with problems and opportunities of operating units. Haigh (2001) has demonstrated that there were those in both the managerial hierarchy and consultancy work who were equally keen to use this vision to further their own interests. Although these ideas were most fully developed in the USA, they had a profound influence on large, bureaucratic, scientifically-oriented firms in the UK. However, neither the hardware nor the software of the 1960s could meet the aspirations of the systems men and the promised "de-layering" of management had to await the development of further machine power and more refined software in the 1990s. Moreover, the increasing financial, economic and political uncertainty began to undermine the confidence of those companies, like BP, that had made significant use of sophisticated mathematical techniques in business planning.[54] In turn, technologically sophisticated firms turned increasingly to simulations rather than optimisation in planning their future in an increasingly insecure world economy. These were important steps for the future, just like the creation of large databases, but produced limited real benefits in the turbulent conditions of the 1970s. Although the accretion of business computing power and powerful corporate central planning staffs appears very Galbraithian, in reality *The New Industrial State* was very far from realisation.

7
Bank Automation

This chapter provides a case study of the broader developments in Chapter 6. The banks were large-scale employers of clerical labour in both small units (the typical branch) and much larger, specialised "office factories" (head office departments, notably in cheque clearing). They had been pioneers of interwar office mechanisation and placed themselves at the technical frontier of large-scale computing in the 1960s. Computers were introduced to reduce staffing pressures but bank employment rose continuously until the mid-1970s. Banks began and ended the computer race with conservative technical choices but flirted with more experimental hardware and software in the mid-1960s. To some extent, the banks were victims of the software crisis noted in Chapter 6, but were also in part responsible for the disappointing impact of automation before 1973. This chapter begins by surveying the banks' staffing problem in the 1950s and then the partial successes with the new computer technology in the early 1960s. The third section examines the banks' difficulties with third generation computing. The fourth looks at some of the new products that became possible after the introduction of computers, and particularly the cash card/credit card. Finally, British experience is compared with that in the USA.

Rising costs, mechanisation and its limits

Before 1970, high street, or retail, banks operated according to simple business rules. They took deposits, usually from personal customers, and lent money, usually to businesses. However, as business and personal customers began to use their accounts more frequently (roughly from 1918), the volume of work rose, notably in recording transactions and processing cheques. Before computers, cheques had to be sorted, bundled and totalled several times in the journey from the receiving to the issuing branch. Bankers were thus concerned with their own internal procedures and those used in the wider banking network, organised through the Committee of London Clearing Banks (CLCB). Bank processing systems were established in the years 1917–30, when "the big five" (Barclays, Lloyds, the Midland, National Provincial and the Westminster) were created by amalgamation and each developed strong central control of office procedures. Senior managers had a keen eye for cost saving and from the late 1920s turned to mechanisation and feminisation to undertake the rising tide of routine work in large city branches and head office departments (Wardley 2000: 81–8; Holmes and Green 1986: 161, 190; Ackrill and Hannah 2001: 77–9; Rouse 1933: 238). Under the cartel and with encouragement from the Bank of England, the retail banks operated a common interest rate on deposits from customers and on loans to the discount market (Griffiths 1973: 7–11). The banks did compete – for larger business clients and, by extending branch networks, to win more personal and small business customers (Holmes and Green 1986: 160–74, 190–2; Ackrill and Hannah 2001: 90–108).

The Second World War had a substantial impact on bank technology and labour. The loss of male bank clerks to the armed services led to some branch closures and the substantial introduction of "temporary" female staff, some of whom retained their roles postwar. In all banks the stock of office machinery ran down as a result of wartime controls and difficult supply conditions until 1950.[1] When more normal economic conditions returned as shortages disappeared and controls were relaxed, the banks found it difficult to regain their interwar self-confidence. Postwar prosperity intensified longstanding difficulties and brought some new business problems.

First, rising affluence and creeping inflation encouraged customers to use their accounts yet more intensively. The number of cheques increased very rapidly (Table 7.1), raising account processing costs. The banks also found fiercer competition in both deposits and lending. Building societies captured growing shares of middle and working class savings. The value of the banks' current and savings accounts barely kept pace with inflation (Table 7.1). On the lending side, government pressures limited bank advances to industry as part of anti-inflationary policy. Banks left personal lending to the building societies (for house purchase) and hire purchase companies (for credit sales of consumer durables). The banks' own investments, particularly

Table 7.1   Growth of accounts and cheque use in British retail banks, 1946–66

	Value of current accounts £ millions	Value of deposit accounts £ millions	Value of cheques cleared in year £ millions	Volume of cheques cleared in year millions of items
Jan. 1946	3,315	1,594	69,011	
Jan. 1951	4,181	2,078	108,773	331
Dec. 1956	4,270	2,386	160,889	
Dec. 1961	4,166	2,711	242,348	438*
Dec. 1966	4,905	4,597	552,000	574

Note: * Dec. 1960
Sources: *Barclays Bank Review*, statistical appendices; *The Times*, monthly report on clearings.

holdings of government bonds, also performed poorly, eroding their underlying financial strength (Capie and Billings 2001: 229–30). The banks' financial positions were sustained by the low levels of default on industrial lending, itself the product of Bank of England pressure to limit advances to priority cases. In short, there were strains in bank finances in the 1950s.

The banks looked to generate new business, as they had in the inter-war years, by labour-intensive extension of the branch network. This implied a big recruiting drive, especially for school leavers. The banks told the Board of Trade:

Recruitment policy must be based on the requirements of the Banking industry, which demands that the main intake of male staff should be in the lower age bracket in order that training from youth can be given in the Banks' specialised requirements. In the case of female staff, the main need for the Banks is for young women to operate the machines that now form a large part of their system, and experience has shown that this work is entirely unsuitable for older women.[2]

Unfortunately, a career in banking had become less attractive to male school leavers. Throughout the 1950s, bank chairmen regularly complained about the quality of their male intake (*The Banker* 1963a: 548). Turnover was also very high by interwar standards, and the banks lost not only those with little aptitude but also some of their brighter prospects. In the 1960s, staffing levels became so critical that they recruited "over-age" and, almost by definition, low quality male staff, especially in London (NBPI 1969b: App. G). Attempts at "tiering" entrants to reward (and, it was hoped, retain) potential managers met

Table 7.2   Lloyds Bank staffing position, 1945–69

	Total staff	Percent female	Percent of female staff leaving in year
Dec. 1945	13,920	44	8*
Dec. 1951	17,690	41	17†
Dec. 1959	20,160	47	20
Dec. 1969	32,510	52	28‡

Notes:
* figure for 1938
† average of 1949–51
‡ figure for London in this year was 30 percent
Source: Winton 1982: 150–1, 166, 190.

some success but graduate recruitment failed abjectly (*The Banker* 1963a: 549–51; 1966a: 29–31; NBPI 1965: 4, 15–16; Ackrill and Hannah 2001: 157–8). Quality thresholds were lower for female staff, and all banks recruited heavily. The Midland, for example, engaged more than 1,000 female school leavers each year from 1958 to 1961, when single females under the age of 20 comprised 16 percent of its total staff.[3] But retention was a problem. The figures of female staff turnover for Lloyds are given in Table 7.2, and show a gradually accelerating rate. For banking as a whole, the problem was worse in London than elsewhere and, by general consensus, female staff turnover rates were slightly above those of comparable employers (*The Banker* 1961; Winton 1982: 151; NBPI 1969b: 5).

To improve recruitment and retention, banks improved starting salaries, especially for females. Lloyds calculated that between 1952 and 1960 the pay for a 17-year-old recruit had risen by 94 percent, whereas that for a 31-year-old had grown by only 69 percent (Winton 1982: 165). For young women, Lloyds, the first to make decisive shifts in its gender balance after 1945, led the way by introducing in 1946 equal pay for female recruits, removed the marriage bar (in October 1949) and freed female staff from pension contributions before the age of 25. The equal pay provisions gradually extended up the age scale so that by the mid-1960s equal pay was granted up to the age of 22, 23 or 24 (depending on the bank) and again after promotion to "appointed staff" level. All banks introduced London weightings in the 1940s and consistently kept them ahead of those paid by the civil service.[4]

Raising pay altered the economics of mechanisation. The banks bought ledger-posting machines for smaller provincial branches and in

November 1959 the Midland became the *first* British bank to extend mechanised book-keeping to its entire network, having converted 300 branches in 13 months.[5] But mechanisation did not solve the problem of staff turnover, as is evident in Table 7.2. It also brought other problems, notably growing pressure on space. The average branch could easily accommodate a ledger posting machine and peripherals. But the big office machines were noisy, hot, bulky and unpopular with staff.[6] When assembled *en masse* in head office machining rooms or back offices of the major London branches, they created an unpleasant working environment and, with the associated peripheral equipment, ate up space.[7] Rents in the City and the West End of London made it essential for the banks to find more compact, operator-friendly alternatives (Ackrill and Hannah 2001: 330; Vine 1967). The suppliers were aware of the situation, as they judged that a generation of equipment was approaching renewal.[8] For Britain's leading retail banks, decisions on techniques of production were becoming very urgent by the late 1950s.

Banks and automation with second generation computers

Long before they introduced computers, British banks understood the potential of automation. The British Bankers' Association told the Board of Trade automation enquiry that they needed to automate cheque clearing, branch book-keeping and the specialised accounting systems at head office to curb the growth of labour costs and, interestingly, to tilt the gender balance back towards men.[9] In the 1950s, British banks were keen observers of US technical trends, especially in San Francisco, where Bank of America (BoA) had pioneered the use of computers in book-keeping and cheque clearing.[10] The US banking system's agreement on standards for cheque automation was carefully watched in the UK, where the CLCB established an electronics committee to establish its own standards. It had to agree the size of cheques, the quality of the paper on which they were printed, the systems of coding (for banks, their branches and the customer account number), and how and where this information should be attached to the cheque (Booth 2002: 314–16). This took time, and provoked increasing impatience from banks on both sides of the Atlantic.[11]

It is perhaps surprising that before 1960 no British bank followed BoA by computerising routine clerical work. There were three main reasons. First, automated cheque clearing was the first priority; half of all bank staff in the 1950s was employed directly or indirectly on cheque clearing (Simpson 1967: 510). Unless deposited at the branch where credit and debit accounts were held, cheques had to be sorted by hand, bundled and tallied on adding machines several times in the clearing process. It was dull, repetitive work (invariably undertaken by young female clerks, both in branches and at head office) and consequently eminently suitable to automation. Secondly, the banks were not convinced until 1959–60 that computer technology was sufficiently reliable for bank book-keeping. It made sense to continue with punched-card machines until clearer signs that computer technology was more mature. Finally, clerical labour tended to be relatively more expensive in the USA than in the UK.

By the late 1950s, however, British banks were champing at the bit. Glyn Mills was the first British bank to use a (LEO) computer to administer its accounts for army and RAF officers (see Chapter 6) from the LEO bureau so Martins was the first English bank to install its own computer, with a rented Ferranti Pegasus 2 in its South Audley Street, Liverpool, branch in January 1960.[12] In July, the Westminster demonstrated computer accounting in one of its City branches using a LEO II, but ordered a Pegasus 2. Barclays, which announced the first firm computer order, chose an EMI EMIDEC 1100, with which it planned to operate the accounts of several London branches from a central location in Drummond Street. Of the main English banks, only Lloyds and the Westminster Bank bought from US suppliers. Lloyds installed three IBM 305s, initially at its Pall Mall branch, but it quickly expanded to make the Pall Mall branch its London computer centre. The Westminster bought an IBM 1401, with a cheque reader/sorter from the same supplier. The Midland, characteristically a little late on the scene, opted for the English Electric KDF 8, not least because English Electric banked with the Midland and Sir Archibald Forbes was director of both companies. It, too, established a London computer centre to handle the accounts of the larger London branches.

British banks stepped cautiously into the computer age. They formed small groups of programmers, in part from their own staff resources and in part from the hardware suppliers (Booth 2004: 285–6, 289–95). The banks tended to automate existing practices, adapting their ledger posting machines to produce output – punched-cards or tape – that could be used as input for the computer to update account details in the form of a number of "runs", each to record changes to some aspect of the account details. Accuracy checks were built into every stage. As the scale of processing increased "computer centres" began to proliferate, first in

London and then the Midlands, North-West and North-East. Updating invariably occurred overnight, so that accurate account details could be delivered to the branch for the opening of business on the following day. Delivery of input to and output from the computer centres varied greatly. Barclays used a teleprinter, but more common was by van, though Bank of Scotland was first to transmit data through the public telephone lines.[13] However, until the capacity of data transmission and the speed and power of processors could be increased, bank automation would remain regional rather than national in scope.

By the mid-1960s, the banks had created, in large part from their own staff resources, workable automated systems to operate where staffing and cost pressures were most acute. The Midland even managed to overtake the pack, meeting all its computing deadlines by the end of 1966 and becoming the first British bank to open a computer centre outside London. This was achieved without antagonising staff or customers. At the outset, bank staff were certainly suspicious. The National Union of Bank Employees (NUBE), the independent union in banking, recruited extensively during the 1950s and 1960s, exploiting a number of long-standing staff grievances.[14] But it was unable to make automation a major recruiting issue. In fact, bank workers saw an immediate advantage in computerisation, which reduced compulsory overtime at branch reporting times and when interest rates were changed (Buckler 1964: 439). There is some, not very reliable, evidence that labour turnover fell in computerised branches.[15] In fact, the main doubts about the new systems came from branch managers, who no longer had their ledgers for instant review of account details and status (Simpson 1967: 507). Some customers quibbled the introduction of machine-produced statements, but otherwise they saw little change in service standards (Buckler 1964: 437–8).

On the other hand, the staffing position deteriorated. Figure 7.1 shows that employment growth accelerated as computerisation gathered momentum. The volume of work was growing much faster than the labour saving potential of computerisation. With the growth of monthly and quarterly payments of utilities bills, instalment credit payments, mortgages, insurances and other financial services, bank accounts were worked still more intensively. Standing order payments strained the processing systems to the limit. The need for faster progress on cheque clearing, which would also take in standing orders, was becoming very urgent.

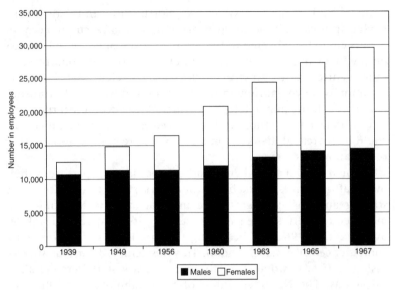

Figure 7.1   Employees of the Midland Bank by gender, 1939–67

Third generation computing and management overreach

1964 was an important stage in the transition to an automated banking system. As noted in the previous chapter, it was the year of the IBM System/360 and the full operational working of American Airlines SABRE system. In the same year, the GPO introduced its first national data communications system, Datel (House of Commons 1969–70a: 322–4). Optimists saw these developments as heralding generally-available, real-time, on-line network computing. Banks rushed to order IBM Series/360s, either like Barclays and National Provincial for the first time, or in the case of the Westminster and Lloyds to upgrade. The Midland decided to remain with its British suppliers, now English Electric LEO (formed by merger in 1963). Early in 1965, the Westminster began to experiment with high-speed data transmission and brought the first provincial branch on-line to its central computer later in the year. These were newsworthy events but, away from the publicity, progress with cheque clearing was disappointingly slow.[16]

The basic idea was very simple. By agreement, cheques were printed with a code line at the bottom, carrying details of the cheque number, customer account number and home branch sort code, in an ink and with a type font that could be read by machine.[17] If the value of the cheque could also be typed onto the cheque, also in machine-readable form (a process known as "encoding"), the precise details of each cheque entering clearing could be read by machine and recorded onto magnetic tape. Each member bank could then produce a magnetic tape with details of cheques presented at one of its branches to be drawn on accounts in other branches of the parent bank and similar tapes with details of accounts to be debited and credited in each of the other member banks. Thus, when the system was fully developed each member bank of the CLCB would send in its own tape to an automated clearing house in which computers would produce from these "input" tapes a further "output" tape for each bank with details, sorted by branch, of the accounts that needed to be changed.

Cheque encoders and reader-sorters had been in operation in a number of banks since 1961 and in 1963 Lloyds went a considerable way to automating its clearing department.[18] However, automated clearing involved large start-up costs and produced few short-term savings. Full benefits would accrue only when all banks had fallen into line, and this process was very slow. The CLCB's estimate for the structure and level of operating costs appears in Table 7.3, and assumed that the volume of cheques cleared would rise at 7.5 percent p.a. for the decade 1964–74. By 1974, the total costs of clearing would fall, and the labour component would plummet. Moreover, in the initial stages staff released from cheque listing and sorting had to be redeployed to

Table 7.3 Anticipated cost structures of different methods of cheque clearing, 1964
(distribution of total costs between three functions)

	Manual system in 1964	Automated system (central encoding) in 1964	Estimates for automated system (branch encoding) in 1974
	A	B	C
Staffing	90	39	24
Premises	6.5	8	3
Machines	3.5	53	73
		Total costs in this system estimated to be 16.6% above those in A	Total costs in this system in 1974 estimated below those in A

Source: HSBCGA, London, Acc 200/677, Report, CLCB Clearing automation sub-committee.

encoding, which had to be undertaken in each bank's head office clearing department because encoding machines were so expensive. The CLCB wanted manufacturers to produce a much cheaper encoding unit to allow every bank to encode cheques as they were received at the branch. Branch encoders were finally supplied, but late, and the first generation had a mixed service record. The reader/sorters did not work entirely as anticipated either.[19] Lloyds, the bank with most experience in cheque clearing, complained that even after six years of automated clearing, approximately one-eighth of items presented could not be cleared automatically.[20] Savings came, but late in the day.

The early estimates of staff savings were not fanciful. Independently, the Midland estimated that automatic capture of information from computerised clearing of cheques and standing orders would account for 60 to 70 percent of branch work.[21] This calculation reflected months of intensive study of branch workloads and clerical staffing needs.[22] US studies showed realised labour savings of a similar magnitude.[23] The CLCB accepted the principle of magnetic tape exchange in 1965.[24] The following year, it agreed to process standing orders through similar systems, and the year after that to establish an Inter-Bank Computer Clearing Centre.[25]

In discussions of automation in British banking circles, the balance shifted from the conservatives to the progressives in 1965–6. Progressives among the banks' automation experts, centred on a new Inter-Bank Research Bureau, looked to "chequeless" banking and much more sophisticated communications systems, but British banks began to overstretch themselves in a computer race during the mid-1960s.[26] In part, they had built a bubble of optimism after their success with second-generation computing. In part, overreach was externally induced by pressures from the computer suppliers for bigger, better systems and from the government, which had reached a very dim view of the banks' ability to manage their rapidly growing workforce. But pressure also came from within.

Chapter 6 hinted at a tacit but "unholy" alliance between computer producers, who proclaimed the huge management potential of third generation computers and "systems men" within firms, who championed massive data banks and integrated management information systems that they would supervise. The Midland's systems analysts quickly grasped the potential of third generation machines to create a huge management information system. They hoped "to provide a centralised accounting and information service to all branches of the bank. This will be achieved by the linking of branches and Head Office departments to the computer system so that the resulting complex can be regarded as one entity".[27] Built into this single system were much improved managerial information, elaborate checking and reporting systems and tougher central control over the discretion of branch managers, especially on lending and the management of advances (Booth 2004: 288) The Midland was by no means alone; Barclays was subject to similar internal pressures (Ackrill and Hannah 2001: 333).

Unfortunately, any tendency towards excess ambition in UK banks was amplified by a competitive war among US computer manufacturers. As noted above, IBM secured orders from four of the British "big five" for System/360 machines in 1964–5. The capital cost of putting an entire branch network on-line was enormous, and the central processing unit represented less than half the total. The biggest single element was for branch terminal units, and it was scarcely surprising that Burroughs, the leading manufacturer in this area, should bid for mainframe contracts. As noted in Chapter 2, Burroughs sold aggressively. For the National Provincial and Barclays, it produced bids for the entire system of central processor and branch terminals that undercut IBM significantly.[28] Both banks contracted to purchase the huge Burroughs 8500, which was still in the development stage. The Midland was also persuaded to cancel its order for third generation English Electric LEO Systems 4 machines in favour of Burroughs, in this instance two 6500 computers, which were also in the development stage. Burroughs persuaded the Midland that there would be fewer problems in linking Burroughs terminal units to a Burroughs central processor than to the machines on order (and already in difficulty with performance criteria and delivery schedules).[29] Changing hardware suppliers at this stage can be understood only in the context of a strong belief in two propositions – the bigger the central processor the better and that competitive pressures were hardening and the bank with the best real-time, on-line system would win.

The Conservative government became keen to increase competitive disciplines in 1961, when the banks broke Selwyn Lloyd's "pay pause". It used threats of state-sponsored competition to bring the banks into line. In 1959, the Radcliffe Committee (1959: 44) raised the issue of the lack of banking facilities for working class customers. Retail banks were very ambivalent about extending their services down the social scale. They feared the cost of offering intensively used accounts with small underlying balances, but were at the same time concerned that a large-scale "working class bank" would erode their business and establish itself as a viable competitor (*The Banker* 1963b). In 1961–2, the Conservative government let it be known that it was considering the establishment of a giro bank by the Post Office.[30] The banks managed to thwart this threat in part by introducing their own credit transfer system, which performed a similar task to a giro system.[31] However, the election in 1964 of a Labour government, dependent for economic success on an effective prices and incomes policy, raised the stakes and its NBPI made the banks a special target (NBPI 1965; 1967; 1968b; 1969b). Its report on bank charges was damning, arguing that the restrictive practices fostered by the cartel caused misallocations of resources both in banking and in the whole system of credit allocation. Its recommendations – that the banks be allowed to compete more freely, that "true" profits should be disclosed and, above all, that the monetary authorities would allow further amalgamations – shook the industry.[32] The Labour government had already set up the Post Office Giro as a computerised, automated bank.[33] The editor of *The Banker* (1966a) was in no doubt that the Post Office Giro posed a real threat, especially its cheap services to businesses.

The retail banks did indeed take the competitive threat seriously, spending heavily to publicise their own credit transfer system, which they renamed the "bank giro".[34] But the banks were more deeply concerned about the market distortions created by the ways that monetary policy had operated (Moran 1986: 41–7). The growth of new wholesale markets (Eurodollars, sterling and dollar certificates of deposit and the inter-bank market in sterling deposits) encouraged innovation, notably the fringe, or secondary, banks (that is, outside the regulatory jurisdiction of the Bank of England) to make lending commitments that the clearing banks could not enter because of the curbs on advances (Kynaston 2001: 268–87, 395–414). Banking was a contestable market, despite its durable and officially sanctioned cartel, and there were many within the industry who believed that full-blooded competition rather than uneven administrative guidance was the best way forward.

Moran (1986: 29–54, quote 53–4) notes that the new financial instruments, new markets and new institutions "endangered the privacy, informality and freedom from partisan political argument ...of [the] esoteric politics [of banking] ... Esoteric politics is ... a fragile social form. It can only be practised by small, socially cohesive elites so united that internal differences show themselves merely as limited technical arguments. The complexities of modern policy making destroy cohesion, privacy and informality". For their part, the banks were convinced that competition would be fierce and ultimately hinge upon IT systems, as was evident in recent US experience. The message was reinforced by the computer manufacturers, who were offering ever more powerful bangs per buck. The vision of the banks' own systems men of vast integrated management information systems pointed in the same direction, and was also promoted by hardware firms, software developers, leading business schools and leading management consultants. Overreach was almost inevitable.

Overreach certainly occurred. All the banks hoped to bring on-line systems into operation in 1968–9, certainly before 15 February, 1971, the date chosen (in 1966) for Britain's conversion to decimal currency. The Midland, for example, planned to put all its branches on-line by November 1968 and to create a centralised data store and management information system by October 1969.[35] Completion of the first phase was delayed until mid-1975, and the path-breaking management information system was never finished. Barclays also failed to complete a full on-line branch network before decimalisation. The merger of the National Provincial and Westminster banks delayed their respective timetables for on-line computing, to reconcile two initially incompatible systems. Only Lloyds managed to connect all branches to its two computer centres (in the City of London and Birmingham) on time (Booth 2004: 279; Ackrill and Hannah 2001: 334; Winton 1982: 187–8).

At one level, it is possible to explain the success of Lloyds simply by continuity. It started with IBM and was not enticed away to Burroughs. The Burroughs threat encouraged IBM to offer heavy support to Lloyds, in the same way that it was supporting BoA through its changeover to IBM 360s.[36] Also, the decisions made by the other three banks to work with Burroughs were unfortunate. Burroughs was not able to deliver the B8500 to either Barclays or the National Westminster (Ackrill and Hannah 2001: 334). Barclays eventually received two B6500s, the machines that the Midland had ordered. These did not work well either. The software crisis, noted in Chapter 6, hit Burroughs hard.[37] The B6500s were also well behind schedule, and in 1967 the Midland was forced to take the still smaller B5500 to begin systems work and testing. But problems quickly emerged in programming the B5500 even for batch processing, generating enormous friction between the bank and its hardware supplier (Booth 2004: 291–5).

However, the banks had to share the blame. As was evident in the previous chapter, the science-based firms like ICI, BP and Shell also experienced the software crisis but managed it better than most British banks. These firms had more experience with computer-based management tools, notably linear programming, and had developed a stronger core of specialist expertise within the organisation. The banks, on the other hand, had managed with a handful of bankers-turned-programmers, supplemented by similar numbers from hardware firms. This had been sufficient for second generation systems, but not for the increased volumes and complexity of work required for the third generation. Lloyds drew on IBM's commercial need to make on-line systems work, but the banks supplied by Burroughs had to be more self-sufficient. They found it almost impossible to secure programmers from the external labour market and had to cease internal training because IT staff had so little time. The problems were most severe at managerial level. Deadlines slipped for trivial reasons, but the cumulative impact was to put projects way behind schedule and compress timetables to an impossible extent. Managers struggled against staff shortages, hardware faults, software underperformance and incompatibilities and understandably became overwhelmed.

Barclays had to return to IBM and thereafter, it used tried and tested machines (Ackrill and Hannah 2001: 335). For the Midland, the lessons were equally harsh. The machines that it cancelled, the English Electric 4/70 and 4/50 were technically very good, especially for the real-time, multi-programming applications needed by the bank.[38] The Burroughs technology that it bought required a very long development time, but eventually did work reliably (*Midbank Chronicle* 1974). The Midland also withdrew from the technological frontier to the tried and tested. However, British banks were not alone as will be seen below.

New products

US retail banks soon saw the potential of computers to create new services. Larger banks offered customers a variety of accounting operations, payroll management, the analysis of income and expenditure flows and even timetabling for state schools (O'Brien 1968: 51–2). Yavitz (1967: 49–51, 113–17) cites the case of (what he calls) "Manufacturers National Bank", which established a separate division, the "Automated Services Center", to sell computerised services to other bank divisions and outside clients on a fully commercial basis. Larger US banks followed similar strategies especially when legal changes allowed them to purchase the stock of service corporations; several bought computer service bureaux (O'Brien 1968: 12). This was, however, for the larger US banks; medium-sized and small banks lacked the internal capacity to extend computerisation beyond immediate internal needs.

British banks, with their concentrated structure, centralised O&M and systems analysis capabilities were also able to exploit excess capacity on their computers once core tasks had been automated. Like "Manufacturers National", Barclays created a new division, "Computer Services", to utilise spare computing capacity, with such success that it merged with ICL's computer bureau, supplying commercial and technical services to outside clients (Tuke and Gillman 1972: 90). The Midland established a similar venture. More routine was Lloyds' extension of computing to much of its work for commercial clients (the executor and trustee department, the registrar's department and in foreign exchange dealing) (Winton 1982: 188; Holmes and Green 1986: 229). However, the cartel and government administrative guidance placed some of the main revenue earners for US banks, notably mortgages, insurance and credit instalment payments, off limits in Britain.

One US product, however, translated more easily to the UK, the credit card. US bank credit cards spread rapidly in the 1950s and within a decade became dominated by two rival groups, the Interbank Card Association, with its Mastercharge/Mastercard and the pioneer, National BankAmericard Inc., with Visa (Coopey 2004). BoA's card was from the outset based on computer processing and, after an uncertain start, became highly successful and was franchised for other US banks. This violated interstate banking laws and BoA shifted its emphasis to expansion overseas (McKenney *et al.* 1995: 67–8). Barclays licensed the BoA card, marketed it as the "Barclaycard" in February 1966 and also used computer processing, without which it would have been entirely uneconomic (*The Banker* 1966b; Ackrill and Hannah 2001: 185–90, 337–8). It was bold to issue credit cards to any credit-worthy customer whether or not already with the bank, especially amid rising concerns about credit-fuelled inflation. Barclays argued that the credit card was yet another measure to expand their customer base and to cap costs by offering a cheaper alternative to the cheque (Thomson 1966). The other British banks had to follow suit and established the Joint Credit Card Company and the Access card, aligned with ICA and MasterCard (Coopey 2004).

Barclays followed this innovation in June 1967 with the world's first cash dispenser installed outside its Enfield branch to allow customers to withdraw cash at any time (Tuke and Gillman 1972: 90). Despite initial fears about the reliability of the technology, these machines spread very rapidly, and the first on-line cash dispenser was installed by Lloyds in 1972.[39] The introduction and development of these machines was closely connected to another aspect of the banks' labour problem, the issue of Saturday morning work. It was difficult to perfect the technology of dispensing cash when a customer inserted a card or a voucher into a machine, but the banks worked with the National Physical Laboratory, and in 1966–7 had two reliable prototypes.[40] The first, developed by De La Rue, dispensed £10 when activated by a voucher, issued by the banks. The voucher had a magnetic ink code line and was fed into clearing like an ordinary cheque. Barclays were given exclusive rights to exploit the machine for a limited period. The second, from Chubb and Sons Lock and Safe Company, needed the customer to insert a card and a code number before delivering cash. The machine gave out cash and kept the card, in effect limiting the customer's borrowing. A final machine, developed by a small electronics company, Speytech, with risk capital provided by the Midland, was unique in that it was designed for multiple drawings (ten, each of £20), thus granting the customer a substantial line of credit. The NPL reported security concerns with both cards, which could be forged easily, and suggested that risks would fall if the dispenser were linked on-line to a computer holding account and code details. Despite reservations about the amount of credit and the security issues, Midland went ahead with multiple-drawing cash dispenser because it was more economic than the single shot machines (where handling and postage costs were very significant) and had great publicity value when Saturday closure was announced.[41] Significantly, the *Financial Times* headlined its report of the decision "Instant cash when banks are shut".[42] Like cheque clearing, cash machines were introduced with a long-term view to efficiency gains and, in this case, a short-term publicity need.

Comparison with retail banking in the USA

US bank automation evolved in entirely different structures and patterns of operation. Regulations of the late 1920s and early 1930s, precluded inter-state banking and many states, like Illinois, allowed only unit banks, whereas others, like California, permitted state-wide branch banking (Bordo *et al.* 1995: 11–17). The regulations introduced after the banking crisis of 1930–3 imposed costs which became burdensome in postwar conditions so that, nationally, retail banks lost out to non-bank financial institutions, such as savings and loan associations and credit unions (Yavitz 1967: Table 2.1). Nevertheless, the booming economy of California in the 1940s and early 1950s helped make BoA the world's largest bank.[43] Its growth was spectacular. In 1950, the bank managed more than 4.6 million current, savings and Timeplan loan accounts, with current accounts growing at a rate of 23,000 per month. Cheque use was far more common in the USA than in the UK, and processing costs grew rapidly.[44] In a standard 40-person BoA branch, approximately ten staff, mainly young women between the ages of 18 and 24, would be engaged full-time on sorting, bundling and adding cheques. Turnover rates for this grade of staff could be 100 percent per annum.

In 1950, BoA and the Stanford Research Institute began a feasibility study of automatic bookkeeping and automatic cheque processing, which culminated five years later in the creation of ERMA (Electronic Recording Machine Accounting), an electronic machine to read and process cheques, and the installation in the San Francisco branch of an IBM 702 to undertake basic bookkeeping. The American Bankers' Association chose the ERMA technology over rival punched-card systems as its network standard and by 1962, in the eyes of experienced IT observers, BoA was two years ahead of rivals in automation and achieved commercial success. Automation allowed it to open branches, and reap the rewards in new business, in smaller communities than had previously been economic, resulting in a rising market share. With a highly sympathetic (and computer literate) chief executive, BoA used new communications networks to extend automation to as many of the domestic (i.e. California-based) activities as possible, allowing the re-planning of branch interiors to give more space to sales, pushing profitability even higher. Among the new financial products was a credit card, which after a disastrous initial period, was re-launched to huge acclaim (McKenney *et al.* 1995: 66–8). The goal of automation was to drive down costs in domestic banking to fund BoA's overseas expansion.

Following, BoA's lead, the proliferation of computers through the banking system after 1960 was quite astounding. By the end of 1963, almost every bank with assets in excess of $500 million had its own computer installation, as did 85 percent of those with assets of between $100 and $500 million and 52 percent of banks with assets of $50 and $100 million. But very significantly in 1963–4 this represented less than 3 percent of all US banks; and for the 77 percent of US banks in the smallest size categories, the only prospect of computerisation in bookkeeping or cheque-clearing lay in using bureau or agency services (Yavitz 1967: 27–9; O'Brien 1968: 8–9). In one respect, therefore, British retail banks were ahead in the mid-1960s; even under second generation batch processing, a much larger proportion of the UK network was automated. However, major US banks provided a wider range of automated services, principally in current account banking, mortgage loans, consumer loans, trust management, credit cards and savings accounts, but automation had been applied to customer services such as payroll management, billing and account reconciliation (O'Brien 1968: ch. 2). In turn, this allowed innovations (such as BoA's entry into microwave communications circuits and the more general establishment of electronic data processing centres by US banks) that had no, or limited, parallels in the UK.[45] Big US banks developed a much larger corps of computer specialists and systems men than did UK banks, and not surprisingly the rush into third generation computing was as spectacular as in the UK (O'Brien 1968: 13–14).

BoA decided in November 1965 to switch to IBM 360/65s, having earlier managed the change from the original IBM 702s to the later, second generation 7070s highly successfully. Unfortunately, the change to System/360s was taxing, despite the best efforts of the bank's huge systems and equipment research team and massive support from IBM (McKenney *et al.* 1995: 78–83). The System/360 operating system did not function effectively and could not multi-task. In the effort to de-bug the programs, the bank had to mobilise computer specialists from all parts of the organisation, sacrificing new business and new project development. It took more than three years to bring the system to work approximately as planned. The internal assessment of the conversion was sober indeed:

> The inescapable conclusion was that the massive conversion effort had failed because of software problems. The [internal] report reviewed all the decisions, including the new plan and the cost [to] the bank of programming and outside help. By May [1968] the total direct reprogramming effort was estimated at 167 man-years at a cost of $165 million, of which at least 37.4 man-years, valued at $363,834, had been lost – a costly effort.

Finally, stung by the failures with System/360, senior BoA senior executives became technologically conservative and, like Barclays and the Midland, withdrew from cutting edge innovation into "tried and true" systems. BoA also found that second generation expertise did not provide a springboard to exploit the third, and it was overtaken in its domestic market during the 1980s by competitors with on-line cash machines and new automated loan products.[46] BoA was not alone; the learning curve was flat for all US firms involved in third generation computing. In 1969–70, US industry had its hands full in getting third generation systems started; no bank had created an integrated management information system or even made third generation systems work effectively.[47]

US banks were however ahead in preparing the transition towards electronic banking. The American Bankers' Association organised a series of "automation conferences" in the mid-1960s, anticipating "checkless banking" organised around a "universal credit card" which would enable customers to draw money from their accounts anywhere in the US, or even "cashless, checkless banking" when all payments would be made electronically through terminals located in retail establishments, hotels and the like (Oettinger 1964; Case 1965; Rader 1965). Indeed, the first point-of-sale electronic funds transfer was established in March 1966 in Wilmington, Delaware.[48] In the following year, the American Bankers' Association created a group to design a system of customer identification, and in effect to invent the international standards for point-of-sale transactions just as it had earlier established the rules for the automation of cheque clearing (O'Brien 1968: 21). British bankers attached to the Inter-Bank Research Bureau followed these developments closely but British banks in general were stuck in the transitional mud from second to third generation computing and further developments had to await the mid-1970s.

Conclusion

The simple question to ask about bank automation is: did it make banks more efficient? Unfortunately, simple questions can be very difficult to answer. Efficiency is usually measured by changes over time in the level of output per worker, but output is very difficult to measure in the service sector (Mason *et al.* 2000: 121–2; Smith 1989: 76–82). In very broad terms, there are three ways of measuring output of retail banks. The first is the "national accounts approach", which seeks to measure value added by subtracting the costs to factors of production employed in the industry from revenues earned by it. The estimates for the wider financial services industry (banking, insurance and finance) in Table 7.4 suggest that productivity grew slowly in the 1950s, decelerated further in the early 1960s and fell thereafter. This is the traditional picture of the performance of British banks during the long postwar boom. But there were substantial falls in the length of the normal working week and significant changes in the gender balance of employment in financial services. Making due allowances would raise the rate of labour productivity.

Table 7.4   The performance of British banking, insurance and financial services, 1950–73 (national accounts approach)

	1950–60	1960–4	1964–73	1973–9
Growth of output (%)	44.6	17.7	60	14.4
Growth of employment (%)	25.5	15	65.3	13.9
Growth of output per worker (% p.a.)	1.8	0.7	–0.7	0.1

Sources: Feinstein 1972: Tables 53 and 59; CSO, *United Kingdom National Accounts*, various years; *Annual Abstract of Statistics*, various years.

The second method is the "service units" approach, which constructs an output measure based on the number of products (accounts, clearings, cash and credit card transactions, etc.) weighted to produce a single series. This is preferable for two reasons. We can measure banking alone and it also captures the struggle to cope with the increasing use of accounts, representing higher service quality, which slips through the net of the national accounts approach. Unfortunately it is also the method for which the data are most fragmentary. The NBPI (1967: 51; 1969b: 1) devised a sophisticated "service unit" measure that revealed rising productivity in the 1960s, exceeding 3.5 percent in 1967–8, though the Board regarded this performance as disappointing. We can be reasonably confident of this rather different picture of bank performance since in commercial services it is not unusual for "service unit" methods to show faster productivity growth than the "national accounts approach" (Smith 1989: 76).

The final method is the "intermediation approach", which treats banks as intermediators between lenders and borrowers rather than as producers of financial services. The method, outlined in detail in the note to Table 7.5, is better suited to broad international comparison, rather than measuring the impact of specific changes in production technology. Table 7.5 gives the results of Anglo-US comparisons in financial services, broadly defined. These suggest a significant productivity lead by the USA in the 1950s, which opened further in the 1960s and early 1970s. This is not inconsistent with the picture painted above of automation in banking in the two countries.

The inconclusiveness of these various measures has encouraged historians to search for alternatives. In their study of Barclays, Ackrill and Hannah (2001: Fig. 7.6) suggest that the value of balance sheet assets per worker might be a better guide to productivity. However, this seems to be a better record of the changing accounting conventions

Table 7.5 Estimates of comparative US/UK labour productivity in banking, insurance and finance, 1950–73
(UK = 100 in each year) (financial intermediation approach)

	1950	1960	1964	1973
Level of relative output per employee in the USA	154.9	153.1	172.5	205.7

Notes and sources: The method is taken from Broadberry 1997b: 26. The method takes the ratio of the money supply to national income as a measure of the degree of financial intermediation. The figures for net national product and M2 are taken from Friedman and Schwartz 1982: Tables 4.8 and 4.9. The relative quantity of financial services is obtained from the relative size of NNP (converted at the exchange rate, see ONS 2002: Table 5.1), multiplied by the relative degree of financial intermediation. This is divided by the relative size of employment in financial services (for the UK from the *Annual Abstract of Statistics*, and for the USA from US Department of Commerce, *Statistical Abstract of the United States*, various years.

and the technology of banking rather than of productivity.[49] It might be better therefore to approach the question of the impact of new technology in banking from the other end: are there studies of technical change in the sector from which parallels might be drawn? Haynes and Thompson have examined the impact on productivity in building societies of the introduction of cash dispensers.[50] They discovered substantial productivity gains, with lags to allow for customer behaviour to adapt to the new methods of delivering the service. Their findings can be applied to the pattern of change in postwar banking if we attribute lags in productivity change to learning by the banks rather than learning by customers and equally importantly place technical change in its economic and political context.

Bank automation was not a Bravermanian story (outlined in Chapter 6) of ruthless exploitation of labour by powerful employers. Bank executives were not in control. Their customers demanded ever more frequent use of account facilities, which forced the banks to supply continuously improved service quality, with charges that were adjusted discontinuously and were eroded by inflation. Bank managers were reluctant to use the classic method of curbing demand, a big price rise, because they feared, in the event rightly, the government response. To meet this irresistible demand from customers, the banks had an insatiable demand for new recruits, primarily to undertake routine work. Bank clerks, especially the young females performing the most mundane tasks, had ways of evading labour intensification and tighter managerial controls – by quitting. Bank executives turned to IT out of weakness in relation to their customers, their workers and government.[51] Office machine suppliers initially served the banks well, but the learning curve from second generation computing was foreshortened by the banks' decisions to jump into the third. The reasons for that leap were understandable, each new category of equipment – on-line systems, cheque reader-sorters and clearing by magnetic tape exchange, cash dispensers – promised mouth-watering labour economies from the most unpopular tasks. But the time taken to realise these goals was much longer than boards of directors wanted. The lags represented the inevitable results of innovation into uncharted areas, where progress is determined largely by empirical and iterative methods. Even making third generation mainframes batch process at the speed of second generation machines took man-years of programming effort. Constant innovation was needed, and some combinations of bank and supplier were better placed to make these critical adjustments than others.

Might it have been better for banks to have sat on the sidelines until the technology had been "run in" and performance problems had been resolved? Arguably this is what British and most medium-sized US banks did in the 1950s. Such a wait-and-see position implies confidence that the wider economic and social environment will remain relatively stable for the period of technological "de-bugging". Bank executives of the 1950s may have made these calculations, in the 1960s the balance favoured leaping rather than waiting. They sensed the steady erosion of the cartel and the growth of internal competition. Second, there were very concrete illustrations of companies that had reaped first mover advantages through investment in IT, with technology suppliers only too keen to emphasise the massive potential of their products. Third, the small groups of banker-computer specialists were well-placed to counsel ambition. They were buoyed by the successes with second generation systems and networked into computer circles in which real-time operations, integrated management information systems and multi-tasking were the common currency. Finally, the pressure from government, by no means all hostile, pointed to a new regime of open competition among large, powerful retail banks. What better way of unleashing the new era than by stealing a technological march? It was an intuitive rather than a rational decision to proceed, but the potential long-term payoffs were substantial.

The productivity gains of the 1980s evident in Table 7.4 were achieved with the infrastructure and ideas established in the period 1960–75. It is certainly true that processing power, the potential of software and digital communications networks continued to develop rapidly and the regulatory framework was transformed in the 1980s. Nevertheless, the core of the new system (the on-line network, electronic clearing of cheques and other vouchers, increasing central control of all commercial transactions) was laid in the drive to exploit third generation computing after 1965. Two examples illustrate the point. Regional processing centres are a direct development of the systems established in the 1960s. On-line computing allowed each of the big four to move from four or five computer centres in the batch-process phase to one or two for real-time operation. Simultaneously, on-line systems allowed greater central control over lending decisions in the branch. The Midland, for example, required all lending decisions to be tested via the on-line system against centrally-imposed criteria and those that did not pass were submitted for head office approval. By 1975, the Midland was experimenting with regional processing centres for lending decisions, thus taking the paperwork as well as the decision-making capacity from the branch manager and achieving scale economies in routine processing, and other banks followed (Holmes and Green 1986: 300; Leyshon and Pollard 2000: 205). Equally interesting is the development of much more targeted marketing by banks in the 1980s and 1990s with the use of credit scoring software and huge customer databases to target their marketing efforts and increase the speed and effectiveness of new product development (Leyshon and Thrift 1999; Marshall and Richardson 1996: 1844–8). The Midland was again a pioneer especially after the appointment of Eugene Lockhart, an American from an information systems consultancy, to a senior executive position. This certainly was not a story of organic growth from seeds planted in the later 1960s, but shows how further development of processing power and the speed and sophistication of communications networks allowed the ideas of the "systems men" of the 1960s to be realised. The fundamental element in their vision of the potential of IT was that firms should compile, both from their own operations and from agents (credit rating agencies in the 1990s), vast "data banks" of information to allow more enlightened production and marketing decisions. Systems men distrusted the practical, personal knowledge of line managers, be they foremen making production decisions or bank branch managers making lending decisions. They preferred the principle of developing software to sort and interrogate data to eliminate quirky decisions and centralise control.[52] In banking, at least, the failure of management information systems in the 1960s and 1970s did not prevent the centre from strengthening its controls over line (branch) managers. The databases may have been started from scratch in the 1980s, but the underlying principle of central erosion of local discretion was built into automated systems from the very start. However, it is impossible to decompose the productivity gains of the 1980s into those caused by the foundations laid in the period 1965–75 and those caused by developments in competition policy, IT and the labour market in the 1980s. It is sufficient to recognise that the efficiency gains of the 1980s would have been much less significant without infrastructure and corporate learning cemented in the establishment of third generation systems.

8
Japanisation

The emergence of Japan as one of the world's economic powers in the 1970s and 1980s astounded the developed world. Okumura (1989) estimated that Japan's contribution to world GDP grew from just 2 percent in 1967 to more than 10 percent in 1987. Japanese economic growth rates were unprecedented; according to Maddison (1995: Table D-1a) average Japanese incomes in 1950 were approximately 18 percent of those in the USA, and reached 82 percent in 1989. This enormous achievement rested upon a steep technological learning curve in manufacturing. In 1950, Japan specialised in relatively unsophisticated goods such as textiles and clothing but moved rapidly up the scale of technological sophistication, to sewing machines, watches, transistor radios, cameras, motorcycles, televisions, automobiles and so on. Japanese firms dominated the protected domestic market and then aggressively sought opportunities overseas.[1] The story of Honda's domination of world motorcycle production and its near elimination of the British industry demonstrates the combination of assertive marketing and world class production (Koerner 1995; Boston Consulting Group 1975; Pascale 1996). Similarly Japanese electronics firms laid waste European television manufacturing capacity (Owen 1999: 276–82).

However, the USA was the main market for Japanese exports and Japan built a strongly favourable balance of trade which even strengthened after Japan revalued the yen by 14 percent against the dollar in 1971. Diplomatic friction between Japan and other developed countries began to increase. From the 1970s, the Americans (and then the Europeans) resorted to protection against Japanese manufacturing power.[2] This defensive strategy had limited effect as Japanese products were increasingly perceived as of high quality, technologically sophisticated and well-matched to consumer needs. Their market penetration seemed resistant to both protectionism and *endaka* (the steep rise in the international value of the yen), which was forced on Japan in 1984. In the next five years, Japan's trade surplus more than doubled, its corporate profitability rose by 30 percent and Fuji Bank reported that Japanese firms had reduced the break-even point for the profitability of exports from US\$1 = Y210 in 1985 to US\$1 = Y114 in 1988.[3]

To make matters even more difficult for American and European producers, there was no real consensus among analysts of the fundamental causes of Japanese industrial success. Katz (1998: 290–306) has surveyed very efficiently the main themes in the American literature on Japanese economic performance, but even this fails to capture the bewilderment about the roots of Japanese economic power. On the one hand, there were those, like Chalmers Johnson (1982) who believed that the Japanese developmental state had ignored the laws of comparative advantage and had established internationally competitive industries through close collaboration between government, industry and the financial system. Abegglen's (1970) coining of the term "Japan Inc." put this approach into popular consciousness. However, there were equally influential, equally persuasive analyses of Japanese strength framed within the context of orthodox market economics (Patrick and Rosovsky 1976). This fundamental inability to pin down the sources of Japanese manufacturing competence formed the perfect seedbed for myth-making. We have already noted in Chapter 1 the tendency of analysts and opinion-makers to focus on one aspect after another of the "Japanese system" and for many new ideas in production management to be associated with Japan for no obvious reason.[4]

20/20 hindsight is a wonderful, if somewhat dangerous, sense. We now know that western preoccupation with Japanese economic, social, political and industrial characteristics intensified as the Japanese economy spectacularly ran out of steam. In the twenty-first century, our shorthand for the Japanese economic system is less "the miracle economy" than "the system that soured".[5] As evidence of the commercial difficulties of Japanese companies has accumulated and deeper understanding of Japanese manufacturing has developed, "Japolatory" (see Chapter 1) seems quaint, misplaced and dated.[6] This is not, of course, to suggest that all the compliments paid to the Japanese system were misplaced, but British and American reactions reveal as much about their own perceptions of weakness and vulnerability as signs of Japanese strength. American reactions are particularly instructive as this was the first challenge to US industrial supremacy that could not simply be brushed aside as the exploitation of US technologies by a low wage economy.[7]

American responses were as cataclysmic as anything witnessed in a British technology scare.[8] Instead of careful analysis, US opinion ploughed into a British-style culture of declinism: publishers began to issue texts on "the coming crash of the American economy" (Kurtzman 1988), the trajectory of "American decline" (Bernstein and Adler 1994) and, most enticingly, a guide on how to prevent the USA from becoming a third world country (Luttwak 1993)! The press focused initially upon fears of permanent damage to the skill base and the tension between unions and employers at the "neo-Darwinian workplace" (Bix 2000: 276–83), but television really set the mood. An NBC programme, "If Japan Can, Why Can't We?" on 24 June, 1980 brought home to middle America the nature and extent of the Japanese challenge to American manufacturing supremacy. It is regarded as one of the most successful documentaries in American television history and associated the problems of the "rustbelt economy" with the rise of Japanese industrial strength (Locke 1996: 167–8). The programme emphasised the quality advantages that Japanese products enjoyed and featured the work of W. Edwards Deming, who had taken the American statistical quality control (SQC) technique to Japan in the reconstruction period. Deming had had enormous impact on Japanese quality control methods, but SQC tended to be forgotten by US manufacturing.

The business schools were slower to react and initially kept a stiff upper lip; Japanese strengths were recognised but lay in doing the basics well.[9] The early analyses of the power of Japanese manufacturing concentrated on quality circles (Leonard and Sasser 1982; Takeuchi and Quelch 1983; Garvin 1983) and cost reduction through better management of inventories and the supply chain (Mather and Blodgett 1984; Armstrong 1985; Aggarwal 1985; Porter and Millar 1985). However, as the volume of literature on Japan increased, American managerial self-confidence ebbed away. The pivotal text was the report of the MIT IMVP (Womack *et al.* 1990) which credited Japanese producers with a new technique of manufacture, lean production, which had enormous advantages over American Fordist mass production:

> Lean production ... is "lean" because it uses less of everything compared with mass production – half the human effort in the factory, half the manufacturing space, half the investment in tools, half the engineering hours to develop a new product in half the time. Also it requires keeping far less than half the needed inventory on site,

results in many fewer defects, and produces a greater and ever growing variety of products (Womack *et al.* 1990: 13).

The accuracy of this account will be considered below, but for such an eminent, well-resourced group to have spoken so disparagingly of US managerial skills was a body-blow for the American management profession.[10] Others followed quickly: Lazonick (1991: 12) wrote of "the rise and decline of US managed capitalism".

This division of view between Japanisation as a menu of techniques from which emulators might draw, and Japanisation as a complete, integrated system of production exactly mirrors debates over the nature of Americanisation half a century earlier. The definition of Japanisation is not easy.

What is "Japanisation"?

Oliver and Wilkinson (1992: ch. 2) define Japanisation in four distinct areas: manufacturing methods; organisational structures and systems; personnel practices; and environmental factors, under which they group supplier relations, unions and the political context. The main Japanese manufacturing methods are: total quality control (making the entire workforce responsible for the maintenance of product quality) and its adjuncts, quality circles and statistical quality control (SQC); just-in-time production (JIT) under which goods are produced and delivered exactly when required and the firm carries minimal stocks of work in progress; *kaizen*, the philosophy of continuous improvement in products and processes, which again involves the entire workforce; and cellular rather than linear organisation of production almost invariably undertaken by teams of workers. The main organisational structures and systems identified are: different approaches to management accounting and product development, both of which require project teams. In personnel practices, the main Japanese innovations are presented as: lifetime employment and company-based welfare to cement worker loyalty to the employer; careful selection and induction processes accompanied by training and re-training throughout the employee's working life; flexible work practices, with "skill" as defined in the UK and the USA virtually unknown in Japan; seniority-based pay systems; long working hours; and elaborate systems of communication between managers and workers. Finally, in the wider environment they identify: enterprise unions; the dual economy, with a big role for "peripheral" workers in major companies, who would be hired and fired to meet fluctuations in demand and protect the lifetime employment of core workers; longer-term relationships between major firms and their suppliers than is customary in the West; a tradition of government support for industry; and institutions of long-term financing so that companies are able to escape the short-term horizons of British and American firms imposed by stock market finance. Oliver and Wilkinson overlook another distinctive element of Japanese production that was noticed in the West, the extravagant use of lightweight, programmable N/C machine tools. This aspect was a prominent part of the "flexible specialisation" agenda (see the discussion in Chapter 1) and has since featured much more in the literature on "flexible manufacturing systems" (FMS) than in debates on "Japanisation", where the use of programmable industrial robots was briefly mentioned.[11]

This is a very long menu and significant parts of the personnel agenda were already very familiar to British and American companies. If lifetime employment was uncommon, long-term commitment to a single company was not (Addison 1986: 406–8), nor was the segmentation of labour markets between core and peripheral workers, and the case studies in previous chapters have drawn attention to the efforts of British and American companies to break down craft demarcations and achieve more flexible working by tradesmen.[12] Indeed, in a celebrated defence of American management Peters and Waterman (1982) argued that most of the qualities identified as Japanese could be found in excellent *American* companies, among whom they numbered DEC, Hewlett Packard, IBM, Procter and Gamble and many more. Indeed, they described excellent American companies as "lean" (Peters and Waterman 1982: 15) long before the IMVP. Even statistical quality control is much less distinctively Japanese than the "Japanisation" literature allows. SQC was developed in the 1930s at Bell Laboratories by a group led by Walter Shewhart as a method of identifying variations in quality in products emerging from any manufacturing process that was not random but came, for example, from excessive wear on a tool or a machine that was out of adjustment, and if not corrected would cause those products to fall outside allowable tolerances. SQC places the responsibility for quality control on the operative, who has to sample output on a regular basis and use basic statistical techniques to decide when a process needed to be shut down and reset. With the assistance of W. Edwards Deming, this process was applied to American wartime production (Locke 1996: 149–50) and played a central part in the managerial techniques that the US Technical Assistance and Productivity Programme sought to disseminate to its allies during the Marshall Aid era (Tiratsoo and Tomlinson 1998a: 125–9). The Japanese were certainly impressed by the potential of SQC, and invited Deming and other quality experts to Japan on a regular basis. As Japanese manufacturers fine-tuned the technique, it fell largely into disuse in both the USA and the UK, where it had anyway been difficult to establish. However, a survey from 1987 of British companies' take-up of "Japanese" management techniques found a small but significant core (c. 7 percent of the total) that had adopted SQC before 1942, long before any Japanese interest (Oliver and Wilkinson 1989: 81).

There are similar problems with the parentage of FMS, which may be regarded as the next stage from the N/C machine tools considered in Chapter 4. The US government's Office of Technology Assessment (1984: 60–2) defined FMS as "a production unit capable of producing a range of discrete products with a minimum of manual intervention. It consists of production equipment workstations (machine tools or other equipment for fabrication, assembly or treatment) linked by a materials handling system to move parts from one workstation to another, and it operates as an integrated system under full programmable control". FMS is probably best understood as an umbrella term for a whole range of computerised design and manufacturing techniques, each with its own acronym.[13] FMS was initially developed in the USA, with Rockwell International probably the pioneer, and American firms had the longest experience of operating such systems (Mansfield 1993: 150; Jones 1991: 240). But, the celebrated Scottish production engineer, Theo Williamson (see Chapter 4), also independently developed pioneer FMSs for Molins in the later 1960s (Feilden 1995: 526–9). However, there is little doubt that FMS developed most extensively in Japanese firms. Whether this arose from the dominance of Japanese firms in the production of robotics (Bowonder and Miyake 1994), the extent to which programmable automation complemented Japanese employment practices (Jones 1991: 243–4), the strength of the Japanese automobile, machine tools and electronics industries (three of the four major users of FMS, with aerospace) (Mansfield 1993:151), or because Japanese firms had lower target rates of return (Mansfield 1993: 158) is unclear. It is clear, however, that the FMS had diverse origins but became closely associated with the Japanese industrial system in the minds of propagandists for reform in Europe and North America.

The rather problematic parentage of some of these "Japanese" techniques and structures might suggest that it was the combination of techniques that distinguished the Japanese approach, but great care is needed. As Oliver and Wilkinson (1992: 53–67) note in their discussion of "environmental factors", Japanese production and management techniques evolved in a specific historical context in which political and economic conditions were very different from those in the UK and the USA. Even Japanese satellite firms in Europe and North America found it virtually impossible to operate fully-fledged JIT systems because they sourced so much from Japan that regular deliveries of small quantities of parts and materials was impractical and uneconomic.[14] The interim conclusion must be, therefore, that Japanese firms adopted management strategies that were certainly not unknown in the West, but pursued them more intensively and in combination. This is, however, only an interim conclusion. As will be argued below, so much of what has passed for analysis of Japanese techniques has focused upon a single producer, Toyota, which has been as active in shaping its image as was Ford in the 1950s (Chapter 4 above). There is a myth of the Toyota production system, just as there was a myth of the achievements of Ford's automation in the 1950s. Before examining the case study of automobiles, we return to the model developed in earlier chapters to assess the potential for international diffusion of Japanese methods.

The context for diffusion

Earlier chapters made the case for analysing international diffusion in three overlapping levels the global; national; and enterprise dimensions. At the global level, three factors were identified: the Cold War; the size of the international productivity gap; and the "world role" to which policy-makers aspired. Much had changed since the 1950s. Although the Cold War was intensified in the Reagan presidency and military spending soared, weapons systems had become so complex that few, if any, applications to the problems faced by civilian industry resulted. There was, however, a real Japanese element to Cold War pressures. The maverick Japanese politician, Shintaro Ishihara (1991: 19–22), pointed out that the next generation of US missile warheads would depend upon Japanese semiconductors and this gave the Japanese enormous power over the USA. The Pentagon's alarm bells rang very clearly and prompted enormous efforts to revitalise American research and development in semiconductors and prevent Japanese firms from passing the technology to the USSR. There was always a strategic edge to American concerns about Japanese high technology industry.

However, productivity measurement suggested that in aggregate there was little cause for American concern. Maddison's growth accounts for the Japan, the UK and the USA (Table 8.1) show the USA with a continuing, substantial productivity lead, with the UK in second place and Japan third.

The order was different within the various branches of manufacturing (Table 8.2), but again the USA held a productivity lead over Japan in all branches, except in machinery, transport equipment and electrical, where Japan overtook the USA in 1980 and by the end of the decade had a near 20 percent lead in value added per hour worked. By 1979, Japan had a productivity lead over the UK in many branches of manufacturing, which was relatively small except in metals and the engineering group. These were scarcely unambiguous signals for the British to re-model their industry along Japanese lines, much less for the Americans. The notion that the Japanese had pioneered a new, ultra-efficient method of creating value in manufacturing (cf. Lazonick 1990; Womack *et al.* 1990) cannot withstand even modest statistical probing.

When the interest in Japanese methods really sparked, both Britain and America were under new governments seeking to restore national prestige. The Reagan government came to office after the international humiliations of the late 1970s and at a time of economic crisis. In the UK, the Conservatives based much of their appeal at the 1979 general election on a commitment to reverse Britain's relative economic decline. Both governments needed to rejuvenate manufacturing industry and Japanese competitive strength in the very prominent industries of vehicles, consumer electronics and machine tools pointed to an obvious example to follow. Both the Thatcher and Reagan governments encouraged Japanese FDI to circumvent the voluntary export

Table 8.1   GDP per worker-hour, 1950–89
(1985 US relative prices)

	1950	1973	1989
Japan	1.69	9.12	15.18
United Kingdom	6.49	13.36	18.55
United States	11.39	19.92	23.87

Source: Maddison 1991: Table C.11.

Table 8.2 Value added per hour worked in major branches of manufacturing, 1973–89

	1973			1979			1989		
	Japan	UK	USA	Japan	UK	USA	Japan	UK	USA
Food, drink, tobacco	28	40	100	29	41	100	25	49	100
Textiles, clothing, leather	75	62	100	79	56	100	62	65	100
Chemicals, oil, rubber, plastics	64	65	100	93	71	100	92	79	100
Metals, metal products	76	43	100	100	47	100	98	67	100
Machinery, transport equipment, electrical	58	61	100	96	61	100	118	59	100
Other manufacturing	40	46	100	44	48	100	68	60	100
All manufacturing	57	52	100	72	54	100	81	61	100

Source: van Ark 1993: Appendix Tables IV.4 and IV.9.

quotas of the EEC and the USA and the steady appreciation of the yen during the 1980s. Japanese FDI was underwritten by bilateral trade agreements from the mid-1980s to the early 1990s (Strange 1993: 54–8). Thus, the "global balance" was less favourable for international technology transmission in the 1980s than in the 1950s, but the efforts of both British and American governments to revitalise their industrial bases, albeit by different methods, encouraged Japanese FDI.

There were substantial changes, too, at the national level. Chapter 3 identified two significant trends in Britain's national politics of production. On the one hand, crisis avoidance helped create the conditions for national negotiations over pay and productivity while, on the other, the post-Donovan reforms helped decentralise bargaining. In the era of "Japanisation", the decentralising forces triumphed. As part of the programme to revitalise manufacturing, the Conservative governments of 1979–97 refused to discuss macroeconomic policy with the unions and enacted a series of measures designed to reduce trade union power at the point of production. After 1979, conservative governments dispensed with a national politics of production.

There were however consistent patterns. The combination of anti-union legislation and high unemployment gave employers an unprecedented opportunity to restructure workplace relations in the early 1980s but many firms, especially in manufacturing, struggled to seize these opportunities. In the judgement of Kessler and Bayliss (1992: 240–1, quote p. 241) the unions undoubtedly lost power and influence and management authority was asserted but the extent of change varied between sectors of the economy. Parts of the "new realism" in industrial relations favoured faster technical change:

> While the unions' basic purpose has not changed, they have certainly sought, rather belatedly perhaps, to the realities of the changed environment in which they have to operate ... [T]here has been a growing acceptance of some of the legal constraints imposed upon them. There has been a greater awareness of the more competitive environment in which firms have to operate and they have been more receptive to the introduction of new technology. Unions have also recognised that they need actively to recruit new members and that in order to do so they need to make themselves more attractive and to provide new services.

The second common element in the national production politics of the early 1980s was accelerating automation. Gallie and collaborators

(1998: 292) have noted that in the second half of the 1980s the proportion of British employees working with automated or computerised equipment had risen from 39 percent to 56 percent and that these new technologies were associated with increased skill requirements. Thirdly, the fiercely competitive markets of the 1980s encouraged firms to seek more commitment from their employees and they experimented with an extensive portfolio of "human resource management" techniques (HRM), through which employers sought to communicate with their employees more directly than through collective bargaining (Purcell 1991; Sisson 1993).[15] HRM comprises a battery of techniques, embracing, at one extreme, the design of highly individual pay and incentive schemes for each worker and, at the other, fostering of teamwork on the Japanese pattern. The common core is that the firm should seek to nourish and develop the human resources at its disposal and thereby to secure new levels of commitment from employees to the firm's goals.[16] More generally, employers used the new possibilities of technological control and the "individualism" of HRM to extend the monitoring and control of their workers (Gallie *et al.* 1998). However, it is essential to repeat that this was not a formal national politics of production, rather an accumulation of decentralised enterprise strategies that were made possible by the changing political and economic environment of the 1980s and 1990s.

Chapter 3 suggested that the distinctive US pattern of decentralised, formal "workplace contractualism" encountered difficulties in the 1970s as firms began to count the twin costs of their limited ability to respond quickly to more rapidly changing markets and the direct expense of a top-heavy management structure. Just as in the UK, the imperatives were to reduce costs, to create greater flexibility within the firm and to enhance employee commitment to the firm. If we take the last first, Mroczkowski (1984) described a range of HRM initiatives adopted by US firms in the 1970s with the aim of both controlling costs and increasing worker commitment to the employer. Among the more interesting were profit-sharing plans and "quality of working life" (QWL) programmes. Profit-sharing began in non-union firms during the high inflation years of the early 1970s as a managerially-imposed method of limiting wage rises but gradually extended into union contracts to satisfy workers' increasing desire to participate in the management of their companies (Mroczkowski 1984: 48–9).[17] QWL initiatives had an even longer history and were adopted by GE in its dispute with the machinists using N/C machine tools.[18] In August 1968 GE agreed with the union a pilot programme during which it would study how best to utilise the technology and the workers would play a much greater role in the organisation of work within the shop (Noble 1984: 278–323). This was, in effect, a QWL initiative and contained most of the basic elements of such programmes.[19] HRM and QWL spread rapidly in American industry from the 1970s (Meyer and Cooke 1993: 534).

Just as in the UK, many employers also attempted to drive down the real wage and re-draw the effort bargain through a federal-government-inspired policy, "concession bargaining". This involved "wage cuts, wage freezes, 'premature renegotiation', an easing of work restrictions and a variety of other contractual innovations" and involved approximately three million workers by 1984 (Addison 1986: 391–3, quote p. 391). In return for a loan guarantee to ease the threat of bankruptcy at Chrysler in 1979, the federal government insisted that both employers and unions make bargaining concessions. The UAW made substantial compromises on wages and benefits which the other major automobile companies sought and thereafter "concession bargaining" spread widely. Similar results followed the deregulation policy of the Carter and Reagan years. Workers in the industries involved experienced falling base salaries and benefits, higher unemployment and much reduced security. Thus, government policy edged the American bargaining system towards lower wages, higher effort and job segmentation into core and peripheral groups (Addison 1986: 407–10).

At the industry and enterprise levels, the case study chapters have emphasised the importance of personal and corporate networks with innovators in the lead nation and the activities of "change agents" in the follower countries. From the later 1960s, market pressures showed British and American entrepreneurs that they needed to find out much more about Japanese methods of production, and by the mid-1970s they could see that Japanese penetration of their domestic markets rested upon rather more than cheap labour.[20] The flow of senior executives, production engineers and trade union officials to Japan in the 1980s, while not as strong as the tide to the USA in the early 1950s, was nonetheless considerable (Womack *et al.* 1990: 237). In addition, Japanese consumer electronics companies operating in the UK acted as shop-windows for the new methods and certainly influenced the operations of indigenous firms (Brech and Sharp 1984).[21] Networks were vitally important. Locke (1996: 166–7) suggests that American firms with close contact to Japanese firms were first to adopt the new techniques.[22] Japanese companies were also keen to establish joint ventures with European and

American companies with the exchange of technology and production methods in return for access to host marketing channels (Turner *et al.* 1987). On balance, the networks linking American and Japanese firms were probably stronger and longer established than those involving British companies.[23]

Among change agents, none is better known than Deming. The NBC documentary noted above finished with an extended discussion of Deming's work in fostering SQC in Japanese manufacturing and almost immediately Deming was invited to advise major US corporations (Locke 1996: 168–9). There is no equivalent in the UK; the most senior academic interpreter of Japanese industrial methods to British audiences, Ronald Dore, joined the "brain drain" to the USA. A case might be made for John Parnaby, who moved from academic life to become Manufacturing Director for Lucas Industries, from where he proselytised for Japanese production methods within the group. Lucas itself was much studied and became a case study for an Open University module on the structure and design of manufacturing systems (Oliver and Wilkinson 1992: 90–8). Even without a prominent focal point, British interest in Japanese methods expanded rapidly.

The potential obstacles to increasing Japanese influence were limited. As noted above, managers rushed to learn about "Japanese" methods as they recognised the competitive strength of Sony, Hitachi, Toyota and Nissan. Governments backed Japanese FDI. Organised labour might potentially have been a problem in the UK as the Japanese model of company unionism did not sit easily with British union traditions and there were doubts whether Japanese firms would tolerate dual allegiance (to company and independent trade union) among their workers (Oliver and Wilkinson 1992: 280–2). However, in the new realism of the 1980s, a number of British unions, notably the engineers (AEEU) and the electricians (EETPU) concluded single union deals with Japanese companies.[24] However, British workers have not given the degree of commitment that Japanese companies expect at home (Guest and Dewe 1991; Stephenson 1996). Conflict was not uncommon and the majority of workers in single union plants showed allegiance to neither union nor company.[25] Although strikes in Japanese owned or joint ventures were rare and labour turnover was very low, the level of worker identity with the company was weak.

This review of the conditions for international technology transmission in the late 1970s and 1980s is necessarily brief but it should be clear that, for the UK at least, there was some potential for the successful transmission of new ideas. In parts of manufacturing there was a productivity gap between Japanese and British performance, albeit much smaller than the Anglo-American gap of the 1950s. British unions were on the defensive and British workers were desperate for jobs as unemployment remained high and persistent. Japanese FDI was encouraged and brought satellite factories and joint ventures as carriers of at least a hybrid version of Japanese techniques.[26] For American manufacturing, the potential of Japanisation is less easily identified. While the political context was similar to that in the UK, with entrepreneurial confidence low, labour on the defensive and the media keen to amplify the sense of national insecurity, the economic conditions were very different. America had a productivity *lead* over Japan in most of manufacturing; Japan's lead was confined to the engineering industries and was so small as to indicate limited potential for major learning. And yet American self-confidence had been badly dented by Japanese competition. The assessments of the business schools, academics and the media were mixed but there was enough gloom to convince American firms that they needed to find the key to Japanese success and adapt it to American conditions. "Lean production" in the automobile industry was at the centre of this stage.

Automobiles

Although there have been many accounts of Japanese automobile production, there are real differences in detail about its essential elements. There is also the problem of sorting myth from reality. The car has such an iconic position in modern culture it is unsurprising that its manufacture should on occasion have the status of heroic enterprise. The Ford system of production at Highland Park and the River Rouge came to symbolise both the ultimate in productive efficiency and the oppression of man by machine and Henry Ford was simultaneously the saviour of mankind by "inventing" "new" methods of production and the "great dictator" who subjugated man to machine.[27] It is equally obvious that producers who seek to adapt Fordist mass production should emphasise the differences from the tyranny of the assembly line and underplay the similarities. We must not forget that methods of production can be a powerful selling feature in the fiercely competitive war between auto-makers. Chapters 1 and 4 noted Ford's efforts to sell a modest car range by emphasising automated production. Fiat's efforts to add lustre to the ordinary Ritmo/Strada with a classic advertising campaign featuring the Robogate welding processes ("hand-built by robots") took the genre to new heights. Similarly, Toyota coined "the Toyota production system" as a method of emphasising the firm's maturity and productive excellence; (carefully) guided tours of the Takaoka factory are the most unlikely tourist attraction in central Japan. Finally, the most powerful accounts of Japan's manufacturing system (Piore and Sabel 1984; Cusumano 1986; Womack *et al.* 1990) are manifestos, calls to "Wake up America" in which subtle exaggeration, illustrative rather than representative data and (over) simplification are justifiable rhetorical techniques. This section of the chapter concentrates first on trying to sort myth from reality in the Toyota production system in order to be better placed to examine the claimed efficiency advantages of lean production. In this debunking exercise, we make much use of the work published by Karel Williams and his varied team of collaborators (Williams *et al.* 1987b; Williams *et al.* 1994) whose academic purpose seems to be to pour large amounts of cold water onto over-ambitious theories of production. As noted in Chapter 4 above, the great strength of this team is its flexibility and ability to mobilise a range of specialist analytical skills and its determination to maintain the highest standards of forensic investigation. From this base, we can begin to understand the efforts of US and UK firms to adopt Japanisation.

At the centre of Toyota's account of its production system are three interrelated techniques; the *kanban* system of pull-through flow production, cellular layouts and teamwork, and close relationships with the supply chain. The essence of *kanban* is that "parts would only be produced at each previous step to supply the immediate demand of the next step. The mechanism was the containers carrying parts to the next step. As each container was used up, it was sent back to the previous step, and this became the automatic signal to make more parts" (Womack *et al.* 1990: 62). Thus, stocks of work in progress are kept to a minimum, but parts, whether from external suppliers or from within the factory, are needed very frequently and in small numbers. In theory, final assembly, rather than a rigid production schedule, controls the ordering and re-ordering of parts, but Toyota used a system of setting production schedules and smoothing throughput over a monthly cycle (Oliver and Wilkinson 1992) and the whole system operated in the fortunate condition of a domestic market that had not reached saturation levels.[28] Even in favourable market conditions, pull-through flow is very difficult to establish, but it was achieved by BMC until the early 1960s (Chapter 4 above) and, most famously of all, by Henry Ford, at Highland Park as demand for the Model T grew very rapidly between 1909 and 1916 (Williams *et al.* 1994: 96–107). Both earlier successes relied, however, as much on the ability to sell as much as to produce, and the Williams team (1994: 116–20) argue strongly that Toyota's postwar success is founded more on the company's "Americanised" sales policies than on its productive excellence. This is perhaps taking iconoclastic argument too far, but successful automobile companies must combine excellence in sales with excellence in production.

The basic idea behind cellular production is to group machines required for the machining operations or the production of subassemblies into a U-shaped cell. This allows a worker to perform several different operations as the work goes around the cell and for individual workers to assist other members of the group who are falling behind. As the Toyota system developed with interconnected cells in honeycomb layouts, it enabled multi-skilled workers to transfer between cells. The system thus requires flexible, multi-skilled workers who work in teams rather than as individuals and good communications to re-direct workers to bottlenecks in the production process and, in turn, implies systems of employment to select, train, reward and retain such workers. Thus, the manifesto for lean production emphasises reciprocal obligations and mechanisms to commit workers and managers to the company's goals (Womack *et al.* 1990: 99–100). However, there is a considerable element of myth in this version of the Toyota production system. First, much of Toyota's assembly plant that is very conventional, as a long quote from Williams *et al.* (1994: 114) reveals:

> If we then ask: where and how is cellular and *kanban* applied, the mystery deepens because much of what Toyota does do across its short span is fairly orthodox. Thus, despite Ohno's well-known scepticism about high-speed machines, Toyota has, since 1956, operated transfer lines for engine and gearbox machining; Toyota's automatic transfer machines are apparently orthodox, apart from some attention to work-station position ... [T]he sections of [Toyota's Takaoka assembly plant] which we toured in 1988 and 1990 were different in detail but similar in principle to Western factories; thus the final-assembly track at Takaoka featured the "Fordist" refinement of reverse tracking component trays to eliminate "walking to pick up" as well as *andons* [information display boards] above the track but was in every other way an orthodox line.

The basic principles had not changed when the author visited Takaoka in 2004. Second, the literature on Toyota's employment system also emphasises the physical demands. Kamata's (1983) autobiographical account emphasises the intensity and physical stress of working for Toyota. Japanese workers work long hours, are rarely absent from work and are expected to work unpaid before the formal start of shift time and during breaks as required.

Finally, Toyota's account of its production system focuses on its management of the supply chain. Toyota sources a far larger proportion of the total value of its cars from external sources than European and American rivals, and so purchaser-supplier links are critical. In the early postwar years Japanese automobile assemblers were faced with shortages of parts and friction with their suppliers over quality, price and capacity (Ueda 2004: 98–9). Resolving these problems brought the assemblers and parts suppliers into close and complex relationships, involving financial, technological and human resource development but was underwritten by the extraordinarily rapid growth in domestic demand for automobiles.[29] Both frequent re-supply of parts and careful management of the supply chain are competitive strengths, but are not necessarily Japanese. Brief mention was made in Chapter 4 of BMC's version of JIT, which "replaced conventional bulk supply of parts by a new system of issuing a complete set or 'kit' of components from a central 'marshalling yard', with the mechanised flow of materials from station to station eventually controlled by Hollerith punched-card readers in each department according to a master schedule" (Zeitlin 2000c: 20–2, quote p. 20). This system gave Longbridge great flexibility in production, reduced stocks of work-in-progress and achieved extremely impressive stock/turnover ratios in some departments. Equally, close management of the supply chain has European precedents. Volvo, which also had to decentralise production and develop complementary resources in its own supply network, developed lasting relationships and organised a network in which parts and materials were processed in several "tiers" of suppliers (Kinch 1995).

The Williams team (1994: 59–60) argue, however that the real advantage to Toyota of its supply chain has been overlooked. Japanese assemblers, and Toyota in particular, make very extensive use of small companies in which wages are comparatively low. Just over one quarter of automobile employment in Japan is in firms with less than 100 employees, and wages in this sector are approximately 50 percent of those in the assemblers. Elsewhere, assemblers cannot match the advantage of such low wages over such a large proportion of the supply chain.

This discussion suggests that Toyota indeed enjoys a productivity and competitive edge over its rivals but which rests significantly on contingent factors (the long, almost uninterrupted expansion of Japanese domestic demand for cars in the postwar period, its ability to exploit cheap wages in its supply chain and its ability to drive workers, in turn aided by the long expansion of domestic demand allowing the company to give secure employment to its core workforce) rather than on the management and organisational techniques embodied in the Toyota production system. This suggestion sits very uneasily with the idea that lean production can be learned and provides a benchmark of performance for non-Japanese producers (Womack *et al.* 1990: 256–7).

Womack and collaborators claimed that lean production on average is twice as efficient as mass production by comparing a "representative" Japanese plant (Toyota's Takaoka assembly plant) with a "classic mass production" facility (the GM plant at Framingham, Massachusetts). As noted in Chapter 1, this conclusion was rapidly taken up and embellished by other business analysts. As well as being very influential, this conclusion is remarkable because it seems to be undermined by figures elsewhere in the IMVP report (Womack *et al.* 1990: Fig. 4.3), which are reproduced here as Table 8.3.

Japanese plants in Japan clearly have a much smaller productivity lead over American companies than the bald 2:1 headline productivity gap suggests. Womack *et al.* (1990: 84–5, 244–5) have three answers: US companies have closed poorly-performing plants like Framingham; have introduced elements of lean production into those that remain; and there is considerable diversity within each geographical group. However, the whole statistical exercise underlying the figures in Table 8.3 is problematic as the raw figures are "adjusted" for various

Table 8.3   Assembly hours per "standard" vehicle for volume car producers, 1989

	Best	Weighted Average	Worst
Japanese-owned plant in Japan	13.2	16.8	25.9
Japanese-owned plant in N. America*	18.8	20.9	25.5
US-owned plant in N. America	18.6	24.9	30.7
US- and Japanese-owned plant in Europe	22.8	35.3	57.6
European-owned plant in Europe	22.8	35.5	55.7
Plants in NICs†	25.7	41.0	78.7

Notes:
* Includes joint venture plant with US firms
† Mexico, Brazil, Taiwan and Korea
Source: Womack *et al.* 1990: Figure 4.3.

differences in output, capacity utilisation, working hours and the range of productive tasks undertaken. The results are accordingly very sensitive to the number and extent of the adjustments and say more about manipulation of the data than underlying productivity differences. Williams and colleagues (1994: 206–45) have found less problematic ways to measure productive and financial performance and present very different conclusions.[30] They compare the main Japanese and American volume producers and propose a far more complex picture of relative performance. They suggest that until the late 1970s, the advantage of the Japanese producers lay primarily in much cheaper labour costs, but when Japanese labour costs rose in the 1980s they reduced the number of hours to build each vehicle (Williams *et al.* 1994: Tables 4.3 and 10.2). By the late-1980s, the Japanese required fewer hours to build a vehicle than the American majors, but the lead was comparatively small, especially when the American industry worked to full capacity.[31] The closeness of these physical productivity statistics means that the balance of competitive advantage rested much more heavily on relative wage levels and structural differences than is commonly believed (Williams *et al.* 1994: 216). By the 1990s, Toyota outperformed its rivals in both productivity and financial terms, but little separated other Japanese firms and the US volume producers, as Tables 8.4 and 8.5 suggest.

In sum, Williams and colleagues ascribe Toyota's productivity lead to the excellence and innovativeness of aspects of its production system (1994: 54, 130), but see the foundation of Toyota's competitiveness in its sales effort, the relatively low pay in its supply chain and in the

Table 8.4 Company value added per employee (US$000)

	Honda	Nissan	Toyota	Chrysler	Ford	GM
1983	38.3	28.0	41.1	54.0	43.6	44.4
1984	40.5	26.3	41.8	43.4	49.8	44.4
1985	59.3	37.8	59.6	67.1	56.1	45.4
1986	83.5	47.6	71.3	69.9	60.7	42.7
1987	87.4	63.0	85.7	75.5	77.7	44.9
1988	84.2	63.3	90.7	65.3	86.5	53.7
1989	68.2	59.9	83.9	73.1	83.5	53.1
1990	73.7	65.2	103.8	68.1	76.1	44.3
1991	79.5	69.5	112.9	70.0	68.9	44.4

Source: Williams *et al.* 1994: Table 10.3.

Table 8.5 Company cashflow per vehicle produced
(US$000)

	Honda	Nissan	Toyota	Chrysler	Ford US	GM US
1984	1.03	0.40	0.56	0.46	1.03	1.29
1985	1.40	0.51	0.81	1.40	1.19	1.20
1986	1.92	0.60	0.97	1.45	1.33	1.08
1987	1.49	0.74	1.13	1.53	1.74	1.20
1988	1.55	0.93	1.14	1.31	1.98	1.68
1989	1.11	0.70	1.09	0.95	1.95	1.54
1990	1.22	0.79	1.31	0.94	1.57	0.70
1991	1.32	0.77	1.43	0.54	0.93	0.57

Source: Williams *et al.* 1994: Table 10.4.

long arduous hours of work in its own factories (1994: 97, 116–19). On one point they are unambiguously clear; there was little for American car producers in Japanisation. As early as the 1970s, Ford, GM and Chrysler were already very efficient in terms of hours to build a vehicle and their growing competitiveness difficulties were rooted in American social conventions on wages, hours and effort. With this foundation, we can appraise the efforts of British and American car producers to cope with Japanese competition.

Ford led the US response.[32] It learned about Japanese methods from two sources. First, Bill Hayden, the head of Ford Europe, visited Japan in 1978 and returned "in a state of shock" at what he had seen and initiated an "After Japan" programme to close the gap (Starkey and McKinlay 1989). Subsequent analyses within Ford Europe were convinced that their handicaps lay in the combination of design, build complexity, schedule instability and the consequent low level of mechanisation and automation (Tolliday 1991: 101–2). Simultaneously, in the face of a severe deterioration in US Ford's domestic market position, senior executives (with UAW leaders) visited the Hiroshima plant of Mazda, with which they had concluded a commercial deal in 1979. Womack *et al.* (1990: 237) suggest that this "productivity team" concluded that Japan's advantage lay in lean production. However, both Ford Europe and Ford US began their "After Japan" strategies with attempts to redraw the effort bargain and cheapen labour costs.

In the USA, a window was opened by the federal government's insistence on "concession bargaining" (see above). Katz (1984) notes that employers secured local work rule changes (to increase worker flexibility and redraw the effort bargain), greater worker involvement in decision-making, reductions in wage rates and substantial workforce cutbacks.[33] Whereas employer labour costs per hour rose dramatically in every other car producing country between 1985 and 1991, those in the USA actually fell (Williams *et al.* 1994: Table 4.3). The efforts to commit workers more fully to the enterprise and increasing flexibility may look like Japanisation, but they occurred within a framework of intensification and slower development of training than in Europe and Japan (Kochan and Weinstein 1994: 491).

Ford Europe attempted a more ambitious blend of new and traditional approaches.[34] It was difficult to simplify design and production engineering as Hayden requested because of market pressures (Tolliday 1991: 102). More progress was made in reducing stocks of work in progress, and Ford tried hard to rationalise its supply chain and foster quality improvement.[35] More traditionally, in labour relations the main priorities were a restoration of workplace discipline (imposed both by managerial and technological control) and increased shopfloor effort (Tolliday 1991: 102–3). This tough management drive was met by equally fierce worker resistance, especially at the Halewood plant. Thereafter, management changed tack and concentrated on negotiated flexibility as part of a programme of breaking down demarcations, introducing teamwork and greater use of temporary workers that applied not only to the UK but to other European and American plant (Oliver and Wilkinson 1992: 111). By this time, the American automobile firms had "domesticated" parts of the employee relations agenda of Japanisation as "employee involvement", and it was under the banner of EI that Ford management worldwide attempted to extend greater worker responsibility for quality, basic maintenance and stock handling.[36] In 1985, Ford UK succeeded in negotiating major reforms of the highly rigid and complex job classifications: "With the agreement of union leaderships, archaic demarcation lines were eliminated and broader job roles were established with the intention of creating a more flexible workforce, intensifying capital usage, and ensuring greater continuity of production. The 1985 contract negotiations included the novel departure of increasing the wage rate for the acquisition of supplementary skills rather than greater output" (Foreman-Peck *et al.* 1995: 237). Whereas US Ford workers accepted major changes in remuneration, the effort bargain and work practices because of the dire market and financial position of their company, the profitability of Ford UK after 1985 increased worker suspicion of fundamental changes in work organisation. Mistrust spilled over into a major strike in 1988, which took both the company and the unions by surprise and was settled only by allowing local negotiations on changes in work practices (Oliver and Wilkinson 1992: 110–12). This may seem a triumph for worker Luddism, but the thrust of Ford's industrial relations strategy "After Japan" was muddled (Foreman-Peck *et al.* 1995: 236) and rested upon a deeply flawed policy towards union recognition that had left the firm with poorly-developed links between national and shopfloor organisation (Tolliday 1991: 109).

More briefly, a similar pattern emerged in BL/Rover. The company faced enormous financial difficulties in the mid-1970s as poorly designed models exacerbated the market problems noted in Chapter 4, constricting already inadequate investment still further and exacerbating already deteriorating industrial relations. The company appealed in 1974 to the newly-elected Labour government for financial assistance and drew up a recovery plan with the National Enterprise Board.[37] A key stage in the "Japanisation" of BL/Rover was the appointment in October 1977 of Michael Edwardes as chairman and managing director. He saw the technical and financial limitations in BL's new model programme and was convinced that both management and labour needed to be shaken up (Edwardes 1983: 95). To develop new models, he favoured links first with Renault, then General Motors and, finally when these two sets of negotiations failed, with Honda.

For Edwardes (1983: 181), the priority was to "regain control of the company" from the unions, and the strategy involved extensive plant closures, new work practices, much revised staffing levels and very confrontational industrial relations (Foreman-Peck *et al.* 1995: 245; Williams *et al.* 1987b: 33–4). From April 1980, management had virtually complete control over working practices, with trade union control over manning levels and work speeds more or less eliminated (Willman and Winch 1987: 170). It targeted and broke "traditional" customs and practices, but without any attempt at worker participation or involvement (Oliver and Wilkinson 1992: 102). The strategy of strengthening supervisory authority continued into the mid-1980s.

On the other hand, the Honda link called increasingly for very rapid changes in methods of production and industrial relations policies that were inconsistent with "macho-management". Like most vehicle assemblers, BL/Rover sought to rationalise its supply chain and conclude long-term contracts with favoured suppliers who could meet the requirements of frequent deliveries of parts manufactured to the highest quality standards. The relative instability of British demand patterns in effect meant that the burden of stock-holding was passed from assembler to supplier (Oliver and Wilkinson 1992: 199–203). Smaller companies in the supply chain felt particularly aggrieved.[38] In industrial relations, the increasing formalisation of the Rover-Honda link in the later 1980s took Rover's strategy further away from a control agenda towards flexibility and employee involvement (Rose and Woolley 1992).[39] Rover's "New Deal" in 1992 marked

> workforce acceptance of total flexibility, continuous improvement and single table bargaining arrangements for blue and white collar employees ... [and] despite the [TGWU's] denial that [this agreement] constituted a sharp break with past industrial relations practices, the cumulative impact of developments during the 1980s was colossal. By 1992 Rover's union negotiators accepted the inevitability of lean production. The agenda was marked by accommodation, grudging perhaps, rather than total opposition (Foreman-Peck *et al.* 1995: 234–5).

Thus, the downturn in the market for cars of the early 1980s unleashed intense pressures for cost reduction in American and European producers. Given the depth of the cyclical downturn, producers pursued every source of cost reduction. It has become part of the literature to distinguish between traditional Fordist responses, such as tightening managerial control over labour, and "lean production" responses, such as stock reduction, quality circles and more active management of the supply chain. However, such polarisation is problematic. Work intensification was an integral part of "Japanisation", as recruits to the British factories of Nissan, Komatsu and "K Electric" could attest.[40] As noted above, close purchaser-supplier relations, low-stock production and SQM were all practised in the UK well before they were taken up by Japanese producers. The general thrust of British managerial strategy was to impose cost reduction, whether on suppliers or workers and in both the UK and the USA the greatest burden of adjustment to new competitive pressures fell upon displaced workers. In many ways, this is consistent with the "lessons of lean production", which were that labour costs were vitally important in trying to compete with Toyota. It is impossible to avoid the conclusion that the case for lean production was grossly oversold in the IMVP report and that American producers had little to gain and much to lose from wholesale emulation of the Toyota production system. For British firms, lean production held more promise, but it was never likely to be a panacea for all ills, as the record of Lucas Industries illustrates.[41] These rather modest conclusions on the potential for lean production gain force from being entirely

consistent with calculations of the productivity gap in Tables 8.1 and
8.2 and with the method outlined in the earlier chapters.

Conclusion

In the early 1980s, American manufacturing experienced the
full force of an international technology scare for the first time.
American public opinion had long faced the idea that rapid technical advance in domestic industry could cause periodic phases of
"technological unemployment" (Bix 2000). It was unprepared for
the idea that technological change was too slow to prevent displacement through international competition. Opinion was especially
unprepared for the idea that jobs could not be saved by protectionist
devices. The reaction was still more intense in the next round of
severe job losses of 1990–1. In a labour market that had increasingly
emphasised the survival of the fittest there was a "blame the victim
mentality" (Bix 2000: 282–3). Political commentators warned of the
increasing strains ahead. Robert Reich (1992: 190–210) warned that
society would polarise between the "symbolic analysts" – the consultants, bankers, lawyers, and scientists who worked in the high-
powered information-age sector and ordinary workers, with the
latter consistently falling further behind. The last rites of American
capitalism were pronounced.

There is little doubt that public opinion over-reacted to the signs of
strain in American capitalism. The impact of trend and cycle were not
distinguished clearly enough, nor were the contingent (the need to
switch resources from oil-intensive industries in the aftermath of OPEC 1
and 2) from the fundamental (the combined impact of progressive
automation making productive industry increasingly footloose and high
wages and ossified systems of industrial relations making production at
home less financially attractive). But in this febrile atmosphere, it was
easy to see American managers as scapegoats and the "Japanese" system
of production as the salvation for all of America's problems. US managers had gone so far up the Fordist blind alley that it would take the
best part of a decade to reorient them on the true path of lean production (Womack *et al.* 1990: 256–7). But lean production had been flavour
of the month only after the failure of quality circles, and would remain
in the public eye only until displaced by EI and the next quick fixes for
competitive difficulty. These are symptoms of lack of self-confidence and
vividly illustrate the collapse of the American management mystique
(Locke 1996).

Predictably, American managers reacted in a somewhat schizophrenic fashion. In the crises of the early 1980s and early 1990s, they contained losses by major redundancies and also used the political opportunities created by the Chrysler rescue to intensify effort, reduce real wages and pare unit labour costs. This drive represented a typically "Taylorist" and "Fordist" response and a reasonably rational response to the situation that faced them. Simultaneously, they were carried along by the whims and fashions of business schools and loyally implemented the changing portfolio of initiatives to become more Japanese. These initiatives were by no means worthless, especially where, like EI and other HRM/ Japanisation hybrids the goal was to intensify worker effort, but the rapidity of change could only have baffled and worried employees.

British opinion was more temperate, as it had been at the time of the automation scare of the 1950s, but was also carried along by the changing currents of American ideas. As in the USA, the main thrust of British firms in response to the competitive difficulties of the early 1980s was to implement major redundancies and to find ways of reducing labour costs (Gregg and Wadsworth 1995). It has also been suggested that British firms secured more intensive use of workers' time (Edwards and Whitson 1991) but the evidence is mixed (Guest 1990). British managers also had more to gain from selective implementation of Japanese approaches, and adjusted their techniques accordingly. There is evidence of greater British than American interest in quality circles, but the results were disappointing (Bradley and Hill 1983; Hill 1991). More pragmatically, there were signs that employers sought more flexible working arrangements, though more in response to competitive pressures than to strategic considerations (Hunter *et al.* 1993). These mixed responses were rational; in both countries there were multiple problems to be faced and managers necessarily had to pursue eclectic and opportunistic strategies.

Conclusion

The aim of this book has been to examine the management of technical change in postwar Britain, a period when the British economy was technologically dependent upon the USA. That technological dependence sprang from differences between the countries in relative factor supplies and costs, the relative abundance of raw materials and the vast research and development expenditure available to those American firms engaged in defence-related projects. This is not to suggest that, during the classic automation period, the flow of technology was a one-way street; British firms were active in registering patents in the USA and with Germany dominated foreign patenting in the USA until the early 1960s. However, "in technology, as in so much else, this has been the American century" (Edgerton 1996b: 63–5, quote p. 65). For the health of the British economy, it was essential that British firms should keep abreast of American (and subsequently Japanese) technology and adopt or adapt promising innovations as rapidly as possible.

An investigation into Britain's record in adopting new ideas from abroad must rely heavily upon case study evidence, but there are well-known problems with this method. Case studies can easily become self-contained empirical exercises without significance for the wider population of firms. This study has adopted two methods to avoid the dangers of "bean counting". First, the USA has been used as a reference point against which to judge British developments. Second, the early chapters attempted to build a framework for understanding the processes of international technology transmission in order to provide a context for the case study material. However, neither can be said to eliminate entirely the pitfalls of case study analysis.

Comparisons are notoriously difficult to operationalise because of differences in structures, institutions and culture between the comparators.

In the Anglo-American case the problems are reasonably well-known. The US domestic market was much bigger and wealthier and if the division of labour depends upon the extent of the market, it is not difficult to see why British mangers might question the appropriateness of US innovations to their own situation.[1] Factor prices were also very different in the two countries; with the price of skilled labour in the UK being relatively cheap and becoming more so over time (Prais 1981: 32). American industrialists seem almost to have been driven to substitute capital for labour, even when financial signals were disappointing, confident that such investments would eventually pay for themselves, as was evident from the first part of Chapter 3. The need to "control" for difference is even more obvious when comparing Britain and America together with Japan. As noted in Chapter 8, what we might term the "Japanese system" was created in the specific cultural and political-economic context of postwar Japan and the idea of the advocates of lean production that key parts of the system could be wrested from that context was always optimistic.

When the comparative method becomes difficult to control, the social scientific answer is to build a model and test it. However, the difficulties of applying such a method to the study of technical transfer and the take-up of innovations are considerable. It is not feasible to model more than a small number of innovations, and it is not always clear which will be the most significant until long after the event. In addition to this selection problem, it is now generally accepted that technical change is to a significant extent path dependent, in that current research and development activities are powerfully shaped by technological knowledge inherited from the past (see Rosenberg 1994: 9–23). It is unrealistic to expect that innovations that have been developed in one technological context might be easily transferable to another. In such circumstances, the construction of a formal model is potentially misleading. The solution proposed in Chapter 1 was to construct a framework for organising thoughts, which is some considerable way short of a formal model but serves to focus on the most relevant issues. In short, both the comparison and the analytical framework allow the sort of flexible approach that is necessary when studying the management of technical change but the corollary is that any conclusions are necessarily tentative.

The thrust of the first three chapters was that we might expect international technology transfer to be most rapid when:

- the technology gap between sender and recipient is wide
- the government of the technology "exporting" nation has incentives to encourage transfer

- the government of the technology "importing" nation has similar incentives
- producers in both nations are networked together
- change agents are actively promoting transfers
- there is a national politics of production that at worst does not impede technical change at the enterprise level and at best actually encourages it

Conditions were very favourable for technology transfer from the USA to the UK in the automation period, slightly less so from Japan to the UK during the 1980s, but the limited size of the productivity gap between US and Japanese manufacturing made it improbable that major, systemic transfers would be possible, despite the depth and range of interest in Japanese techniques from the American media, business and academic opinion. It is self-evident that the size of the productivity gap is the most important element in this framework, but it is also evident from the disputes over the alleged advantages of lean production that such measurements are not easy and subject to discretionary decisions that can have enormous implications for the empirical results. This is a problem that has been fully recognised in the wider literature on comparative productivity measurement and usually appears around whether to adjust for differences in the quality of the same general product produced in different countries.[2] In broad terms, there is no real agreement in the literature on which method to favour in principle, and so judgements have to be made on a case-by-case basis.[3]

That there was scope for technology transfer between the USA and the UK in the 1950s is beyond question, and the checklist above suggests that conditions were ripe. The technology gap was sizeable across the whole economy and in manufacturing industry, which the British and American governments most wanted to encourage. There had been strong technological links between some of the larger British and American firms that had become established in the interwar years and agreements to share technology were not uncommon.[4] In the continuous process industries, the interwar years had already seen the emergence of international companies that combined the monitoring of technical developments with the civil engineering expertise to create the factory infrastructure in which these new technologies could be deployed and these trends strengthened over the postwar period (Chapter 5). In engineering the links were less formal but there were obviously international networks of production engineers in both the automotive and machine tool industries to which leading British personalities were connected (Chapter 4). At less elevated levels, American producers of industrial, office and civil engineering machinery had been well represented in the UK since the early twentieth century and their numbers increased under the twin stimuli of British government encouragement and the need to get round the British tariff (Dunning 1998a: 26–31, quote p. 31). Dunning's assessment of the position is well worth inclusion

> The increasing participation of US firms in British manufacturing industry over the past century has been but one aspect of the pattern of demand and supply conditions in the United Kingdom, coming more closely into line with those created in the United States a decade or two decades previously. Both American-styled capital and consumer goods have been increasingly favoured by the British consumer, while more recently, due mainly to external trade difficulties, there has been a growing desire of the UK economy to be independent of dollar originated supplies. In consequence US investment capital has been attracted to the UK, and particularly to those industries which help to raise the level of UK industrial competitiveness and to improve the balance of payments.

The capital goods producers are particularly important as their products carried US production technologies into British manufacturing and services (as was illustrated in Chapter 2 above). Given the difficulties that both manufacturing and service sector employers had in attracting and retaining clerical and secretarial staff, the growth of the US-owned office machinery suppliers was important in averting a crisis in clerical and administrative work.[5] These comments, albeit at lower levels of inward investment, would equally apply to changing British tastes towards Japanese consumer electronics, cars and machine tools from the later 1970s and the desire of British governments to do something about the growing deficit on international trade in manufactured goods from the early 1980s (Strange 1993: 108–273, esp. 212–34). In these conditions, we might expect the larger firms to have ready access to innovations in production and management.

The case study chapters suggest that the larger firms were relatively successful in deploying new technologies. This is scarcely surprising as automation and lean production were, for the most part, for the larger scale producers. In the continuous flow industries only the larger firms had the resources to afford the huge capital costs involved in investment in the new plant. They enjoyed better links to the high technology producers in the USA, whether through their commercial dealings with the design engineering companies or at the corporate level, in many cases going back to the interwar period and the era of international cartels. These could be especially important in technology transfer, as the English Electric/RCA technology-sharing agreement illustrated (Chapter 2). The larger firms were also heavily engaged in scientific and technical research, especially in the continuous flow industries. Accordingly, they were among the leaders in using computers to process data in the research context. Their growing corps of computer-literate scientific and technical personnel was active in the adoption of computerised technologies for the management of major industrial processes and in management decision-making. Shell, BP and ICI were among the world's leaders in the application of operations research and other optimisation techniques to business decision-making. British Steel also used these techniques in optimising their furnace operations and output mixes. These large companies shared a culture of scientific solutions to technical and business problems and their highly bureaucratised structures made them heavy users of business machines in stock control, wage calculations and other routine clerical tasks; IBM was keen to ensure that the transition from its punched-card machines to its computers was easy and frictionless.

For the smaller firms, the falling prices of instrumentation and process control technology in the 1950s when combined with the greater availability of bulk materials handling allowed a variety of industries to shift from batch to continuous processing in some part of their operations or to enhance already well-established automatic plants.[6] Many branches of the food and drink processors bought their control, measurement and bulk handling equipment from American suppliers, US satellites located in the UK or from British firms making American equipment under licence. A typical response from the non-automaters came from the Master Bakers: "The average member of this Association is not affected by automation. No doubt, certain bakeries who, up to now, have not introduced much automatic machinery would be pleased to do so if the difficulties regarding the raising of capital were eased". Other bakers' trade associations gave similar replies.[7] Other food and drink processors complained at the long delivery times for equipment, which was another great disincentive for the smaller producers. Thus, although continuous process technology was most suitable for the largest firms that could purchase complete production systems from international design engineers (and became more so when instrumentation and computer control were brought together in the mid-1960s), there were gains that smaller firms could and did realise.

In engineering, the situation was subtly different. The "big stuff" in this case was the big ATMs to achieve scale economies in the repetitive machining of engine and gearbox parts and the transfer presses to bulk produce engine pressings. British production engineers showed both their excellence and their limitations. In the best example, the Longbridge factory of Austin/BMC, the production engineering represented creative adaptation of a very high order and the development of a more "flexible mass production" than was achieved in Detroit. However, BMC did not rationalise its body shells and the level of automation in pressing, welding and painting was disappointing. This was based on careful calculation of the economics of transfer presses (see Graves 1955: 33–6), and a strong belief that it faced a fragmented market and needed a full range of body shells to defend its market share. Interestingly, exactly the same considerations inhibited Ford Europe from simplifying the design and engineering of its range (reducing "build complexity") in its "After Japan" phase (Tolliday 1991: 101–2). Beneath this "big stuff", smaller rotary transfer machines were widely adopted in many branches of engineering.

However the automation technology that was expected to revolutionise smaller firms, N/C machine tools, reached only a tiny fraction of the anticipated market. As noted in Chapter 4, Noble (1984) explains limited diffusion in the USA by the capture of the technology by the military-industrial-educational complex and leading innovation away from commercial uses. The British case calls this conclusion into question. Britain's N/C machine tool "industry" also followed a similar path, producing very expensive machines whose main use was in the precision, cost-plus work in aerospace and other high-quality batch processes. In the UK, record-payback, the alternative to N/C technology upon which so much of Noble's argument hinges, failed because of lack of commercial interest from machine tool users rather than the nefarious influences of military planners. It is worth noting that the N/C technology of the 1950s developed into industrial robotics, with broad application in engineering, and flexible manufacturing systems, which tended to be found in the same types of high-precision, small-batch jobs as N/C technology in the 1960s.

The most disappointing aspect of automation technology in the UK was in the office. The larger, more bureaucratic firms saw in ever more powerful computers a vision of tighter control of the enterprise from the boardroom (the intention of management information systems) or head office (as in bank automation). But the software and hardware available in the 1960s and 1970s were slow to supply the functionality that systems analysts had hoped for. Management information systems, promised in the early 1960s, were not delivered until the later 1980s (Rosen and Baroudi 1992). Driven by fashion, employers in both the UK and the USA ordered systems that were far more powerful than they needed for the routine tasks that they wished to automate, or else, like the banks, they overreached themselves. For the great majority of clerical employers, computerisation was a side-show, a distraction from the main issues, which were to consolidate, mechanise, bureaucratise and develop the skills of their clerical and secretarial staff. Sales of office machinery certainly rose, but many office employers continued to rely more on labour than machines and tended to poach staff from those organisations, like the banks, that had in the 1950s become skilled recruiters and trainers of young female clerks. Service sector employers had little opposition from their workers when mechanising and automating office work; new technology was seen as a potential solution to the drudgery of many aspects of routine clerical work.

Worker opposition was always more likely in the manufacturing sector, but it was surprising just how much freedom employers had in implementing new automated technologies. In Chapter 4, the success of Austin/BMC managers in managing the very cyclically sensitive demand for cars was noted, despite the reputation of both the industry and the Longbridge factory for disturbed industrial relations (Turner et al. 1967: 235–8). The most notable example of conflict over the introduction of new technologies lay in the adoption of N/C machine tools in the USA (Chapter 4 above). More generally, automation blurred the boundaries between established skills especially in maintenance work. Both British and American firms at the leading edge of automation attempted to negotiate flexibility agreements with their skilled workers and to create more broadly competent craftsmen.[8] Given the craftist mentalities of British and American skilled workers, it is hardly surprising that they should insist on their job property rights under conventional management systems. Demarcation rules among maintenance workers did not render automation projects uneconomic, but made the management of maintenance work more difficult and expensive. However, in the changing market and political context of Britain in the early 1980s, with mangers having to re-think their approach to industrial relations in the light of the growing interest in Japanisation, important agreements were reached on craft flexibility within wider HRM initiatives (see Young 1986). In the new political and economic context of the mid-1980s, there were new opportunities to build flexibility with "responsible autonomy" (Friedman 1990), that is restructuring the management of skilled work to allow the workers more involvement and participation in how work was organised while improving communications between managers and workers to discuss and overcome problems.

This seems to suggest that technical change occurs in bursts when external economic circumstances permit. Indeed, by focusing on "technology scares", this study has emphasised discontinuities. But continuities are equally obvious. In automobiles, for example, the introduction of industrial robots in the 1970s and 1980s was really an attempt to remove bottlenecks in the welding and paint shops which had been created by the pace of automation on the pressing and machining lines in the 1950s and 1960s (Maielli 2007). Some union leaders saw the innovations in HRM as consistent with the traditions of their own organisation and the wider labour movement, though there was equally strong "rejectionist" opinion (Bacon and Storey 1996: 60–4). Unfortunately, the export of "pop management" from the USA to the UK has exaggerated the discontinuities and imparted its own fashion consciousness to the management of technical change during the 1980s, but similar swings and shifts were evident in office automation two decades earlier (Chapters 6 and 8 above). The growth of the management education industry has not been without its critics from within. Thus, Robert S. Kaplan, former Dean of Carnegie-Mellon Business School, noted that the research output of American business schools had contributed nothing to the understanding of quality control or the information-based management revolution. Others have criticised the expensively-paid professors of management who charge astronomically high consultancy fees and provide only the most superficial diagnoses of company problems (both reported by Locke 1996: 227–9). The pressure on business analysts to offer instant assessments of strategic options has merely exposed the "herd instinct" among academic/consultants. Opinions have changed with frightening speed and what was said last year has been instantly forgotten. It is no real wonder that managers have felt somewhat bewildered and that the real value of innovations, especially those concerned with Japanisation, have been under-explored.

Notes

Chapter 1   The Political Economy of Technical Change

1 For an assessment of the scare and the reaction to it, the best sources remain Saul 1960; Searle 1971. More generally on the British economy and the record of technological innovation (in the widest sense) see Nicholas 2004; Marrison 1996: 1–221; Pollard 1989: 1–57; Wilson 1995: 62–132.

2 On rationalisation in Britain, see Garside 1990: 203–39; Hannah 1976: 27–53; Tomlinson 1994a: 104–11, 1277–35. On Germany, see Brady 1993; Nolan 1994. By far the best discussion of debate on the impact of innovation and technological change in the USA is Bix 2000: chs. 1–6. See also Mumford 1934.

3 The standard text on the British economy in the 1950s contains two references to automation (more exactly to "automation"). The first is linked to union fears and redundancy, and the second to redundancy strikes and negotiations for safeguards against unemployment: Worswick and Ady 1962: 31, 503.

4 Most famously, John Diebold, whose book automation (1952) did much to stoke the fires of public interest.

5 A key contribution came in articles by Peter Drucker (1955a; 1955b; 1955c) in *Harper's Magazine*, which predicted that automation would stabilise output (but not prices) and thus employment. However, there were many prepared to disagree. The CIO called a conference in the same month to discuss the impact on labour. One contributor, Walter S. Buckingham, predicted that heavy localised unemployment would result, as the closure rate of plants would increase as a small number of producers adopted automated methods, pushing more traditional producers out of business and producing ghost towns CIOCEP 1955: 40.

6 University of Warwick, Modern Records Centre, MSS 36, A93 (i), "Automation: A Report to the UAW-CIO Economic and Collective Bargaining Conference held in Detroit, Michigan, 12–13 November, 1954: A Resolution on Automation", undated: 12 [archive cited hereafter as MRC].

7 *Ibid*: 18.

8 There were strike waves in 1943–4, 1945–6, 1949–50 and concerned more than the bread-and-butter issues of wages and hours, entering issues of control and managerial prerogatives: see Noble 1984: 24–33; Korpi and Shalev (1979: Table II) categorise industrial conflict in postwar USA as slightly worse than in the UK.

9 Henry G. Riter (1955), the President of NAM, argued "That's the pity of it – that one man who controls one union can hold industry at bay. I trust I won't sound facetious if I say – Walter Raleigh spread a cloak under the feet of Good Queen Bess, but Walter Reuther is doing his best to pull the rug from under all of us".

10 Hagley archive, NAM papers, Acc 1411, Series I, Box 104, "Amendments to the NAM Position Statement on Industrial Relations, March 1955, folios 1 and 11" [collection cited hereafter as Hagley, NAM].

11 Hagley, NAM Acc 1412, Series VII, Box 147, Folder Guaranteed Annual Wage – 1, 1954, Memo from Sybyl S. Patterson, Director, Employee Relations Division, 20 April, 1954, "Tentative Framework for a New NAM Campaign on 'Steady Work for Steady Pay Versus the Guaranteed Annual Wage'"; Folder Guaranteed Annual Wage – 2, 1954, NAM, Employee Relations Division, *The Guaranteed Annual Wage and its Implications for a Free Economy*, New York, NAM, February 1954.

12 It was estimated that in 1956, the US would graduate 27,000 engineers and 50,000 technicians whereas Soviet universities and institutes would produce 45,000 engineers and 1,600,000 technicians of comparable quality. US Congress 1955: 40 (Evidence of Walter S. Buckingham).

13 A graphic example of this thinking came in an address by Benjamin F. Fairless (1955), Chairman of the Board, United States Steel Corporation, to a local chamber of commerce: "[Technology] is our salvation. It is the one great advantage that we have, and we must, I think, preserve it at all costs; for our native ability to design, build and to use the world's most productive machines, provides, today, our last, best hope of enjoying a peaceful tomorrow! But recently, I have been much disturbed – as you, no doubt, have also been – by the sudden appearance, in this country, of a great propaganda campaign which is clearly calculated to discourage and retard the technological progress on which our freedom and the safety of our homes depend. This campaign is based wholly on the psychology of fear. It is designed to frighten our people into a belief that the new machines which are being developed now will destroy the jobs of thousands of workers and leave them destitute. And unless I am badly mistaken – as I sincerely hope I am – this propaganda is proving effective both in the ranks and in the leadership of labour".

14 UK National Archives Public Records Office, BT190/2, NPACI 42nd meeting, 28 May, 1954 [hereafter archive cited as NAPRO]; "Business Notes", *The Economist* 171 (5 June 1954): 821–2.

15 NAPRO BT 190/2, NPACI 42nd meeting; "Invest in Success", *The Economist* 173 (16 Oct. 1954).

16 MRC, Confederation of British Industry and predecessors archive MSS 200/B/3/2/C1162, part 1, BEC file on "The Automated Factory"; MRC, TUC Archive: MSS 292/571.81/1, TUC file on automation. The latter contains letters on automation by Fletcher, secretary of the production department, to the International Ladies' Garment Workers' Union, Walter Reuther of the UAW, the US Textile Workers' Union, the CIO Department of Education and Research and the American Management Association.

17 *Ibid.* extract from *The Railway Review*, 12 November, 1954 pointing out the concerns of US workers, particularly in power generation.

18 The TUC noted the scope for automatic control mechanisms in industry and the "almost unlimited potential" of electronics in processing business data: MRC MSS 292/571.81/5a, Scientific Advisory Committee, 1/1.

19 ASSET 1956: 9. The United Pattern Makers' Association wanted more investment to introduce automation more speedily: MRC MSS 292/571.81/5a,

Scientific Advisory Committee, 1/1, "Trade Union Congress Resolutions, 2 February 1956".

20 "Automatic processes and electronic controls were stated to be commonplace in the steel, chemical and oil industries and were being increasingly used in office work...Nevertheless, where automation was known to have been introduced little, if any, redundancy had occurred, it having been possible to absorb it through labour turnover and restricted labour recruitment". *Ibid*, Scientific Advisory Committee, 1.

21 *Ibid*, Scientific Advisory Committee, 2/3.

22 Here the union record was rather patchy. The Tobacco Workers' Union, which had seen considerable changes in methods of production, had been unable to press joint consultation. The National Union of General and Municipal Workers, on the other hand, had generally been consulted over automatic processes in chemicals, car manufacture, steel, tarmac, plate and sheet glass, and glass containers. *Ibid*.

23 *Ibid*, and MRC MSS 292/571.81/5b, "NUBE: report on office management conference", undated.

24 On over-heating, see *The Economist* (19 February, 1955), p. 604; on monetary policy, see Howson 1994: 236–7. Internal Treasury advice was more circumspect than Butler's policy: NAPRO T171/450, Hall, "The Budgetary Problem in 1955", 13 December, 1954.

25 NAPRO T171/456, Hall to Bridges, 30 Aug. 1955; Hall to Butler, 1 Sept. 1955; Dow 1964: 79, 155.

26 Details from NAPRO LAB 10/1445, "Background Note"; NAPRO CAB134/1193, Cabinet Committee on Automation, AC(56)7, revise, Annexe.

27 *Ibid*. Lyddon 1996: 190–1; Turner *et al.* 1967: 240, 262–3.

28 *Daily Herald*, "Car Workers Vote to Stay Out Against Automation", 1 May, 1956; *Daily Telegraph*, "Communist link in car strike. Party activity at Standards. Orders given to fight automation", 2 May, 1956; *Daily Herald*, "Automation Firm Sacks 2,600 men", 31 May, 1956.

29 *The Manchester Guardian*, for example, reported the story as a "short time dispute" ("Strike at Standards", 27 April, 1956) but also reported on "Car workers' underlying fear of automation", 26 April, 1956. *The Times*, on the other hand, managed to make automation an issue while recognising that it was not: "Union policy on automation. Issue in Standard strike. Discussion by men's leaders urged", 2 May, 1956. *The Financial Times* chose to describe it in terms of a dispute over short time working under a headline claiming that it was a test case on automation: "A Test Case", 11 June, 1956.

30 *Daily Worker*, "Standard vanguard", 2 May, 1956; *Coventry Evening Telegraph*, "Strike issue obscured", 4 May, 1956.

31 See, for example, *Daily Telegraph*, "Strike threat over car firm short time", 5 March, 1956.

32 "Personal message from the Managing Director to all hourly-paid employees", 30 May, 1956. Copy in NAPRO LAB10/1445.

33 An automatic transfer machine, or an "in-line" machine, undertook several operations that were planned to take approximately the same time. Increasingly these machines were linked together by devices that moved the workpiece from one tool to the next and clamped it in position for the various machining operations until a large number of machines were linked together (Rolt 1965: 238).

34 N/C machine tools comprised an electronic control system, programmed by instructions keyed into paper or magnetic tape or punched cards, and a machine tool. The control system activated controllers to move the workpiece or the cutting tool to cut to commands in the control program. The machine tool could be of any type and the cutting operations could vary between the relatively simple and the complex. In theory N/C machines allowed complex tasks to be overseen by relatively less skilled workers (Rolt 1965: 241–3).

35 "A feedback control system is a control system which tends to maintain a prescribed relationship of one system variable to another by comparing functions of these variables and using differences as a means of control". The "closed loop" implies no human intervention so that the system regulates itself, AIEE 1951.

36 Among the first to produce published results was the Yale University Technology Project. Its principal researcher, Charles R. Walker (1950), had already examined changing technology at the Ellwood works of US Steel, before his study of automation in steel (Walker 1957). The Project also examined power plants and other industries: Mann and Hoffman (1956).

37 These included *Instruments in Industry*, begun I June 1954, for instrumentation producers. It was followed in October 1954 by *Process Control*, aimed at users of automatic control technology. In January 1955 came *Instruments in Industry*, subtitled the *British Journal of Instrumentation, Automation and Process Control*. In early 1956, *Process Control* became *Process Control and Automation*, soon followed by the merger with the recently launched *Automation* to become *Automation (incorporating Instruments in Industry)*.

38 See NAPRO DSIR 17/564, AC(55–6)70, "Future DSIR Provision for Support of Research in the Field of Human Factors in Industry". 19 Apr. 1956, Annexes B and D. Among the published studies were PEP 1957; DSIR 1957; Davison *et al.* 1958.

39 The Board asked directly about the country of origin of the equipment, so imported machinery and control mechanisms can be eliminated from the cross-checking exercise.

40 NAPRO BT64/4801. The replies were received in the Board in the period from October 1956 to mid-February 1957. They varied from very brief to enormously detailed and extensive.

41 The treatment of the food industry, many parts of which were introducing continuous flow processes, was particularly impressive in this respect: *ibid*, Reason to Wright, 9 January, 1957.

42 These data represent the state of the debate, rather than accurate measurements of the damage done to US industry. They are often peak-to-trough measurements, and so exaggerate the extent of the problems. They are taken from Locke 1996: 160–1.

43 This analysis has been vigorously criticised as gross over-simplification by Williams *et al.* (1987b). They particularly dispute the idea that production techniques can be so easily differentiated.

44 Multi-modelling means the production of assemblies, like axles, in batches with tool changeovers in between, and mixed modelling means sending two or more models of different, and maybe unrelated, types down the same assembly line: Williams *et al.* 1994: 22.

45 Piore and Sabel's (1984: 205–20, 223–6) list of craft-based flexible manufacturing are specialty steels in mini-mills, specialty chemicals, textiles in the Prato district of Italy, and Japanese machine tools. They also suggest that the trajectory of Japanese expansion was about to favour small- and medium-sized firms.

46 One of the characteristics of this literature has been the sharp differences of view on the precise location of Japanese strength. A number of authorities have suggested that Japanese strength lay deep in Japanese culture (for example, Pascale and Athos 1982; Morishima 1982). Others have identified close collaboration with government resulting in unfair trading practices (Wolf 1985; James 1989) or strategic marketing (Wong *et al.* 1987), Japanese manufacturing methods (Schonberger 1982; 1985), personnel practices (Hayes 1981) and strategic planning (Wheelwright 1981).

47 Compare, for example, the positive case put forward by Lee (1990: 176–7) with the more measured views of Supple (1962: 85) and Coleman (1987: 151). For a review of the debate, see Wilson 1995: 15–18.

48 For the former position, see Zeitlin 1995: 277–86; Broadberry 1997a: 1, 14–16, 81, 89; Lewchuk 1987. For the alternative view, see the contributions in Kipping and Bjarnar 1998. More recent work by Zeitlin (2000a: 11–20) seems to accept many of the points of criticism.

49 For Bank of England attempts to exaggerate external weakness to further its own goals of tighter controls on domestic spending and faster progress to convertibility, see Booth 2000.

50 For the formulation of this approach see Olson 1986; 1996; Batstone 1986; Calmfors and Driffil 1988. For critiques, see Paqué 1996; Booth *et al.* 1997.

51 Monitoring mechanisms allow both sides to check on a continuous basis that bargains are being kept. Eichengreen's best example is the German co-determination policy that mandated the appointment of a labour representative to the board of all corporations of significant size. Bonding mechanisms were available on agreement but would be lost in the event of reneging. Eichengreen's examples include tax and transfer systems to encourage investment by employers and extensions of social security in return for wage moderation by organised labour. Finally, co-ordinating mechanisms ensure that the strong do not exploit their strength to the disadvantage of the weak (employers or workers) and are epitomised in centralised bargaining, Eichengreen 1996: 45–50.

Chapter 2 World Roles and International Technology Transfer

1 Redmond and Smith estimate the cost of Project Whirlwind at $8 million against an original estimate of $200,000, and Flamm (1987: 176) suggests that the full cost of SAGE was $8 billion.

2 The SAGE project provided IBM with half-a-billion dollars in the 1950s and at its peak about 20 per cent of the company's workforce: Watson and Petrie 1990: 230.

3 This discussion of the development of N/C machine tools is taken from Noble 1984: 96–143.

4 Noble (1984: 135–7) cites an unpublished economic appraisal by MIT Management School economists, Robert Gregory and Thomas Atwater.

5 See the cabinet discussion of the terms of the US loan and Dalton's paper on its terms: NAPRO Cab 128/4, 6 Nov. 1945, 29 Nov. 1945; Cab 129/5, "Financial Agreement with the USA", 28 Nov. 1945.

6 The best accounts of the loan negotiations are the Keynes papers (Moggridge 1979) and Pressnell's (1986) official history. For the Chancellor of the Exchequer's increasingly pessimistic view of the prospects of meeting the convertibility requirements, see Dalton 1962: 74–86.

7 On the general expectation of devaluation, see NAPRO T 236/2398, "The Future of Sterling", R.W.B. Clarke, 27 Feb. 1948, and other memoranda by Clarke, Bolton and others in this file.

8 The extremely erratic performance of the productivity gap for "mining", for example, can be explained by Britain's dependence for energy (since "mining" includes the extraction of coal, oil and natural gas) on old, deep coal mines, with narrow, faulted seams, whereas US coal mining enjoyed wider, more accessible seams and easy oil and gas extraction. When the UK began to exploit North Sea hydrocarbons and closed its least efficient coal mines the productivity differential narrowed impressively after 1973.

9 Details from Science Museum, International Computers Limited archive [hereafter SM ICL], 1/32, "RCA/English Electric Information Sharing Agreement", 20 Feb. 1963.

10 SM ICL 1/23 LEO Computers Management Meeting, 21 Sept. 1962; SM ICL 1/34 "[EE-LEO] Development Co-ordination Committee", meeting 14 Mar. 1963. The RCA random access technology failed, costing EE-LEO more major contracts: SM ICL 1/37, EE-LEO Management Meeting, 9 Feb. 1965.

11 The Iron and Steel report (AACP 1952: 16–21), for example, listed a range of technical improvements on the size of furnaces, closure of smaller British works, improvements in transport networks both within the steel plant and that which linked the works with raw material supply and markets, improvements in raw material qualities and points of detail in furnace design that appear very relevant to British conditions in addition to the more vague, amorphous tendency to see the efficiency of the US steel industry as one aspect of the high-wage/high-productivity ethos of US industry.

12 NAPRO CAB 124/1798, Fraser to Hailsham, 5 March 1959.

13 *Ibid*, Norman Brooke to Hailsham, 19 March 1959 (reporting that there was little to be gained from a "college of automation"). However, *The Times* of 4 May 1959 reported (from the *Engineering Industries Journal*) on talks between Cranfield, the Electronic Engineering Association and the National Union of Manufacturers' Advisory Service on the college of automation. Even the idea of a government-sponsored conference to examine the case was scotched by officials: *ibid*, Murray to Part, 15 Dec. 1959.

14 Charles Babbage Institute, University of Minnesota, Burroughs Archive: CBI 90, Series 48, Box 4, Folder 1, Travis to Eppert, 24 Jan. 1967 [hereafter CBI 90]. Irven Travis recalled that Burroughs had made inquiries about work in progress at the Moore School, where he was director of research, in early 1947. Burroughs concluded a contract with the Moore School for basic research into electronic computing techniques with applications to office work in August 1947. After a period as consultant to Burroughs, Travis joined the company as head of research on March 1949. Just over a year

later, Burroughs Research Group had 69 employees, at an annual payroll of almost $300,000.

15 CBI 90, Series 10, John S. Coleman Biography Box 6, file 2, *McGraw-Hill Digest, Business, Engineering, Industry*, August 1952. *Ibid*, Box 6, file 1: *Nation's Business*, April 1956 (both features on Coleman).

16 CBI 90, Series 51, Box 1, Folder 5, "Import Licences for Burroughs Sensimatic Typewriters", 20 Mar. 1958.

17 CBI 90, Series 48, Box 3, Folder 10, "A History of Burroughs Corporation", undated but late 1978 or early 1979.

18 Royal Bank of Scotland Group Archives: GB 1502/WD/366/13, "Notes of a Meeting with Burroughs", 12 Jan. 1960; *Ibid*. "Notes of a Meeting with Burroughs", 10 Jan 1961 [hereafter archive is cited as RBSGA].

19 RBSGA, GB 1502/WD/366/13, "Electronic Sub-Committee held on Friday 19, June 1959".

20 Bill Lonergan, project manager for the Electrodata division of Burroughs in the late 1950s, described the VRC as the "ledger-snatcher", "a monster", "clearly not the right way to do things. It was a dinosaur". Charles Babbage Institute, Oral Histories, "Burroughs B5000 Conference I", 6 September 1985 (folio 16).

21 *Computer Weekly*, "Burroughs Launch Big Machine in the UK", 9 Feb. 1967.

22 "3 New Branches Open in Britain" and "B2500 and B3500 Systems Featured", *Burroughs B-Line International Edition*, 3 August 1965.

23 On costings, see the comparative estimates for an IBM-based and a Burroughs system for the National Westminster Bank, in which Burroughs undercut IBM by a small margin: RBSGA, 021979, "Notes for the Chairman; Computer Developments", 1 May 1968; for reference to the record of the B5500 in US banks, see HSBC Group Archives London, Acc 200/223, E.V. McGlone (Burroughs) to W.G. Kneale (Midland Bank), 24 January 1968; on the (alleged) superior compatibility of Burroughs central processors and terminal computers, *ibid*, "Note for the Management Committee: Project 70, Central Processors", 25 January, 1968 [hereafter archive referred to as HSBCGA, London].

Chapter 3   National Politics of Productivity and Technical Change

1 On the growing trend to see judgements on government competence in economic policy as the key to electoral choices, see Butler and Stokes 1969: 402.

2 Bix (2000: 127) notes the range of weekly and monthly publications and novels that expressed concern about unemployment in the 1930s. She also notes: "Science fiction writers of the 1930s transformed the old Puritan work ethic into a Machine Age morality play. Honest labour represented the foundation of humans' self-respect and motivation, and if the future advance of technology robbed men of those values, life would disintegrate".

3 Reuther was the "most effective anti-Communist in the postwar years": Renshaw 1991: 108.

4 Details from "History, some economic arguments and problems posed by GAW, alternatives to supplementation of unemployment compensation;

background working paper on union demands for guaranteed wages" by Thomas F. Johnson, United States Chamber of Commerce, 25 September, 1953, Hagley Library, NAM papers, Acc 1412, Series VII, Box 147.

5   The voice of moderation within the NAM belonged to Sybyl S. Patterson, Director, Employee Relations Division. See her "Tentative Framework for a New NAM Campaign on 'Steady Work for Steady Pay Versus the Guaranteed Annual Wage'", 20 April, 1954. *Ibid.*

6   The term "financial Dunkirk" was coined by Keynes in July 1945: Moggridge 1979: 374.

7   For a good survey of the debates on planning of the 1930s and 1940s and their influence on the Attlee government's thinking on planning and controls, see Tomlinson 1997b: ch. 6. For political differences on control policy after 1948, see Kelly 2002: ch. 5.

8   The debates over the strategic direction of the British economy have been enlivened since the mid-1980s by the publication of Correlli Barnett's polemics against the wartime coalition (1986) and the Attlee governments' economic policies (1995). Barnett's interpretations of his sources have been heavily criticised (see Harris 1991; Edgerton 1991; Tomlinson 1997a). The criticism of Barnett reached its high point in the argument that British governments had indeed pursued an active policy to promote productivity in the 1940s (Tiratsoo and Tomlinson 1993; Tomlinson 1997b: 68–166). This perspective has, in turn, been criticised by those who would have preferred a more intensive competition policy (Broadberry and Crafts 1996).

9   The volume of work on economic policy during the transition to peacetime "normality" is enormous. In addition to titles already mentioned, note Dow 1964; Middlemas 1983.

10 On government and industry during wartime, see Ashworth 1991: 6–26; Tomlinson 1994a: 192–7. For discussion of the network of wartime controls, see Hancock and Gowing 1949; Chester 1952a. On the development of more centralised, national uniform, social welfare provision before and during the war, see the essays collected in Smith 1986 and also Titmuss 1950.

11 The best sources on the political context are: Tomlinson 1997b: 263–305; Morgan 1984: 85–93. On the administrative context, see Alford *et al.* 1992: 21–5.

12 On the wartime role of the union leadership, see Clegg 1994: 165–258; Barnes and Reid 1982. On the radical criticism of employers, see Croucher 1982; Hinton 1994.

13 The unions agreed to suspend many of their established trade practices for the duration of the war, but even the more radical unions contemplated a new postwar political economy in which industry, both publicly and privately owned, would be run according to national goals rather than for private profit. The engineers, for example, began to contemplate a system in which unions would not need to mount defensive work rules and aggressive pay bargaining: see the AEU quoted by Booth 1996: 46.

14 Excess demand for labour lasted until late 1947 and the adjustments to macroeconomic policy following the coal and foreign exchange crises of that year (Dow and Dicks-Mireaux 1958). Excess demand arose from the inability of controls to hold back pent-up demand from consumers and

firms, low interest rates and a general determination within the government and the Treasury to avoid cutting demand when an international slump was thought to be imminent (Cairncross 1987: 409–45; Tomlinson 1997b: 211–27).

15 In a now-celebrated memorandum for cabinet, Harold Wilson, President of the Board of Trade, noted that the Attlee government had little theoretical or practical understanding of how to manage the private sector in a socialist economy: NAPRO CAB124/1200, "The State and Private Industry", 4 May, 1950.

16 MRC, MSS.292/557.1/2, NPACI (GC side) 1/1, 28 September, 1948; 4/2, 30 March, 1950.

17 The scale of food subsidies became the critical issue for the government in 1947, as inflationary pressures mounted and the cost to the Treasury of pegging the cost of basic foods in the shops began to rise rapidly. The cost of food subsidies was pegged in 1947 and cut after devaluation in 1949: Cairncross 1987: 333–53, 409–26; Rollings 1988: 290–1. On the struggle within the union movement, see Panitch 1976: 30–40.

18 On trade union anti-Communism, see Stevens 1999: 170–6; on the efforts of the Attlee government to bolster that drive, see Davis Smith 1990: 98–105.

19 According to Tiratsoo and Tomlinson (1998b: 22) unemployment averaged 1.7 per cent per annum, inflation averaged 3.3 per cent and the current account showed a small average surplus of £38.5 millions.

20 The analysis emerges in various papers in the Economic Section's file on long-term economic prospects: NAPRO T230/267, Long-term economic planning: "Economic Policy, 1953/57", undated; "Potentialities of the UK economy 1953–57", 17 June, 1953; Hall to Gilbert, 16 Dec. 1954 "Long-term economic survey".

21 NAPRO BT 190/2, NPACI, 42nd meeting, 28 May, 1954.

22 The TUC Economic Committee was certainly aware of the strength of German and Japanese competition in British markets, and came close to accepting that radical change was needed in trade union structures: MRC MSS.292/560.1/10, TUC Economic Committee 5/1, 10 February, 1954. See also Middlemas 1983: 226–33.

23 The papers of the Cabinet committee on industrial relations of July 1955 are in NAPRO CAB 134/1273.

24 The white paper had originally been scheduled for 1952, but a variety of short-term problems (notably fears that publication would produce an adverse response on the foreign exchanges) had postponed publication on at least three occasions: NAPRO T267/7, "The government and wages", paras. 10–11, 93–106.

25 NAPRO CAB 128/25, CC51(52); NAPRO CAB 134/1229, EP(56) 17th meeting.

26 NAPRO CAB 129/81, C(56)118.

27 Macmillan held a dinner party for senior advisers, at least one of whom had good links to the EEF to discuss current economic problems, including the engineering pay claim: Cairncross 1991: 58–60.

28 NAPRO LAB 10/652, NJAC 40th (special) meeting; NAPRO BT 190/2, NPACI 33rd meeting; Clegg and Adams 1957: 27–34; Davis Smith 1990: 119–23. See below for discussion of government poll ratings.

29 NAPRO T230/579, "Economic Growth and National Efficiency", July 1961. The file begins with a cutting from the Financial Times of 14 Sept. 1960 by F.W. Paish, "Growth of the British Economy". For a longer version of the case for running the economy with higher average unemployment, see Paish 1966: 309–36.

30 MRC MSS.200/F/3/E3/3/21 E.191.61.

31 For a favourable view of Woodcock (against that of his many critics), see Taylor 1999; 2000: 14–15, 150–5.

32 MRC MSS.292B/560.1/1, Economic Committee 4, 11 January, 1961; *ibid*, Economic Committee 4/2, 11 January, 1961; for TUC opposition to wages policy, ibid, Economic Committee 6, 8 March, 1961.

33 MRC MSS.292B/560.1/1, Economic Committee 5/3, 8 February, 1961.

34 MRC MSS.292B/560.1/2, Economic Committee 11/5, 9 August, 1961; MRC MSS.292B/560.1/3, Economic Committee (Special) 1, 27 September, 1961; *ibid*, Economic Committee 3, 8 November, 1961.

35 NAPRO PREM 11/4069, Selwyn Lloyd to TUC Economic Committee, 10 January, 1961.

36 MRC.MSS.292B/560.1/3, Economic Committee 5, 10 and 17 January, 1962.

37 On the disappointing productivity outcomes of the Fawley agreements, see Ahlstrand 1990. On the limited impact of NEDC on British political economy, see Ringe and Rollings 2000: 350. On the failure of NEDC to stimulate trade union reform, see Taylor 1999. The new interest in growth planning by large-scale industry did, however, contribute to the reform of the ways in which industrial opinion was represented to government and the public. Grant and Marsh (1977: 25) argue that the new politics of growth and planning were extremely important in the merger of the three main representative bodies of British management to form the Confederation of British Industry in 1965.

38 The balance of payments statistics produced at the time showed a large current account deficit, which the government duly exploited. However, subsequent revisions suggest that the deficit was only 40 percent of that estimated at the time and was more or less eliminated in 1965: ONS 2002: Table 1.17.

39 The course of the TUC's deliberations can be seen in the papers for the Economic Committee in the first quarter of 1965: MRC MSS.292B/560.1/9, Economic Committees of 7 December, 1964 (special), 5 (13 January, 1965), 6 (25 January, 1965), 7 (10 February, 1965) and 8 (1 March, 1965). MRC MSS.292B/560.1/10, Economic Committees 9 (10 March, 1965), 10 (17 March, 1965), 11 (5 April, 1965) and 12 (14 April, 1965).

40 Most authorities agree that President Johnson's Treasury Secretary, Henry Fowler, pressured the Chancellor of the Exchequer to replace the voluntary incomes policy with something more robust. The IMF and the OECD held similar views: Panitch 1976: 86–7; Taylor 1993: 136–7; Jones 1987: 70–1.

41 The most readable account of this period is Taylor 1993: 126–76. On the Prime Minister's threat to see unemployment rise to 2 million to use market pressures to curb wage growth, see pp. 139–40.

42 *The Times*, "Standing Ovation for Prime Minister", 2 Oct. 1968: 4.

43 The dominant intellectual influence on the royal commission was undoubtedly the Oxford University voluntarist approach to industrial relations,

represented on the commission by H.A. Clegg and by Allan Flanders and Alan Fox in its working papers. But there were also two prominent labour reporters, Andrew Shonfield and Eric Wigham, and representatives of the main vested interests.

44 All the members signed the main report, four added a "supplementary note"' and Shonfield produced a vigorous "note of reservation", arguing for state intervention into pay bargaining in the national interest.

45 See the discussion of the Industrial Relations Act of 1971 by some of the leading participants in the symposium organised by the Institute of Contemporary British History in Feb. 1988 (ICBH 1988).

46 For academic studies, see Pratten 1976; Prais 1981; Davies and Caves 1987. Popular studies include Allen 1979. Perhaps the best example of polemic is Joseph 1979. The best forensic discussion of this literature is Nichols 1986.

47 See also Melling's (2007) discussion of the ruthlessness with which senior executives of US automobile producers could strike at attempts by junior management to seek independent union organisation.

48 This argument obviously owes much to Middlemas (1986). Middlemas (1979) has also argued that the origins of crisis concertation go back to the strikes of the Edwardian era.

49 Woodward (1991: Fig. 6.5) shows that Britain's inflation rate was very close to the OECD average for the period 1950–70, as might be expected under a regime of pegged exchange rates such as Bretton Woods. Stout (1976) has demonstrated quite clearly that for much of British industry during the long boom the problems were on the side of non-price rather than price competition.

Chapter 4   Automation in Engineering

1 The classic differentiation between "mass production" and "flexible specialisation" was made by Piore and Sabel 1984. The classic forensic interrogation of these concepts is Williams *et al.* (1987b). The best attempt to modify "mass production/flexible specialisation" into a workable set of distinctions is Scranton (1997). Hereafter, Scranton's vocabulary of "volume" and "specialty" production is used, not least because it has none of the ideological overtones of Piore and Sabel's terminology.

2 Motor cars formed part of the wider group, motor vehicles. The divergence in relative productivity, most evident in 1948/49, is probably due to differences in efficiency in commercial vehicle building in the two countries. In the UK, heavy commercial vehicle makers used batch production techniques to meet the relatively limited demand, whereas US firms faced sufficiently strong markets to justify investment in mass production methods: Bhaskar 1979: 241; Foreman-Peck *et al.* 1995: 106–9; Nevins and Hill 1962: 383, 440.

3 Nevins and Hill 1962: 356. MRC MSS 200/B/3/2/C1162, part 1, R. Webb Sparks to Burton, 19 Aug. 1954.

4 BMC, unlike Renault and Volkswagen, received neither additional state funding, nor major sums from the lucrative US OSP contracts for military R&D and defence production (McGlade 2000: 73).

5 For contemporary criticisms of the Austin-Morris merger, see Adeney 1989: 200–1; Pagnamenta and Overy 1984: 231 (quoting the Company Secretary of MG Motors); Church 1994: 80. On the rationalisation programme, see Williams *et al.* 1994: 136–7.

6 The judgement was made at the time by US and Soviet authorities as well as by British: Buckingham 1961: 37; Strumilin 1957: 56–9. For a long-term, comparative perspective, see Williams *et al.* 1994: 137–41.

7 *Motor Business*, 5 (Dec. 1955): 33; *Autocar* (10 Aug. 1967): 10.

8 Ford worked on a five-year product cycle, but the Minor, introduced in 1948, remained in production until 1971 and the Mini was produced for more than 35 years (Foreman-Peck *et al.* 1995: 129).

9 The British offshoots of Ford and GM produced a limited range of body shells (see below), but were less "Fordist" in this respect than VW (see Abelshauser 1995: 270).

10 Etheridge papers, MRC MSS.202/S/J/3/4/32, Visit to the Volkswagen Works by the Birmingham Productivity Association, 2–3 April, 1963, notes by J.A. Williams.

11 The anti-union senior management of the Longbridge factory had no time for shop stewards but the papers of the plant shop stewards committee reveal continuing contact between the committee and works' managers to resolve production issues throughout the early 1950s. MRC, Etheridge Papers, MSS.202/S/J/1/1, Austin Joint Shop Stewards' Committee Minutes, 1951–3.

12 MRC MSS.202/SP/3, Etheridge's notes (dated 29 Oct. 1962) in reply to questions by Horace W. White, who chaired Etheridge's talk on "Human Relations in Industry" to Bromsgrove Chamber of Commerce.

13 NAPRO LAB 10/1460, Draft notes for the Minister re. Duties of Employers and Unions, 30 June, 1956.

14 In Appendix IV of Board of Trade (1957) producers of automation equipment were asked to indicate their potential markets. The British Electrical and Allied Manufacturers' Association identified the motor, aircraft and steel industries as the principal likely users of automatic welding machines.

15 This estimate compares favourably with that of Diebold in 1955 cited at the end of Chapter 3.

16 Record-playback involved "capturing" on tape the movements of a cutting machine as it performed complex operations under the control of a skilled machinist. This tape could then be edited to remove errors and speed the process, but it was essentially a record of the way that a skilled machinist would undertake the task. The tape could then be replayed every time that this particular task needed to be reproduced. Numerical control, on the other hand, rested upon the skill of the computer programmer to trace the shape to be machined and translate this into movements of the cutting head. This was also embodied in a master tape that could be operated by a semi-skilled machinist (Noble 1979; 1984: 147–52).

17 This paragraph and the next depend heavily on Hamilton (1997).

18 Williamson (1955: 148–9) described the system to the IPE automation conference at Margate.

19 Ferranti was deemed to have the best technical system and the most accurate machine in tests on N/C tools by the USAF in 1957–8. However, GE,

the major user of the MIT system and the holder of many contracts for N/C machine tools, warned of huge cancellation charges for any lost contracts (Feilden 1995: 524).

20 These machines were designated CNC (computer numerical control).

21 The sample sizes were very small, and restricted to makers of pumps, turning machines, turbines and printing machines. The sample thus omitted aerospace (Gebhardt and Hatzold 1974: 29).

22 The Science Research Council noted that British demand for N/C tools grew by 9 per cent p.a. in the 1970s, but that in 1978 N/C types were only 1.5 per cent of the stock of machine tools (see Wilkinson 1983: 4).

23 NAPRO LAB, 18/738, Ministry of Labour, "Shortage of Labour in the Metal-using Industries", Oct. 1961.

24 MRC, MSS.202/S/J/3/2/88, letter from D. Baker, AEU shop steward, North Tool Room, Oct. 1967.

25 Subcontracting was common in both the British and American aerospace industries as one method of overcoming localised shortages of highly skilled labour when order books were tight (Jones 1985: 244).

26 The Society of British Aircraft Constructors told the Board of Trade's (1957: Appendix II) automation inquiry that, "Primarily the reason for introducing automation is to improve aircraft performance by ensuring consistency of components, and by reproducing by servo-controlled machines complicated parts or shapes which could not be attempted by manually controlled machines".

27 In his thesis, Hamilton (1997: 102–4) explained the limited diffusion of N/C machine tools in the UK during the 1960s in terms of entrepreneurial conservatism, but this sits uneasily with Gebhardt and Hatzold's data.

28 The users of computer-controlled machine tools mentioned the USA and Switzerland as additional sources to domestic supply: Board of Trade 1957, Appendix II: 21, 27; on the inability of domestic machine tool makers to meet demand during booms, see NAPRO BT 190/38, NPACI (60)78, "The United Kingdom Machine Tool Industry", 4 May, 1960.

29 MRC MSS.292/615.61/2, TUC Economic Committee, "The Machine Tool Industry", 9 Mar. 1955; MRC.MSS.292/615.61/1, TUC Economic Committee, 11/5, 9 May, 1958.

30 At district level, the resolutions on automation sought job protection and better wages. The president's report to the national committee also took a balanced view: "One cannot prevent industrial evolution; in fact it would be far easier to stay on the incoming tide with one's naked hands. The AEU has never deliberately assumed the character of an obstructionist. Our main and immediate problem is to safeguard the future economic existence of our members ...": (AEU 1956: 186–8, 228–9).

31 MRC MSS.202/S/J/3/2/88, letter from D. Baker, AEU shop steward, North Tool Room, Oct. 1967.

32 Rootes was interested in N/C tools, in part because it had severe problems with skilled workers within its version of the gang system (Tolliday 1986: 217–19). But its own financial problems effectively excluded the company from the early deployment of N/C tools.

33 The Production Engineering Research Association's study (PERA 1963) gave 17 examples of efficient use of N/C machines but only one, an alloy steel connecting rod, of any real relevance to the mass production industries.

34 See Jones 1991: 240–2 for slightly later examples of this same principle of rigid hierarchical control thinking.

35 Although measurement of skill is a conceptual battleground, at least one respectable study (Keefe 1991) has suggested that over the 30 years of experience with N/C technology there has been no discernible reduction in skill levels (measured in a variety of ways) required for machine tool operation.

36 Interestingly, Wilkinson's (1983) study of the introduction of CNC technology in the West Midlands, managers tended to pursue a control strategy (most forcefully in an American-owned machine tool producer) but workers were able to shape operational practices during the debugging stage.

37 BMC's introduction of transfer machines created concerns about job security and position papers from the Communist Party organisation at Longbridge (MRC MSS.202/S/J/3/2/13, file 2, "Automation. What it Means", undated) and vigorous claims for higher wages on newly automated processes (*Ibid*, Longbridge log, 30 Nov. 1955). The issue passed relatively easily for the management.

Chapter 5   The Continuous Flow Industries: Feedback Control and Computerisation

1 The refining of crude oil is a classic example. Burn (1961c: 162–4, 183–5) notes that in the interwar years, oil refining was a simple distillation process, undertaken in batches, that separated the various hydrocarbon compounds according to their boiling points. Refining was undertaken largely at the oilfields, but the improvement in measuring and monitoring instrumentation, which allowed further refining process, and rapid growth in demand after the war encouraged producers to build large refineries in the using countries.

2 See Wiener (1953) and Campbell (1953), for example.

3 Jones (1956: 41–55) included in his evidence to the Congress Sub-committee an appendix from the Bureau of the Census showing significant increases in the real value added in these branches of industry between 1947 and 1954 – by 350 percent in precision instruments, 153 percent in optical instruments, 90 percent in mechanical measuring instruments, 138 percent in electrical measuring instruments.

4 The director of research for the International Chemical Workers Union estimated that in the production of ammonia, levels of capital per production worker were four times the manufacturing average: US Congress 1955: 153.

5 Professor Thomas J. Walsh, Chemical Group Director of the Automation Project and Professor of Chemical Engineering at the Case Institute of Technology, Cleveland, Ohio and Director in evidence to the 1955 Congress automation enquiry: US Congress 1955: 473–91. However, his figure of approximately 700 workers per refinery, independent of scale of production, was contradicted by Nelson's figures (see below).

6 An open loop control system relied upon a human operator responding to changes in readings on measuring devices, interpreting those readings and changing part of the production system.

7 Board of Trade 1957: Appendix II, response of the Association of British Chemicals Manufacturers.

8 This problem was also evident in the UK, where the major oil companies reported: "Individual refineries units are controlled by instrumentation which automatically corrects unit conditions of pressure, temperature and flow ... [but] there is, as yet, no significant amount of interconnection between units in the direction of co-ordinated operation through automatic controls of the refinery operations as a whole." The Association of British Chemical Manufacturers made almost identical points. *Ibid.*

9 Flamm (1988: 65–7) describes the importance of Northrop Aircraft's Snark missile in creating the Bendix G-15 and the Librascope LGP-30, both of which were early small computers that sold in significant quantities and were used in process control applications. Gandy (1992: 90–1) notes that in the UK Ferranti's engineers took the electronics from the Bloodhound missile and used it as the basis of the development of the Argus computer.

10 The capital intensity of production in these industries made adjustment of capacity to demand extremely difficult in any recession. For a discussion of the impact of these influences on efficiency in oil refining, see Lynk 1986.

11 BP and Standard Oil (NJ) reached an agreement to exchange technical data on isomerisation in March 1941 (Bamberg 1994: 245).

12 Shell expanded its Stanlow refinery in the early 1950s, and its catalytic cracker came into operation in 1952. BP's catalytic crackers at Grangemouth, Llandarcy and the Isle of Grain came on stream in 1953. Esso's big refinery at Fawley opened in 1951 and Mobil's new refinery at Coryton began operations in 1953.

13 BP continued to use Kellogg and another US design engineer, Badger, to design and install the process plant for its major refineries (Williams 1984: 323; Bamberg 2000: 230, 288). Esso used the Foster Wheeler Corporation of America and its British affiliate to design and build the Fawley refinery (Flanders 1964: 21).

14 Reference to the increase in the number of standard, "plug-in" components offered by instrumentation firms in the reply to the Board of Trade's automation survey from the Engineering Division of BP: NAPRO BT 64/4801, 25 Nov. 1956

15 We have already noted the evidence of Thomas J. Walsh that in 1954 seven US refineries were under construction, with an average capacity of 57,000 barrels per day. In 1956, Britain had three refineries (Isle of Grain, Stanlow and Fawley) operating at above this average and the biggest, Fawley, in 1954 was twice the 1954 US new refinery average (Burn 1961c: Table 12).

16 Flanders (1964: 80) mentions, *inter alia*, the institutional use of craftsmen's mates, craft demarcation and a reduction of the maintenance and construction workforce by one-third, while simultaneously reducing from 20 per cent to 1 per cent of the time worked by this group.

17 Lynk (1986) notes that British refining capacity adjusted slowly and that operating costs for a sophisticated plant could be 20 per cent higher when running at 70 rather than 90 per cent capacity and the cost penalty was even higher (25 per cent) for a small refinery.

18 Cracking is a "process whereby less volatile components of petroleum undergo complex chemical changes when heated to high temperatures and

put under high pressures, either in the presence or the absence of catalysts. Carbon-to-carbon bonds are broken under these conditions, producing several compounds with lower boiling points too high to fall into the gasoline fractions. Thus complex molecules of high molecular weight are 'cracked' or divided into simpler compounds". Williams 1984: 315 (citing the 1980 *Petroleum Dictionary*).

19 Reader (1975: 322) notes that Du Pont was always suspicious that technical information passed to ICI might leak out to other firms, particularly in the oil industry. Du Pont had a particular aversion to Standard Oil, which made overtures to ICI for collaboration in 1937.

20 Association of British Chemical Manufacturers, Answer to the Board of Trade's letter, NAPRO BT 64/4801, 11 Feb. 1957.

21 "Computer keys ICI Plant to Profits", *The Times*, 1 Jan. 1968: 19 ("Briefly from Industry").

22 Chambers complained of lower tariff protection than both the USA and the EEC, forcing ICI to invest heavily in capacity that far exceeded domestic demand "Review of ICI's Prospects", *The Times*, 1 April, 1966: 19.

23 Robert Jones, "ICI's Management Revolution", *The Times*, 8 Sept. 1970: 23 (on the Gloucester fibres plant).

24 In 1957, the Association of British Chemical Manufacturers had complained of skill shortages across design, maintenance and operative staff. They drew attention particularly to the difficulty of combining mechanical and electrical skills and union resistance to changes in apprenticeship training. NAPRO BT 64/4801, 11 Feb. 1957.

25 Ranieri (1998), for example, notes the impact of the American Rolling Mill Company (ARMCO), a medium-sized steel producer based at Middletown Ohio, on the decision to build Cornigliano, the largest and most modern steel works in Italy. Cornigliano used ARMCO's technology and expertise in modern management techniques.

26 The basic oxygen process was initially developed in the early 1950s for very small-scale operations but after a decade the problems associated with adoption for larger scale production had been overcome (Meyer and Herregat 1974: 158–9).

27 US producers on average had better quality ores and coke, cheaper and more readily available fuel oil, better quality furnace bricks, better layouts and better repair and maintenance regimes for furnaces (AACP 1952: 22–73).

28 Chick (1992: 82) notes that John Craig of Colvilles, who visited the USA during wartime, reached similar conclusions.

29 This position is most associated with Broadberry and Crafts (1996; 2001). Broadberry (1997a: 310) mentions the reference to competition in the AACP report on steel-founding but without reference to the actual competitive framework in the US industry.

30 Haller's (1966: II-193) careful survey of changing technology in steel-making for President Johnson's Commission on Technology and the US Economy concluded that the new systems of production would favour the smaller US producers and might break up what appeared to be a suspiciously stable price structure under the domination of the largest firms.

31 The Joint Iron Council's memorandum to the Board of Trade's automation inquiry identified automation in mould production as the most likely area

of rapid development of automation in its branch of the industry and identified several British innovations, two new German developments (on which it hoped to obtain translations of the technical literature) and films of two American innovations, one of which was considered suitable for computer-control. NAPRO BT/4801, memorandum dated 4 Jan. 1957.

32 The Board of Trade's automation papers contain memoranda from both the Joint Iron Council and the Steel Founders (26 Oct. 1956). The Steel Founders echoed the views of the Joint Iron Council: "new mechanisms and automatic control normally involve new and original design, as well as means of manufacture, and to this extent there will be a gap between idea and application": *ibid.*

33 The British Iron and Steel Research Association, for example, developed process control programs for users inside and outside the industry (House of Commons 1969–70a: 155).

34 The remainder of this and the whole of the next paragraph is based on Owen 1999: 135–47.

35 Pettigrew (1985: 72–3) citing the *Sunday Times* article on ICI of 16 July 1972, "The Case of the Missing Catalyst".

36 Indeed, Milward and Brennan (1996: 240–7) make a good case for the positive effects of protection on Britain's postwar chemicals industry.

37 Reader (1975: 473) notes of ICI's shareholders that "although legally the owners, would at all times have been more exactly described as 'investors', looking for income and capital growth, but not for a part in decision-making, and there have been no private individuals or families, as there have in some American corporations, with holdings great enough to give a decisive voice on policy".

Chapter 6   Office Automation: Computers, Clerical Work and Management Systems

1 The pioneers were: Anderson 1976; Silverstone 1976. More recently, see Bamberg 2000: 324–36, 394–423; Wardley 2000; Ackrill and Hannah 2001: ch. 7; Agar 2003: chs. 5–10.

2 This implies that clerical and secretarial staff possess firm-specific rather than generic skills. The creation of office employment bureaux and the emergence of the office "temp" (see below) might indicate that secretarial staff, in particular, possessed easily transferable generic skills.

3 This should be seen in the context of the discussions of the failure of two professional groups (engineers and "systems men") to control management structures (Armstrong 1984; Haigh 2001).

4 Routh 1980: Table 1.1. Heath and Macdonald (1987: Table 1), on the other hand, include sales staff with clerical workers, and not with the semi-skilled as did Routh. They estimate that "clerical and sales" comprised 16.3 percent of the employed in 1951 (3.7 million workers) and 19.5 percent in 1971 (4.9 million workers).

5 See, for example, the differences of approach between Cohn (1985), who identifies the cost structures of firms as the key, and Lowe (1987: 196–206), who places much more emphasis on the attitudes of individual managers.

See also Thompson 1989: 196–206; Crompton 1997: 6–24; Crompton and Jones 1984: 145–8.

6 Pay excludes non-monetary benefits (sick pay, pension arrangements, etc.), which tended to be much better for white than blue collar workers (Stewart *et al*. 1980: 170–2; Parkin 1971: 24–5; Lockwood 1989: 53–67, 223–4. On the relative decline of female semi-skilled manual earnings, see Routh 1980: Table 2.29.

7 In summer 1967, the Alfred Marks Bureau reported salaries of £1,000 p.a. for 25-year-old secretaries, 50 percent higher than for equivalent staff in Liverpool. By July 1971, it estimated that annual salaries for the same group at £1,000–1,250 and at £1,300 in 1972. *The Times*, "Secretaries Earn More 'Up West'", 4, July, 1967: 22; "Temps for a Change', 8 July, 1971: 20; "Secretaries' record rise", 3 August, 1972: 20.

8 *The Times*, "The 'Super Secretaries'", 22 January, 1969; "Secretaries can earn up to £4,000 a year", 22 July, 1971: 19.

9 Board of Trade 1957: Appendix III (for petrol refiner, excavator-maker (listed under "Contractor's Plant"), multiple shops, Lloyds, banks, insurance companies and local government. The quote is taken from NAPRO BT 64/4801, Reply from the British Insurance Association, 18 February, 1957.

10 See also *The Times*, "Survey examines job changing", 3 January, 1968: 18; *The Times*, "What girls want in jobs", 4 April, 1968: 21.

11 In 1967 it was estimated that there were between 1,500 and 2,000 private employment agencies in Britain: *The Times*, "Towards the jobs revolution", 12 July, 1967. McNally reports that in 1977 there were 5,500, of which the largest single group dealt with office staff: *Women for Hire*, p. 106. Agencies, which had in 1960 considered a city of half a million inhabitants the minimum viable number, were moving to towns of 100,000 by the end of the decade: *The Times*, "A sign of the temps", 20 April, 1970, p. 25.

12 *The Times*, "Keeping it in the family, 2", 16 May, 1969.

13 The NBPI (1968b: 2) found that temporary staff comprised no more than 2–4 percent of all office staff, but were concentrated among younger age groups and in London.

14 Telephones and typewriters spread in commerce and the civil service in the 1890s, but were taken up by the railways, banking and other clerical employments during wartime (Anderson 1976: 56).

15 The earliest tabulating machines, from which bank accounting machines developed, were introduced in 1910 and spread after successful work on the UK 1911 census (Campbell-Kelly 1989: 25–31).

16 Hays *et al*. (1967: 53) note that the ratio of typewriters to population was one to five in the USA, one to 30 in Continental Europe and one to 55 in the UK, with the UK especially poor before 1939.

17 The notes taken by T.R. Thompson and O.W. Standingford on their visit to the USA in May–June 1947 have now been published as Appendix A in Caminer *et al*. 1998: 337–59.

18 See PEP 1957: 39–58; John Hendry 1987; Caminer *et al*. 1998. The second and third sources have excellent details of the agency work undertaken by LEO Computers.

19 MRC, MSS/F/3/51/32/27, "Electronic Computers for Data Processing : Users and Orders", Industrial Management Research Association, 15 April, 1958.

20 The British Computer Society was keen to disseminate ideas for business applications in its very early years. This is evident in the papers read and the comments recorded in the pages of its journal, *The Computer Journal*. Its first volume (1958–9) also carried a series of articles by A.S. Douglas on commercial applications (pp. 69–70, 132–41, 168–71), by T.R. Thompson of LEO (1958–9) and by Gregory and Gearing (1958–9) on US developments. On visits to the USA, see Chapter 7 below.

21 The sources for this paragraph are Board of Trade 1957: Appendix III; NAPRO BT 64/4801, Replies from: British Petroleum, no date; Mobil Oil Company, 15 February, 1957; Esso Petroleum Company, 15 November, 1956; Shell Refining and Marketing Company, 31 October, 1956; MRC MSS/F/F/3/51/32/27, "Electronic computers"; Coopey 1999: 64–5; Hendry 1987: 91–4; Tweedale 1992: 123–7; Gearing [Metal Box] 1958–9; Hickman [Unilever] 1959–60; Warmington [Albert E. Reed Group] 1960–1; Platt [Pilkington Brothers] 1960–1.

22 Agar (2003: Table 8.1) lists almost 30 computer projects identified in Whitehall in February 1958 for completion by early 1964; NAPRO BT 64/4801, Reply from Ministry of Housing and Local Government, 19 February, 1957. The ministry reported that by late 1956 three local authorities had installed computers, nine had placed orders, 17 had computers under consideration and another 17 were at the preliminary stages of considering computers.

23 For example, Diebold 1952: 99–100. For more detail on airline reservation systems, see McKenney *et al.*, 1995: 97–113; Eklund 1994.

24 The SPREAD project that resulted in System/360 has passed into computing folklore: see Pugh *et al.* 1991: chs. 3–5.

25 The UK Atomic Energy Authority undertook such work on ten of its 21 "medium, large or very large machines"; the British Steel Corporation used 11 of its 46 larger machines on scientific and research calculations; and Esso Petroleum used one of its two head office computers for technical work (House of Commons 1969–70a: 39, 144–6; 1969–70b: 228). Bamberg (2000: 410–23) describes the expansion of BP's linear programming activities, its adverse impact on routine data processing and the frustrations of trying to commission the Ferranti Atlas to do the work.

26 Caminer *et al.* 1998: 252–4 (quote p. 254); *The Times*, "£2$\frac{1}{2}$ m. LEO order by G.P.O.", 17 December, 1964: 15.

27 The National Computing Centre reported that only 55 percent of corporate computer owners were satisfied with the return they were gaining, yet 70 percent were planning to extend their commitment (House of Commons 1969–70b: 11).

28 It took five years to right software problems on the ICL System 4/50 (House of Commons 1969–70a: 262).

29 Campbell-Kelly (1989: 238) notes that ICT (a forerunner of ICL) attempted to recruit 100 additional programmers in early 1965, but needed a full year to meet the establishment.

30 The Select Committee was told by the National Computing Centre that less than half the number of trainees needed was emerging each year and that shortfall was almost certain to increase (House of Commons 1969–70b: 14–15).

31 Thus, ICI sought to protect the sunk costs of programming and software development (amounting to an estimated 2,000 man-years of programming) when purchasing new computers in 1964. They chose from the IBM System/360 range to allow them to continue running software developed on the IBM 1401s, which the new machines replaced (House of Commons 1969–70a: 166).

32 This paragraph is based on the evidence of bureaux (House of Commons 1969–70a: 256–88).

33 For the USA see the results of the survey by management consultants, A.T. Kearney, publicised by their president (Schroeder 1971). For the UK see House of Commons 1969–70a: 257.

34 The judgement of management consultants cannot be trusted in this area; as will be seen below, McKinsey had a vested interest in promoting management information systems and Booz-Allen had helped develop the PERT system. The reports' findings are reported in House of Commons 1969–70a: 256, 259.

35 This sort of response came from the Civil Service Department (responsible for staffing and efficiency in the civil service). The managing director of telecommunications at the GPO claimed, "The total computer business has played a very significant part in the productivity of the business. From a manpower point of view we are achieving something of the order of 8.5 per cent improvement in productivity per man. We can see very substantial advantages". The National Coal Board claimed to have saved 3,000 jobs through the use of computers, but to have created half that number in its computer department: House of Commons 1969–70a: 332, 429, 437.

36 For a discussion of the differences between the mass marketers like IBM and those, like the LEO management, who believed that hardware and software needed to be adapted to unique business models, see Baskerville 2003.

37 The SPA is described by Haigh 2001: 18–25. The AMA established a Continuing Seminar on Management Information Systems in 1959, which is described by Gallagher 1961: 7–8, 10.

38 The intellectual manifesto was written by a McKinsey consultant, Richard F. Neuschel (1950).

39 *The Statist*, 19 July, 1964, cited by Bamberg 2000: 410. On the use of operations research in industry, see Hays 1984.

40 For the philosophy, see the minutes of evidence of Computer Technology Ltd., a maker of small, modular computers (House of Commons 1969–70a: 175–7. Agar (2003: 345–7) notes that similar possibilities were under consideration in Whitehall at the same time.

41 Graham Turner (1971b: 110, 152–3, 351, 394, 460–2) lists Royal Dutch Shell, ICI, AEI, Vickers, Dunlop, Rolls Royce as well as the BBC and the Bank of England.

42 On the advice given by US management consultancies in general, see Kipping 1999: 209–10.

43 The report in *The Times* announcing Shell's commitment to a computer-based integrated management information system listed General Motors, Westinghouse, ICI and Rolls Royce as the leaders in linking several very large computers to create very large management information systems: "Management information system for Shell?", 28 June, 1966: 22.

44 House of Commons 1969–70b: 237–40; Turner 1971b: 119; Caminer *et al.* 1998: 103–4, 123–4, 326–7; *The Times*, "Shell-BP switches to Univac system", 11 February, 1969: 24.

45 Maurice Hodgson, former head of the planning department, listed its functions as "providing better information on key questions of strategy: what fields of business ICI ought to be in, where should it concentrate its capital investment, what performance should it expect?" (Turner 1971b: 158). Hodgson became chairman from 1978 to 1982.

46 *Dictionary of National Biography, 1981–85*: 32–3; for the political context of decision-taking on the ICI board see Pettigrew 1985: 461–2. For the limitations of software in ICI in the second half of the 1960s, see House of Commons 1969–70a: 162–3.

47 Pettigrew notes that the intellectual culture of ICI headquarters at Millbank was: "don't rock the boat, don't dig too deep, too fast. This boat has stood the test of time": *Awakening Giant*, p. 459.

48 See also Guest 1961 for a prescient view from the early 1960s.

49 But see Haynes and Thompson 2000 for a view of computers in financial services during the late twentieth century.

50 Bamberg (2000: 410–12) notes the problems faced by BP in commissioning a new Atlas computer from ICT. The machine was ordered (from Ferranti) in 1961, with a commissioning date of January 1964. Full operational use did not begin until June 1966, but performance was unsatisfactory for some time thereafter. In this lengthy interim, the company's data processing department was overwhelmed by the huge amounts of data that would have been used for linear programming on the computer.

51 Even ICI, a firm with a strong scientific/engineering culture, found it necessary to create a directors' computer course for senior managers: House of Commons 1969–70a: 161. In his account of the commercial failure of LEO computers, Hendry (1987: 95) notes that the company sold "a complete computerised office system" that "entailed a complete re-design of [the customer's] office systems", which many potential clients resisted.

52 Remington introduced electric typewriters in 1925 and IBM a much improved machine in 1935. Although production of electric typewriters by British firms was limited, they were available from US firms, both as imports and from offshoots in the UK or elsewhere in Europe (Prais 1981: 229; Hays *et al.* 1967: Table 6).

53 Campbell-Kelly (1992: 133) notes that in Prudential Assurance "many tabulating machines remained in use well into the 1970s, creating what was effectively a museum of punched-card machine technology alongside state-of-the-art IBM System/370 computers of the period".

54 Bamberg's (2000: ch. 16) account of the pioneering and highly successful development within BP of linear programming to inform an increasing range of business decisions, but its demise in the later 1960s is fascinating.

Chapter 7   Bank Automation

1 On wartime allocations, see HSBCGA, London, Acc 262/3, Letters headed "Burroughs Machines", 12 Nov. 1942 and "Burroughs Adding Machines", 1,

2 and 4 June, 1943; for the state of the office machine market in the 1940s, see Campbell-Kelly 1989: 106–10, 127–9.

2 BBA Archive, M.32031/9, CEO meeting, 21 Jan. 1954, min. 1.

3 HSBCGA, London, Acc 658/01, "Salary Registers", various years.

4 In 1967, the NBPI (1968a: App. A) found London weightings in the private sector at c. £150 p.a., rather less by industrial employers, and less still from nationalised industries and the civil service. By the mid-1960s, some banks paid allowances to staff in other major cities; NBPI 1965: 5, 12.

5 HSBCGA, London, Acc 262/5, hand-written note, "Machines Installed 1928–1952 Inclusive", n.d.; "Mechanisation at Midland Bank: thirteen month programme complete", *The Times*, 2 November, 1959.

6 The Midland Bank's staff magazine, *The Midbank Chronicle* (1955), reported the reaction of relief (provincial) staff helping head machine department.

7 A typical installation comprised the key punch, a verifier, an automatic sorter, the tabulator, the interpreter, an interpolator (the principal purpose of which was to inter-sort one related pack of cards into another and to throw out any cards containing designated information), a reproducer (which would copy a set of cards very quickly) and, where necessary, a printer.

8 For Powers-Samas, the main supplier of punched-card equipment to British banks, see Campbell-Kelly 1989: 178; Lloyds was uncertain how and when to replace its ageing Power-Samas machines: Lloyds TSB Archive, 1087: HO/DP/Pla.9

9 NAPRO BT 64/4801, British Bankers' Association, "Automation enquiry", 11 January, 1957.

10 The Midland (1956 and 1961) and Lloyds sent representatives to the USA to check on progress in technology and organisation. On BoA, see McKenney *et al.* 1995: 41–73.

11 The final decisions were announced in 1960, and ended a five-year process for the USA and four for the UK. The main cause of delay was the need to ensure that machines ran reliably (Booth 2002: 315).

12 *The Banker* 1967a; Ackrill and Hannah 2001: 330–1; Lloyds TSB Archive, 9669: HO/DP/Pla/1, "Proposal for branch current account work using IBM 305 RAMAC", n.d.; "IBM proposal for installation of an IBM data processing machines: submission to Lloyds Bank Ltd", no date but March 1960; Booth 2004: 284–6.

13 Ackrill and Hannah (2001: 330) recount Barclays' experiments connecting four branches by the telephone network. For other banks, see *The Banker* 1967a.

14 On NUBE's concerns about automation, see "Saving Labour in Offices", *The Times*, 13 June, 1956: 15.

15 Vine 1967: 504. This is however contradicted by the turnover figures for London in Table 7.2.

16 The automation of cheque clearing had been the primary goal of the CLCB Electronics Committee, established in October 1955. The committee, now known as the Systems and Development Committee, was still at work in 1969. Unfortunately, the committee's papers has not survived within the British Bankers' Association archive at the Guildhall Library. Some papers from 1966 to 1969 have been preserved in HSBCGA, London, Acc 200/176 and Acc 200/677.

17 Account numbering, cheque numbering and sort codes were regularised for the whole system by the deliberations of the CLCB Electronics Committee.
18 *The Banker* 1967a: 497, 499. Details of the CLCB decisions on clearing are taken from a large report from the Clearing Automation Sub-committee of July 1965, held in the HSBCGA, London, Acc 200/677.
19 CLCB, Minutes of the Systems and Development Committee, 26 August, 1966. Copy in HSBCGA, London, Acc 200/176.
20 G.B. Hague to L.M. Mears, n.d. in HSBCGA, London, Acc 200/677.
21 The range of routine tasks to be eliminated is listed in *Midbank Chronicle* 1968; anticipated staff savings had been listed in *Midbank Chronicle* 1967.
22 HSBCGA, London, Acc 262/11, "Report by Branch Work Unit Working Party", February 1967.
23 The CLCB knew that Stanford Research Institute had told the Federal Reserve of similar savings from automated clearing. The banks also knew the benefits of same-day automated clearing while retaining the four-day delay to credit to a customer's account: "Exchange of magnetic tape: cost factors": Report to the Systems and Development Committee by the New Services Working Party, 6 June, 1967 in HSBCGA, London, Acc 200/176.
24 The decision to proceed with the computer bureau for automatic clearing was taken in stages during 1966–7. The progress can be seen in the copies of the Systems and Development Committee papers held in HSBCGA, London, Acc 200/176.
25 Minutes of the Systems and Development Committee, 6 June, 1967, 25 July, 1967, both in HSBCGA, London, Acc 200/176.
26 On chequeless banking, see memo by W. Hopps, 17 July, 1967. The New Services Working Party of the Systems and Development Committee raised with the GPO microwave communications systems, the implications of "touch-tone" telephones for banking and research into voice pattern identification: minutes of the systems and development committee, 21 February, 1967. On early British recognition of the US ASCII standards (March 1967): F.W. Gibson to W. Hopps, 17 July, 1967. All in HSBCGA, London, Acc 200/176.
27 HSBCGA, London, Acc 112/1, P70/25, "System Objectives", 19 Jan. 1967.
28 Ackrill and Hannah 2001: 333–5; *The Banker* 1967a; 1967b; *Financial Times*, "Midland's Computer Switch", 24 February, 1968: 1.
29 HSBCGA, London, Acc 112/1, P70/73A, "Communication Between English Electric Processors and Burroughs Terminals", 5 July, 1967. The decision to lease two Burroughs B5500s and order two B6500s was taken in March 1968 (HSBCGA, London, Acc 200/223, Management Committee Meeting, 7 March, 1968, minute 33).
30 A giro bank is essentially a savings bank with free credit transfer facilities. The threat of a Post Office Giro is discussed by Sharp 1961.
31 BBA M32031/12, CLCB meeting of 1 June, 1961, minute 53.
32 NBPI 1967: 53, 62; Winton 1982: 195–200; Holmes and Green 1986: 242–4; Ackrill and Hannah 2001: 162–3, 171–84; *The Banker* 1967c; 1967d.
33 The GPO ordered English Electric LEO System 4 machines for the giro, a range designed for real-time, multi-access computing: see David Caminer *et al.* 1998: 130–1, 255–6; Campbell-Kelly 1989: 269–70.

34 BBA archive, M32031/17, Chief Executive Officers' meetings 18 Aug. 1966, minute 97; 17 November, 1966, minute 128; 15 Dec. 1966, minute 141. The decision to rename the automatic credit transfer system as the "bank giro" was taken by the CLCB meeting of 19 Jan. 1967, BBA archive M32031/18.

35 HSBCGA, London, Acc 200/223, Management Committee Meeting, 21 Sept. 1967, min. 158, "Project 70: Progress Report".

36 McKenney *et al.* (1995: 79) note that during the transition to the IBM 360s, "there were to be as many outside [primarily IBM] as inside staff reprogramming and building new systems during the transition period".

37 Burroughs' orders, captured from IBM, for airline seat reservation systems from Trans World Airlines and United Airlines also ended in failure and recapture by IBM (McKenney *et al.* 1995: 117–20).

38 Campbell-Kelly (1989: 241–3) describes the real-time, multi-programming software for the 4/50 as "considerably more elegant and advanced" than the IBM System/360 and the 4/70 as a "considerable technical triumph" that performed well in the prestige projects, incidentally including the National Giro Bank, for which it was bought in the later 1960s.

39 N. Nutall, "At Last the True Story of the Hole in the Wall Gang", *The Times*, 27 June, 1992.

40 HSBCGA, London, Acc 200/677, Paper for the Management Committee, "Automated cash dispenser", 17 May, 1967. This paper is the main source for the whole paragraph.

41 Midland's cash dispenser cost about 50 percent more than the Chubb machine, but with substantially (at least 90 percent) lower running costs: HSBCGA, London, Acc 200/677, Note for the Management Committee, "Automated cash dispenser", 26 March, 1968. On the importance of Saturday closing, see HSBCGA, London, Acc 200/677, Note for the Management Committee, "Automated cash dispenser", 26 April, 1967.

42 *Financial Times*, 4 October, 1967; and "Wider use of cash dispensers", 4 November, 1968.

43 Unless otherwise indicated, this paragraph leans heavily upon Fisher and McKenney 1993; McKenney *et al.* 1995: ch. 3.

44 On cheque use in the USA, see Revell 1983: Table 2.1, p. 15.

45 On BoA's telephone service in California, see McKenney *et al.* 1995: 71. The purchase of EDP service centres is discussed by O'Brien 1968: 12. Note also the British computer services bureaux established by Barclays and the Midland discussed above.

46 This paragraph is based on McKenney, *et al.* 1995: 76–84. The quote is taken from p. 82.

47 As reported to a seminar at the Graduate School of Business, Columbia University in early 1969 (Booth 2004: 293).

48 "Next in Banking: Pay Bills by Phone", *Business Week*, 13 Nov. 1965: 82–6.

49 Before the 1960s, bank assets were dominated by their real estate property portfolios that were very conservatively valued. Many banks did not capitalise their office machinery until expenditure on computer installations rose in the 1960s (Capie and Billings 2001: 237–8).

50 Haynes and Thompson (2000: 93–116) found significant productivity gains in financial services from intensive use of cash dispensers.

51 BBA archive, M.32031/19, CLCB special meeting, 28 November, 1968, minute 83.
52 On the centralisation of marketing decision by the banks, see Leyshon and Thrift 1999: 441–2.

Chapter 8   Japanisation

1 However, American academics debated whether the Japanese economy was in fact "export-led", since domestic markets grew at roughly the same pace as exports in the high-growth-era, 1952–73. See the summary of these debates given by Tsuru (1993: 84–6).
2 Trade frictions with the USA induced Japanese firms to establish production bases abroad. Colour televisions were the catalyst for the most severe restrictions, and led in 1977 to an agreement between the governments of Japan and the USA to maintain "orderly market conditions" (i.e. voluntary export restraints by the Japanese). However, this only encouraged Japanese firms to accelerate their foreign direct investment and channel it more towards the advanced capitalist nations rather than in the developing nations of East Asia, where FDI had been concentrated in the 1960s (Tsuru 1993: 184–201).
3 As reported in the *Financial Times*, 20 May, 1989, cited by Oliver and Wilkinson 1992: 4.
4 The association of "flexible specialisation" with Japan was queried in Chapter 1. These points are developed below in the discussion of flexible manufacturing systems (FMS).
5 Katz's (1998: Fig. 1.1) attempt to isolate trends in the postwar growth patterns of the Japanese economy suggest an average growth rate of 9.6 percent per annum between 1956 and 1973, 4.1 percent per annum from 1973 to 1991, and 1 percent per annum from 1992 to 1999. The slow, halting trajectory continued into the first decade of the twenty-first century and only in 2005–6 were there any signs of faster growth.
6 Katz (1998: 3–28) describes the Japanese industrial system after 1973 as "mainframe economics for a PC world". This is a graphic description of the way in which policies and systems that had been appropriate for the protection of infant postwar industries increasingly added to costs, inhibited structural adjustments and undermined Japanese competitiveness and industrial flexibility.
7 In the late 1970s, US analysts identified low Japanese wages as a cause of their competitive problems in the automobile industry but it soon became clear that differences in pay accounted for a relatively small part of cost disadvantages suffered by American firms (Cole and Yakushiji 1984: 119–28).
8 Apocalyptic tones were less evident in the UK, where management and worker self-confidence was already at low levels. The British press carried similar stories of the invincibility of Japanese methods and the *Financial Times* was particularly thorough in its reporting of the issue. British reactions were tempered by the conviction that Japanese inward investment could revitalise British management, and from 1977 the Invest in Britain Bureau of the Department of Trade and Industry was very successful in

attracting Japanese firms to the UK. Strange's (1993: table 5.4) list of Japanese manufacturing affiliates shows a huge expansion after 1984, especially from the automobile and office equipment producers.

9 The earliest reports in the *Harvard Business Review* were certainly of this type. Hayes (1981: 51) pointed out that "The Japanese have achieved their current level of manufacturing excellence mostly by doing simple things but doing them very well and slowly improving all the time". Wheelwright (1981) emphasised that the extraordinary quality control record of major Japanese electronics companies could be transferred to the USA and Weiss (1984: 121), also concentrating on electronics, ascribed the (much) higher levels of labour productivity in Japan to "mundane decisions that managers make". Indeed, he suggested that Hewlett Packard's managerial decision-making was every bit as good as the best of the Japanese (Weiss 1984: 119).

10 Locke (1996: 166), who never knowingly under-sells the difficulties of US management in the 1980s, identified a "near panic that broke out in American management [around 1980] about its ability to survive, much less compete. Since the Americans really did not know what to do, this panic resulted in a hasty search for the secrets of Japanese success."

11 Nissan introduced American-designed Unimates (N/C mechanical arms) on an experimental basis in the 1960s to automate spot and arc welding but found the machines difficult to program accurately and unreliable in practice (Cusumano 1986: 227–9). These problems were however gradually overcome and large-scale deployment began in 1976; by the end of 1983 Nissan had 1,400 such machines, the vast majority in welding operations. Many were developed in-house and had primitive control mechanisms using re-programmable punched tape and microcomputers. Toyota waited until control systems had improved and purchased or developed robots of various sizes that were both inexpensive and more easily programmed to do different jobs (Cusumano 1986: 235).

12 Siebert and Addison (1991: 79) noted that in Japan, the UK and the USA, "highly stable employment is the experience of the average male". They also suggest (1991: 77) that approximately half of the British workforce and 40 percent of the US workforce were in internal labour markets, suggesting a very significant commitment to segmented labour markets in both countries.

13 Shani and colleagues (1992: 91) list CIM (computer-integrated manufacture), CAE (computer-aided engineering), CAD (computer-aided design), CAPP (computer-aided process planning) and MRP II (manufacturing requirements planning).

14 Oliver and Wilkinson (1992: 273–6) note a variety of techniques adopted by Japanese transplant firms in the UK, from on-site manufacture, the establishment of joint ventures with potential suppliers and a more geographically dispersed supply chain than is common in Japan.

15 The HRM techniques to which British firms turned in the 1980s had been developed at least a decade earlier in the USA to counter growing tensions within the American industrial system (Ackers *et al.* 1996b: 5).

16 For a discussion of the role of trade unions under the individualising imperative of (much of) HRM, see Bacon and Storey 1996.

17 Mroczkowski listed Ford, GM, Pan Am, Uniroyal, International Harvester, the New York Daily News and the major steel companies as the major promoters of profit-sharing from the later 1970s.

18 For the background to these problems, see Chapter 4 above.

19 Citing an unpublished paper by Keidel, Mroczkowski (1984: 50–1) classified QWL techniques into five clusters: work redesign (including job enlargement and enrichment, job rotation and modular work groups); pay restructuring (giving blue collar workers salary status, sharing productivity benefits among the workgroup), time rescheduling (flexible working hours, staggered work hours, job sharing), performance development (problem solving, physical redesign) and administrative review (information sharing, procedural change, training). The GE pilot programme embraced most of these elements.

20 In the afterword in the 1990 edition of his classic study of British and Japanese industrial relations, Dore (1973 and 1990: 428) notes the critical reception from eminent British industrial relations specialists to the suggestion in the first edition of his book that Japanese systems of factory organisation had positive lessons for the British system. Enlightened British businessmen were however ahead of the academics at this point. Chapter 5 noted the visit by the Deputy Chairman of British Steel, Monty Finniston, to Japan to see for himself the operation of the giant plants of companies such as Nippon Steel and Kawasaki Steel.

21 It has been argued that many Japanese transplant factories do little more than assemble parts supplied only from Japan. For a discussion of the UK position, see Trevor and Christie 1988.

22 He cites the example of the Xerox Corporation as a fast learner. Its links to Japan came from its British subsidiary, Rank-Xerox, which formed a joint venture with Fuji Film in Japan, Fuji-Xerox. When this company hit competitive difficulties in the early 1970s, it adopted total quality control, which was guided by Japanese executives who had introduced similar systems into Fuji Film in the 1950s. When the Xerox Corporation itself experienced competitive difficulties, experienced staff from Fuji-Xerox piloted the same quality control methods through the American parent.

23 Note Hasegawa's (2004) discussion of the Americanisation of Japanese electronics firms in the 1950s and 1960s, but the subsequent "Japanisation" of Japanese firms and their emergence as strong international competitors in the 1980s. In the Americanisation phase, he notes the importance of formal technology partnerships between, for example, Honeywell and NEC and the Oki Electric Industry and Sperry Rand in general purpose computers, and NEC with Western Electric, GE and Bell Labs in semiconductors.

24 Toshiba's single union agreement with the EETPU at its Ernsettle factory near Plymouth was especially controversial. The factory had been established to manufacture colour televisions by Rank-Toshiba, a joint venture between the British Rank Organisation and the Japanese firm. Toshiba invested £3 million in the enterprise and provided design expertise and technology. Rank provided the management and the engineers. Seven unions were represented at the factory. In late 1980, this joint venture

folded within two years, but for reasons unrelated to the labour force or unions. Toshiba quickly mounted a "rescue" of the factory, with a new production system, much lower production targets and a narrower focus. The press comment at the time focused however on the single-union deal with the EETPU: Strange 1993: 310–11.

25 Garrahan and Stewart (1992) suggest that the apathy towards the union by Nissan workers is scarcely surprising as the AEEU was a marginal organisation within the Sunderland factory, with the Company Council rather than the union the central institution of employee involvement.

26 In particular, Japanese companies took time to build their supply networks and full JIT production. They gradually built a network of British and joint venture suppliers as local content increased.

27 For a discussion of the imagery of the machine in American interwar popular culture, see Bix 2000: 125–42.

28 Mature markets characteristically have slower growth and much more intense cyclical variation than markets that are in the process of "motorisation". The American market exhibited all the characteristics of maturity after 1973, while the Japanese market was still growing until the early 1990s. The European market was in an intermediate position (Williams *et al.* 1994: 67–8).

29 Ueda (2004: 94) divides the supply chain into four parts: suppliers from subsidiary and associate companies – those in which the assembler was the primary shareholder; suppliers within the assembler's keiretsu grouping – those with a capital affiliation to the main group; shitauke group companies – those with no initial capital ties but with a strong business link; other independent suppliers – which may be group members of the suppliers of the other car makers. The degree of leverage depended upon the closeness of the relationship.

30 They favour "motor sector hours to build" to measure national productivity differences and company value added per employee to measure company efficiency. Company financial performance is measured by cashflow per vehicle produced and the management of the flow of production by two measures (work-in-progress/value-added and work-in-progress-plus-raw-materials/value added). These do not need adjustment for the different characteristics of inputs and outputs.

31 Japan overtook the USA in the period 1975–7. Between 1983 and 1989, the American industry took between 12 and 32 per cent more hours than the Japanese. The gap was narrowest during years of brisk demand in the USA and widest during downturns in the domestic market. Thus, the size of the automobile "productivity gap" is much closer to the "major branch average" taken from van Ark that to the "lean production" figure given by the MIT project.

32 Chrysler's reaction was hamstrung by the depth of its financial problems and GM's management structures were overwhelmed. GM established a joint venture with Toyota, the New United Motor Manufacturing Inc., in a former GM plant at Fremont, California but both it and Chrysler pushed through a relatively large number of plant closures as the US market went into recession and costs mounted (Womack *et al.* 1990: 82–4, 244–5).

33 On efforts to build better relationships at the workplace to encourage workers to play a part in resolving production problems and reduce inefficiencies in their own work areas, see Meyer and Cooke 1993: 534–5.

34 This paragraph follows Starkey and McKinlay 1989; Tolliday 1991: 100–7; Oliver and Wilkinson 1992: 105–17.

35 By the early 1990s, Ford UK scored well on its ability to manage work flow effectively (Williams *et al.* 1994: 52).

36 The comments on EI by the US industrial relations expert, Richard B. Freeman (1995: 526–7) are especially revealing: "EI takes many forms and names – teams, quality circles, total quality management and so on – and covers a wide range of issues. There are permanent health and safety committees; there are short-run teams to deal with specific productivity problems; there are peer review committees of disciplinary actions ... Although there is evidence that joint consultative committees (a weak form of employee involvement) have some positive economic effects, *many managements are suspicious that EI may simply be the 'flavour of the month' in the continuing fad of how to succeed in business – replacing last month's panacea of being lean and mean"* (emphasis added).

37 There is no space to consider the intricate politics of the triangular relationship between government, its agent the NEB and the company. The best source is undoubtedly Wilks 1984: 96–117, 205–32.

38 Oliver and Wilkinson (1992: 203) cite the manager of a small presswork company describing JIT [Just in Time] as "Japanese Induced Terror".

39 In 1987, the company negotiated the introduction of team working and total quality management.

40 Line speeds were faster, absences from the assembly lines were much more closely monitored, the company instituted a culture of unpaid work before shifts and during breaks to meet targets and compulsory overtime at short notice was not uncommon (Oliver and Wilkinson 1992: 217–22, 225–9, 234–40).

41 Lucas Industries supplied components to the automobile industry. In 1981, it recorded its first ever loss in more than 100 years of trading and it was clear that it faced structural as well as cyclical problems, not least from the rapid contraction of the British-owned volume car industry. It introduced many new techniques, most notably shifting out of volume production of standardised products into more flexible processes. It adopted the *kanban* system and other elements of JIT production, cellular rather than assembly-line organisation, teamwork, quality control, flexible working and the intensification that is inherent in it and reform of administrative structures (Turnbull 1986; Oliver and Wilkinson 1992: 89–98). Profit levels were restored, but Lucas was still consistently outperformed by its bigger rivals (Foreman-Peck *et al.* 1995: 242). Lean production did not allow firms to escape from market constraints.

Conclusion

1 Of course, it is also obvious that product and process innovations have a powerful ability to widen markets (for a discussion of the classic case of cotton in the British industrial revolution, see Rose 2000: 22–37).

2 For a brief but concise review of the issues, see Broadberry 1997a: 24–5.

3 In the case of the size of the productivity gap between American and Japanese automobile production, the lower estimate is more convincing. The estimates of Williams and colleagues much closer to the results of van Ark (1993), which are known to be reliable, and the comparison at the core of the calculations of Womack and colleagues quite clearly compares best Japanese practice (Takaoka) with worst US (Framingham), and this is no basis for rigorous comparative analysis.

4 Note the links between Marconi and RCA to share patents and process information relating to the production of radio valves (Chapter 2) and that between du Pont and ICI across a very wide range of chemical products (Reader 1975: 48–54; Chapter 5 above).

5 Hays *et al.* (1967: 59) note that the American firms were at the forefront of technical development in the office machinery industry and helped to familiarise the British market with new or improved equipment. They also note (p. 53) that the comparative abundance of clerical workers to 1939 retarded interest in mechanisation in clerical work in the UK, as did the relatively small size of the modal office (see Chapter 6).

6 The information on the smaller firms in food processing is more sporadic and limited than on the larger firms in chemicals and steel, but automatic processes were longer established in the drinks than the food processing side of the industry. The soft drinks makers and the dairies had introduced continuous processing and bottling in the 1930s, but in the mid-1950s the margarine makers, for example, were shifting from a batch system that required 6–8 hours, to a continuous one of only several minutes duration, complete with packing and palletisation of the finished product. NAPRO BT 64/4801, replies to the Board of Trade Questionnaire from the Food Processing Industry, covered by Reason to Healy, covering 7 Dec. 1956.

7 *Ibid*, replies from National Association of Master Bakers, Confectioners and Caterers, Scottish Association of Master Bakers and the Federation of Wholesale and Multiple Bakers. It should be noted however that the Scottish Association also reported on the "high degree of automation already achieved in the breadmaking industry".

8 For British chemicals producers and oil refiners, see Chapter 5. In the 1958–9, Ford's attempts to multi-skill its maintenance workers (and reclassify them as "automation equipment maker and maintenance worker") led to demarcation and "de-skilling" disputes and higher pay for all skilled grades in the plant affected. See the article by Ken Bannon and Nelson Stamp in the collection of essays originally published in the *Monthly Labor Review*: US Department of Labor 1960.

References

Archival sources

Charles Babbage Institute, University of Minnesota
CBI 90, Burroughs Collection

Guildhall Library, City of London
British Bankers' Association Collection

Hagley Museum and Library, Wilmington DE
Acc 1412, National Association of Manufacturers Collection

HSBC Group Archives, London
Midland Bank Papers

Modern Records Centre, University of Warwick
MSS 36, British Iron and Steel Trades Confederation
MSS 200, Confederation of British Industries and Predecessors Collection
MSS 202, Dick Etheridge Papers
MSS 226, Motor Industry Heritage Collection
MSS 292 and 292a, TUC Papers

National Archives, Public Records Office, Kew
Board of Trade
BT 64, Industries and Manufactures
BT 190, National Production Advisory Council on Industry
Cabinet
CAB 124, Lord President of the Council, Minister of Science
CAB 128, Cabinet minutes
CAB 129, Cabinet memoranda
Department of Scientific and Industrial Research
DSIR 17, Registered files
Ministry of Labour
LAB 10, Industrial Relations Department
Prime Ministers' Office
PREM 11, Correspondence and papers, 1951–64
Treasury
T 171, Budget papers
T 230, Economic Section
T 236, Overseas Finance
T 267, Treasury Historical Memoranda

Royal Bank of Scotland Group Archives
Williams Deacons Bank

Science Museum, London
International Computers Limited Collection

Newspapers and the weekly press

Autocar
Business Week
Computer Weekly
Fortune
Harpers' Magazine
Motor Business
The Economist

Coventry Evening Telegraph
Daily Herald
Daily Telegraph
Financial Times
Manchester Guardian
New York Times
The Times

Official publications

Board of Trade (1956). *Report on the Census of Production, 1954*, London, HMSO.
Board of Trade (1957). Automation Enquiry, NA PRO CAB 134/1193, March.
Board of Trade (1967). "Machine Tools", *Board of Trade Journal* (May 19): 1307–9.
CPRS [Central Policy Review Staff] (1975). *The Future of the British Car Industry*, London, HMSO.
DEP [Department of Employment and Productivity] (1969). *In Place of Strife: A Policy for Industrial Relations*, London, HMSO, Cmnd 3888.
Donovan, Lord (1968). Royal Commission on Trade Unions and Employers' Associations, *Report*, London, HMSO, Cmnd 3623.
DSIR [Department of Scientific and Industrial Research] (1956). *Automation: A Report on Technical Trends and their Impact on Management and Labour*, London, HMSO.
DSIR (1957). [Liverpool University] *Men, Steel and Technical Change*, Problems of Progress in Industry, 1, London, HMSO.
DTI [Department of Trade and Industry] (1971). *Report on the Census of Production, 1968*, Industry Reports, London, HMSO.
House of Commons (1969–70a). Select Committee on Science and Technology, Session 1969–70, *The UK Computer Industry*, Volume I, Minutes of Evidence. BPP 1969–70, vol. IX.
House of Commons (1969–70b). Select Committee on Science and Technology, Session 1969–70, *The UK Computer Industry*, Volume II, Appendices. BPP 1969–70, vol. IX.
Ministry of Labour (1965). *Memorandum of Evidence to the Royal Commission on Trade Unions and Employers' Associations*, London, HMSO.
NBPI [National Board for Prices and Incomes] (1965). *Report No. 6: Salaries of Midland Bank Staff*, London, HMSO, Cmnd 2839.
NBPI (1967). *Report No. 34: Bank Charges*, London, HMSO, Cmnd 3292.

NBPI (1968a). *Report No. 44: London Weighting in the Non-industrial Civil Service*, London, HMSO, Cmnd 3436.

NBPI (1968b). *Report No. 89: Office Staff Employment Agencies, Charges and Salaries*, London, HMSO, Cmnd 3828.

NBPI (1969a). *Report No. 122: Fourth General Report, July 1968 to July 1969*, London, HMSO, Cmnd 4130.

NBPI (1969b). *Report No. 106: Pay in the London Clearing Banks*, London, HMSO, Cmnd 3943.

OECD [Organisation for Economic Co-operation and Development] (1970). *Gaps in Technology: Analytical Report*, Paris, OECD.

ONS [Office for National Statistics] (2002). *Economic Trends: Annual Supplement, 2002*, London, HMSO.

Radcliffe, Lord (1959). Committee on the Working of the Monetary System, *Report*, London, HMSO, Cmnd 827.

US Congress (1955). *Automation and Technological Change*, Hearings before the Sub-committee on Economic Stabilisation of the Joint Committee on the Economic Report: 84th Congress, First Session, Washington DC, USGPO.

US Congress (1956). *Instrumentation and Automation*, Hearings before the Subcommittee on Economic Stabilisation of the Joint Economic Committee, 84th Congress, 2nd Session, 12–14 December, 1956, Washington DC, USGPO.

US Congress (1957). *Automation and Recent Trends*, Hearings before the Sub-committee on Economic Stabilisation of the Joint Economic Committee, 85th Congress, 1st Session 14 and 15 November, 1957, Washington DC, USGPO.

US Congress (1960). *Office Automation and Employee Job Security*, Hearings before the Subcommittee on Census and Government Statistics of the Committee on Post Office and Civil Service, House of Representatives, 86th Congress, 2nd Session, 2 and 4 March, 1960, Washington DC, USGPO.

US Department of Commerce (1954). *Census of Manufactures*, Washington DC, USGPO.

US Department of Commerce (1971). *1967 Census of Manufactures: General Summary*, Washington DC, USGPO.

US Department of Labor (1960). *The Impact of Automation: A Collection of Twenty Articles from the* Monthly Labor Review, Washington DC, USGPO.

US Office of Technology Assessment (1984). *Computerised Manufacturing Automation: Employment, Education and the Workplace*, Washington DC, USGPO.

USNCTAEP [United States National Commission on Technology, Automation and Economic Progress] (1966). *Technology and the US Economy*, Appendix Volume 2: The Employment Impact of Technical Change, Washington DC, USGPO.

USPAC [United States, President's Advisory Committee on Labor-Management Policy] (1962). *Report: Benefits and Problems Incident to Automation and Other Technological Advances*, Washington DC, USGPO.

Contemporary "how-to" books and articles, pamphlets, reports, etc.

AACP [Anglo-American Council on Productivity] (1949). *Simplification in British Industry*, London, AACP.

AACP (1952). *Iron and Steel*, London, AACP.

AACP (1953). *Metal-Working Machine Tools*, London, British Productivity Council.

AEU [Amalgamated Engineering Union] (1956). *Report of Proceedings of the 38th National Committee*, London, AEU.

AFL-CIO [American Federation of Labor and Congress of Industrial Organizations] (1956). *Labor Looks at Automation*, Washington DC, AFL-CIO (May) AFL-CIO Publication No. 21.

AFL-CIO (1962). *Automation's Unkept Promise*, Washington DC, AFL-CIO, Industrial Union Department, Publication No. 47 (June) (Hagley pamphlets).

Aggarwal, Sumer C. (1985). "MRP, JIT, OPT, FMS?", *Harvard Business Review* 63/5: 8–16.

AIEE [American Institution of Electrical Engineering] (1951). "Proposed symbols and terms for feedback control systems", *Electrical Engineering* 70 (1951): 905–9.

Alexander, Tom (1969). "Computers Can't Solve Everything", *Fortune* 80 (October): 126–9, 168, 171.

Allen, G.C. (1979). *The British Disease: A Short Essay on the Nature and Causes of the Nation's Lagging Wealth*, London, IEA.

AMA [American Management Association] (1956). *Keeping Pace with Automation: Practical Guides for the Company Executive*, New York, AMA, Special Report, No. 7.

Anderson Consulting (1992). *The Lean Production Benchmarking Project Report*, London, Anderson Consulting.

ASSET [Association of Supervisory Staffs, Executives and Technicians] (1956). *Automation: a Challenge to Trade Unions and Industry*, London, ASSET.

Banker, The (1961). "More overtime at Barclays", *The Banker* 111: 522.

Banker, The (1963a). "Bank Staffs: The Next Thirty Years", *The Banker* 113: 548–53.

Banker, The (1963b). "How much do the Banks want the 'Little Man'?", *The Banker* 113: 400–3.

Banker, The (1966a). "Giro Woos Business", *The Banker* 116: 551.

Banker, The (1966b). "Credit Card from Barclays – Cheque Card from Midland", *The Banker* 96: 72–3.

Banker, The (1967a). "Computer Banking: A Survey", *The Banker* 117: 496–501.

Banker, The (1967b). "Plessey and Burroughs Bid for NP Computer", *The Banker* 117: 1083.

Banker, The (1967c). "Efficiency of the Banks", *The Banker* 117: 486–95.

Banker, The (1967d). "After the PIB Report", *The Banker* 117: 482–503.

Bararb, George J. and Earl B. Hutchins (1963). "Electronic computers and management organisation", *California Management Review* 6: 33–42.

Bayhylle, J.E. (1968). *Productivity Improvements in the Office*, London, Kogan Page (Associates) for the Engineering Employers' Federation.

Benson, Sir Henry (1966). *The Steel Industry*. The Stage 1 Report of the Development Co-ordinating Committee of the British Iron and Steel Federation, London, BISF.

Bezier, P. (1954). "Large Quantity Production: Automation and its Implications for Management", account of a paper presented by Bezier to the European Management Conference, *Automobile Engineer* (Dec.).

Bezier, P. (1955). "Automatic Transfer Machines", in IPE 1955: 73–90.

Boston Consulting Group (1975). *Strategy Alternatives for the British Motor Cycle Industry*, London, HMSO.

Buckingham, Walter S. (1961). *Automation: Its Impact on Business and People*, New York, Harper and Row.

Buckler, E.J.W. (1964). "Automation and the Branch Manager", *The Banker* **114**: 436–40.

Business Week (1951). "How a Robot Factory Should Work" (21 July): 56–60.

Business Week (1952a). "Automation: A Factory Runs Itself" (29 March): 146–50.

Business Week (1952b). "The Coming Industrial Era: The Wholly Automatic Factory" (5 April).

Caminer, D.T. (1958–9). "– And how to Avoid Them", *Computer Journal* **1**: 11–14.

Carron, W.J. (1955). "Automation: Fact not Fiction", *AEU Monthly Journal* **22** (August): 247.

Carter, C.F. (1971). "Trends in Machine Tool Development and Application", *Second International Conference on Product Development and Manufacturing Technology*, University of Strathclyde, Paper 4.

Case, John M. (1965). "How do we get there?", *Proceedings of the National Automation Conference, 1965*, New York, American Bankers' Association.

CCUS [Chamber of Commerce of the United States] (1965). *A New Look at how Machines make Jobs*, Chicago, National Research Bureau; Employee Relations Bureau of Chamber of Commerce of the United States.

Chestnut, Harold (1957). "Feedback Control Systems", in Grabbe 1957: 41–88.

CIOCEP [Congress of Industrial Organisations, Committee on Economic Policy] (1955). *The Challenge of Automation: Papers Delivered at the National Conference on Automation*, Washington DC, Public Affairs Press: 30–44.

Clague, Ewen (1961). "Social and Economic Aspects of Automation", paper given to the Joint Automatic Control Conference, University of Colorado, Boulder, Colorado (28 June) (Hagley pamphlets).

Conservative Party (1968). *Fair Deal at Work*, London, Conservative Party.

Conway, J. (1954). "Trade unions and automation", *AEU Monthly Journal* **21** (October): 426.

Daniel, D. Ronald (1961). "Management information crisis", *Harvard Business Review* **39**/5: 111–21.

Davis, D.J. (1955). Evidence to US Congress 1955: 51–69.

Diebold, John (1952). *Automation: The Advent of the Automatic Factory*, New York, Van Nostrand.

Diebold, John (1958). *Failures in Business Computing and How to Avoid Them*, New York, The Management Science Training Institute.

Diebold, John (1959). *Automation: Its Impact on Business and Labor*, Washington DC, National Planning Association.

Dinning, N. (1955). "Automation: Complacency or Realism?", *AEU Monthly Journal* **22** (August): 246.

Drucker, Peter F. (1955a). "America's Next Twenty Years: The Coming Labor Shortage", *Harpers Magazine* (March).

Drucker, Peter F. (1955b). "The Promise of Automation", *Harpers Magazine* (April).

Drucker, Peter F. (1955c). "America's Next Twenty Years", *Harpers Magazine* (May).

Ewell, James M. (1961). "The Total Systems Concept and How to Organise for it", *Computers and Automation* **10**: 1–11.

Fairbanks, Ralph W. (1952). "Electronics in the Modern Office", *Harvard Business Review* **30**: 83–99.

Fairbanks, Ralph W. (1956). *Successful Office Automation*, Englewood Cliffs, NJ, Prentice-Hall.

Fairless, Benjamin F. (1955). *Our One Indispensable Weapon*, New York, United States Steel Corporation, 1955 (address of a talk at the Greater Johnstown Chamber of Commerce, Johnstown, Pa, 11 February, 1955) (Hagley pamphlets).

Freedman, Audrey (1966). *Impact of Office Automation in the Insurance Industry*, Washington DC, US Department of Labor, Bureau of Labor Statistics (Bulletin No. 1468).

Garvin, David A. (1983). "Quality on the Line", *Harvard Business Review* **61**/5: 64–75.

Gearing, H.W. (1958–9). "Statistical Foundations for Business Forecasts', *Computer Journal* **1**: 59–63.

Goldsmith, J.A. (1959–60). "The State of the Art: (a) Commercial Computers in the United Kingdom", *Computer Journal* **2**: 97–102.

Goodman, Leonard Landon (1957). *Man and Automation*, Harmondsworth, Penguin.

Grabbe, Eugene M. (ed.) (1957). *Automation in Business and Industry*, New York, John Wiley.

Graves, H.J. (1955). "The Automatic Mechanical Project Factory: A Sight of Things to Come", in IPE 1955: 28–38.

Gregory, R.H. and H.W. Gearing (1958–9). "Electronic Computers as Tools for Management in the USA, 1956", *Computer Journal* **1**: 179–91.

Griffith, Frank (1955). "Why Austin Developed Unit Construction Transfer Machines," *The Machinist* (21 Jan.): 107–13.

Griffith, Frank (1961). "Automation in Motor Cars calls for Much Re-thinking," *Financial Times Survey of Electronics and Automation* (23 Jan.).

Guest, L.C. (1961). "A Temperate View of Data Processing and Management Information Systems", in American Management Association, *Advances in EDP and Information Systems*, New York, American Management Association, 1961: 7–13.

Haller, William (1966). "Technological Change in Primary Steelmaking in the United States, 1947–65", in USNCTAEP 1966, Appendix II: II–177–II–200.

Harbour and Associates, Inc. (1992). *The Harbour Report: Competitive Assessment of the North American Automobile Industry*, Detroit, Harbour and Associates.

Hayes, Robert H. (1981). "Why Japanese Factories Work", *Harvard Business Review* **59**/4: 57–66.

Hickman, T.C. (1959–60). "Early Experiences with an EDP System", *Computer Journal* **2**: 152–63.

Hope, K.S. (1961–2). "SABER: A Real-time Problem in Tele-processing", *Computer Journal* **4**: 109–13.

Hugh-Jones, E.M. (1956). *The Push-Button World: Automation Today*, Norman, University of Oklahoma Press.

IPE [Institution of Production Engineers] (1955). *The Automatic Factory: What Does it Mean? Report of the Conference held at Margate, 16–19 June, 1955*, E. & F.N. Spon for The Institution of Production Engineers.

Johnson, William B. (1963). "Integrated Numerical Control: A Positive Management Tool", in Wilson 1963: 459–89.

Jones, Thomas Roy (1956). Evidence to US Congress 1956: 33–71.

Joseph, Keith (1979). *Solving the Union Problem is the Key to Economic Recovery*, London, Centre for Policy Studies.

Kent, A.M. (1955). "Production Engineering Practice", *AEU Monthly Journal* 22 (June): 184.

Knopf, George S. (1963). "Manufacturing Advantages of Numerical Control", in Wilson 1963: 29–49.

Laspe, C.G. (1957). "Process Control in the Petroleum and Chemicals Industries", in Grabbe 1957: 19–55.

Leaver, Eric W. and J J. Brown (1946). "Machines without Men", *Fortune* (November): 165–6, 192–204.

Leonard, Frank S. and W. Earl Sasser (1982). "The Incline of Quality", *Harvard Business Review* 60/5: 153–62.

Lissner, Will (1960). "Foreign Rivalry Rouses Industry", *New York Times* (10 December).

Lissner, Will (1961). "The Automation Race", *Time* (1 September).

Luttwak, Edward N. (1993). *The Endangered American Dream: How to Stop the United States from Becoming a Third World Country and How to Win the Geo-Economic Struggle for Industrial Supremacy*, New York, Simon and Schuster, 1993.

Mann, Floyd C. and L. Richard Hoffman (1956). "Case history in two power plants", in The Technology Project, *Man and Automation*, New Haven, Yale University Press.

Mather, Hal F. and Timothy B. Blodgett (1984). "The Case for Skimpy Inventories", *Harvard Business Review* 62/1: 40–4.

McCallum, I. (1955). "Automatic Control in the Petroleum Industry: A Case Study", in IPE 1955: 107–14.

Midbank Chronicle (1955). "Operation Dividend", *Midbank Chronicle* 5: 14–15.

Midbank Chronicle (1967). "The Future Use of Computers, II", *Midbank Chronicle* 17: 364–5.

Midbank Chronicle (1968). "The Future Use of Computers, VII: Project 70", *Midbank Chronicle* 17: 504–5.

Midbank Chronicle (1974). "Living with the Computer", *Midbank Chronicle* 24: 126–8.

Miller, Robert W. (1962). "How to Plan and Control with PERT", *Harvard Business Review* 40/2: 93–105.

NAM [National Association of Manufacturers] (1962). *Union Demands for Job Security: An Economic Analysis*, New York, NAM Research Department.

Oettinger, Anthony O. (1964). "The Coming Revolution in Banking", *Proceedings of the National Automation Conference, 1964*, New York, American Bankers' Association.

Paschell, William (1958). *Automation and Employment Opportunities for Office Workers: a Report on the Effect of Electronic Computers on Employment of Clerical Workers*, Washington DC, US Department of Labor, Bureau of Labor Statistics (Bulletin No. 1241).

PEP [Political and Economic Planning] (1957). *Case Studies in Automation: Three Studies in Automation*, London, PEP.

PERA [Production Engineering Research Association] (1963). *Numerical Control: An Economic Survey*. Report No. 119, Melton Mowbray, PERA.

Platt, A.J. (1960–1). "The Experience of Applying a Commercial Computer in a British Organisation", *Computer Journal* 3: 185–97.

Priest, Arthur (1955). "Automation Replacing Workers in US Industry", *AEU Monthly Journal* 22 (July): 217.

Puckle, O.S. (1957). "Numerical Control of Machines for Aircraft Manufacture", *Process Control and Automation*, 4/2: 40–6.

Rader, Louis T. (1965). "Automation: America's Deposit on the Future", *Proceedings of the National Automation Conference, 1965*, New York, American Bankers' Association.

Reuther, Walter (1955). Evidence to US Congress 1955: 97–149.

Riter, Henry G. (1955). "GAW in Myth and Reality, an Address to the Graduate School of Banking of the University of Wisconsin, Madison, August 29, 1955" (Hagley pamphlets).

Rouse, H.L. (1933). "A General Review of Six Years of Mechanisation", *The Banker* 27: 238–44.

Sargrove, J.A. and Peter Huggins (1955). "Automatic Inspection: The Anatomy of Conscious Machines", in IPE 1955: 95–106.

Schonberger, Richard J. (1982). *Japanese Manufacturing Techniques: Nine Hidden Lessons in Simplicity*, New York, Free Press.

Schonberger, Richard J. (1985). *World Class Manufacturing*, New York, Free Press.

Schroeder, Walter J. (1971). "The EDP Manager and the Computer Profit Drain", *Computers and Automation* 20: 14–18.

Sharp, B.C. (1961). "The New Credit Transfer Service", *The Banker* 111: 180–5.

Simpson, Douglas (1967). "Problems and Solutions", *The Banker* 117: 507–14.

Smith, Ellis and Frank Allaun (1955). "Automation: engineers face a second industrial revolution", *AEU Monthly Journal* 22 (October): 308–9.

Snyder, John I. Jr. (1963). "The Total Challenge of Automation", Address before the Fifth Constitutional Convention, AFL-CIO (19 November) (Hagley pamphlets).

Stokes, J.A. (1955). "Automatic Electronic Control of Machine Tools", in IPE 1955: 191–7.

Strumilin, S.G. (1957). *Ökonomische Probleme der Automasierung der Produktion*, Berlin, Verlag die Wirtschaft.

Takeuchi, Hirotaka and John A. Quelch (1983). "Quality is More than Making a Good Product", *Harvard Business Review* 61/4: 139–45.

Terborgh, George (1965). *The Automation Hysteria*, Washington DC, Machinery and Allied Products Institute.

Thayer, Leo S. (1963). "The General Economic Aspects", in Wilson 1963: 19–29.

Thomson, John (1966). "The Case for the Credit Card", *The Banker* 116: 444–6.

TUC [Trades Union Congress] (1948a). *Productivity: Report of a Conference of Trade Union Executive Committees*, London, TUC.

TUC (1948b). *Productivity: Report of the General Council*, London, TUC.

TUC (1956). "Trade Unions and Automation", in *Report of Proceedings at the 88th Annual Trades Union Congress*, London, TUC: 512–25.

TUC (1957). *Report of the 89th Annual Trades Union Congress*, London, TUC.

TUC (1965). *Productivity, Prices and Incomes: Report of a Conference of Executives of Affiliated Organisations held on 30th April 1965*, London, TUC.

Vine, Roy (1967). "Why the Banks have gone in for Automation", *The Banker* 117: 501–7.

Warmington, C.B. (1960–1). "The First Year's Production on a Computer, and Future Plans", *Computer Journal* 3: 124–7.

Weinberg, Edgar (1955). "A Review of Automation Technology: The Meaning, Outlook and Implications of America's Most Recent Industrial Development", *Monthly Labor Review* (June): 3–10.

Weiss, Abraham (1955). *What Automation Means to You: A Summary of the Effects of the Second Industrial Revolution on the American Worker*, Washington DC, International Brotherhood of Teamsters, Chauffeurs, Warehousemen and Helpers of America, AFL.

Wilson, Frank (ed.) (1963). *Numerical Control in Manufacturing*, New York, McGraw-Hill.

Woollard, Frank G. (1954). *Principles of Mass and Flow Production*, London, Iliffe.

Woollard, Frank G. (1955). "Machines in the Service of Man", in IPE 1955: 198–206.

Woollard, Frank G. (1956). "Automation in Engineering Production", in E.M. Hugh-Jones (ed.) *Automation in Theory and Practice*, Oxford, Basil Blackwell: 29–47.

Young, A.J. (1955). "Prerequisites of the Automatic Factory", in IPE 1955: 180–90.

Ziebolz, Herbert W. (1957). "Basic Concepts of Industrial Automation and Control", in Grabbe 1957: 131.

Diary, autobiography and memoir

Brooks, Frederick P. (1995). *The Mythical Man-Month: Essays in Software Engineering, Anniversary Edition*, Boston MA, Addison Wesley Longman.

Cairncross, Alec (ed.) (1991). *The Robert Hall Diaries, 1954–1960*, London, Allen and Unwin.

Caminer, David, John Aris, Peter Hermon and Frank Land (1998). *LEO: The Incredible Story of the World's First Business Computer*, New York, McGraw-Hill.

Castle, Barbara (1974). *The Castle Diaries, 1964–70*, London, Weidenfeld and Nicolson.

Dalton, Hugh (1962). *High Tide and After: Memoirs, 1945–60*, London, Muller.

Edwardes, Michael (1983). *Back from the Brink: An Apocalyptic Experience*, London, Collins.

Ishihara, Shintaro (1991). *The Japan that Can Say NO*, New York, Simon and Schuster.

Thornett, Alan (1998). *Inside Cowley. Trade Union Struggle in the 1970s: Who really opened the Door to the Tory Onslaught?*, London, Porcupine Press.

Watson, Thomas Jr. and Peter Petrie (1990). *Father and Son and Co.*, London, Bantam Books.

Books and articles

Abé, Etsuo (1997). "The State as the 'Third Hand': MITI and Japanese Industrial Development after 1945", in Etsuo Abé and Terry Gourvish (eds) *Japanese Success? British Failure? Comparisons in Business Performance since 1945*, Oxford, Oxford University Press: 17–44.

Abegglen, James (1970). "The Economic Growth of Japan", *Scientific American* **222**: 31–5.

Abelshauser, Werner (1995). "Two Kinds of Fordism: On the Differing Roles of the Automobile Industry in the Development of the Two German States", in Shiomi and Wada 1995: 269–96.

Abramovitz, Moses (1986). "Catching Up, Forging Ahead, and Falling Behind", *Journal of Economic History* **46**: 385–406.

Ackers, Peter, Chris Smith and Paul Smith (eds) (1996a). *The New Workplace and Trade Unionism: Critical Perspectives on Work and Organisation*, London, Routledge.

Ackers, Peter, Chris Smith and Paul Smith (1996b). "Against All Odds? British Trade Unions in the New Workplace", in Ackers *et al.* 1996a: 1–40.

Ackrill, Margaret and Leslie Hannah (2001). *Barclays: The Business of Banking, 1690–1996*, Cambridge, Cambridge University Press.

Addison, John T. (1986). "Job Security in the United States: Law, Collective Bargaining, Policy and Practice", *British Journal of Industrial Relations* **24**: 381–418.

Addison, Paul (1975). *The Road to 1945: British Politics and the Second World War*, London, Cape.

Adeney, Martin (1989). *The Motor Makers: The Turbulent History of Britain's Car Industry*, London, Fontana.

Agar, Jon (2003). *The Government Machine: A Revolutionary History of the Computer*, Cambridge MA, MIT Press.

Ahlstrand, Bruce W. (1990). *The Quest for Productivity: A Study of Fawley after Flanders*, Cambridge, Cambridge University Press.

Akera, Atsushi (2002). "IBM's Early Adaptation to Cold War Markets: Cuthbert Hurd and his Applied Science Field Men", *Business History Review* **76** (Winter): 767–802.

Alford, B.W.E., Rodney Lowe, and Neil Rollings (1992). *Economic Planning, 1943–1951: A Guide to Documents in the Public Record Office*, London, HMSO.

Altshuler, Alan, M. Anderson, Daniel Jones, Daniel Roos and James P. Womack (1984). *The Future of the Automobile: The Report of MIT's Automobile Programme*, London, Allen and Unwin.

Amin, Ash (1994). "Post-Fordism: Models, Fantasies and Phantoms of Transition", in Ash Amin (ed.) *Post-Fordism: A Reader*, Oxford, Blackwell: 1–39.

Anderson, Gregory (1976). *Victorian Clerks*, Manchester, Manchester University Press.

Anderson, Gregory (1977). "The Social Economy of Late Victorian Clerks", in Geoffrey Crossick (ed.) *The Lower Middle Class in Britain*, London, Croom Helm: 113–33.

Annals of the History of Computing (1981). **5** (special issue on the SAGE project).

Anshen, Melvin (1960). "The Manager and the Black Box", *Harvard Business Review* **38**/6: 85–92.

Ark, Bart van (1993). *International Comparisons of Output and Productivity: Manufacturing Productivity Performance of Ten Countries from 1950 to 1990*, Groningen, Groningen Growth and Development Centre.

Armstrong, A.G. (1967). "The Motor Industry and the British Economy", *District Bank Review*, (Sept.): 19–40.

Armstrong, David J. (1985). "Sharpening Inventory Management", *Harvard Business Review* **63**/6: 42–50.

238 *References*

Armstrong, Peter (1984). "Engineers, Management and Trust", *Work, Employment and Society* **1**: 421–40.

Ashworth, William (1991). *The State in Business: 1945 to the mid-1980s*, London, Macmillan.

Bacon, Nick and John Storey (1996). "Individualism and Collectivism and the Changing Role of Trade Unions", in Ackers *et al.* 1996a: 41–76.

Bain, George Sayers (1970). *The Growth of White Collar Unionism*, Oxford, Oxford University Press.

Bain, George Sayers (ed.) (1983). *Industrial Relations in Britain*, Oxford, Basil Blackwell.

Balogh, T. (1952). "The International Aspect", in Worswick and Ady 1952: 476–510.

Bamberg, James (1994). *The History of the British Petroleum Company*. Volume 2, *The Anglo-Iranian Years, 1928–1954*, Cambridge, Cambridge University Press.

Bamberg, James (2000). *The History of the British Petroleum Company*. Volume 3, *British Petroleum and Global Oil, 1950–1975, The Challenge of Nationalism*, Cambridge, Cambridge University Press.

Barjot, Dominique (ed.) (2002). *Catching Up With America: Productivity Missions and the Diffusion of American Economic and Technological Influence after the Second World War*, Paris, Presses de l'Unversité de Paris-Sorbonne.

Barnes, Dennis and Eileen Reid (1982). "A New Relationship: Trade Unions in the Second World War", in Ben Pimlott and Chris Cook (eds) *Trade Unions in British Politics*, London, Longman: 149–68.

Barnett, Correlli (1986). *The Audit of War: The Illusion and Reality of Britain as a Great Nation*, Basingstoke, Macmillan.

Barnett, Correlli (1995). *The Lost Victory: British Dreams, British Realities, 1945–1950*, London, Macmillan.

Barr, A.E. De (1973). Contribution to Discussion of Merchant 1973.

Barrell, Ray, Geoff Mason and Mary O'Mahony (eds) (2000). *Productivity, Innovation and Economic Performance*, Cambridge, Cambridge University Press.

Baskerville, Richard (2003). "The LEO Principle: Perspectives on 50 years of Business Computing", *Journal of Strategic Information Systems* **12**: 255–63.

Batstone, Eric (1986). "Labour and Productivity", *Oxford Review of Economic Policy* **2**: 32–43.

Baumol, W.J. (1967). "Macroeconomics of Unbalanced Growth", *American Economic Review* **57**: 415–26.

Baumol, W.J. (1986). "Productivity Growth, Convergence and Welfare: What the Long-run Data Show", *American Economic Review* **76**: 1072–85.

Beauchamp, Ken (1981). "John Sargrove: inventor of the first PCB", *Electronics and Power* (June): 477–83.

Beckerman, Wilfred (1972). "Objectives and Performance: An Overall View", in Wilfred Beckerman (ed.) *The Labour Government's Economic Record, 1964–1970*, London, Duckworth: 44–67.

Beesley, M.E. and G.W. Troup (1961). "The Machine Tool Industry", in Burn 1961a: 359–92.

Bennett, S. (1976). "The Emergence of a Discipline: Automatic Control, 1940–1960", *Automatica* **12**: 113–21.

Bernstein, Michael A. and David E. Adler (eds) (1994). *Understanding American Economic Decline: A Structural and Institutional Approach*, Cambridge, Cambridge University Press.

Beynon, Huw (1973). *Working for Ford*, Harmondsworth, Penguin.

Bhaskar, Krish (1979). *The Future of the UK Motor Industry: An Economic and Financial Analysis of the UK Motor Industry Against a Rapidly-Changing Background for European and Worldwide Motor Manufacturers*, London, Kogan Page.

Biggart, Nicole Woolsey and Gary H. Hamilton (1992). "On the Limits of a Firm-based Theory to Explain Business Networks: The Western Bias of Neo-classical Economics", in Nohria Nitin and Robert C. Eccles (eds) *Networks and Organisations: Structure, Form and Action*, Boston, Harvard Business School Press: 471–90.

Bix, Amy Sue (2000). *Inventing Ourselves out of Jobs? America's Debate over Technological Unemployment, 1929–1981*, Baltimore, Johns Hopkins University Press.

Bjarnar, Ove and Matthias Kipping (1998). "The Marshall Plan and the Transfer of US Management Models to Europe: An Introductory Framework", in Kipping and Bjarnar 1998: 1–17.

Blackaby, F.T. (ed.) (1978a). *British Economic Policy, 1960–74*, Cambridge, Cambridge University Press.

Blackaby, F.T. (1978b). "Narrative, 1960–74", in Blackaby 1978a: 11–76.

Blanchflower, David G. and Richard B. Freeman (1994). "Did the Thatcher Reforms Change British Labour Market Performance?", in Ray Barrell (ed.) *The UK Labour Market: Comparative Aspects and Institutional Developments*, Cambridge, Cambridge University Press: 51–92.

Blank, Stephen (1973). *Industry and Government in Britain: The Federation of British Industries in Politics. 1945–65*, Farnborough, Saxon House.

Booth, Alan (1989). *British Economic Policy, 1931–49: Was There a Keynesian Revolution?*, Hemel Hempstead, Harvester-Wheatsheaf.

Booth, Alan (1996). "Corporate Politics and the Quest for Productivity: The British TUC and the Politics of Industrial Productivity, 1947–60", in Melling and McKinlay 1996: 44–65.

Booth, Alan (2000). "Inflation, Expectations and the Political Economy of Conservative Britain, 1951–64", *Historical Journal* 43: 827–47.

Booth, Alan (2001). "New revisionism and the Keynesian era in British economic policy", *Economic History Review* 54: 346–66.

Booth, Alan (2002). "British Retail Banks, 1955–70: A Case of "Americanisation?", in Matthias Kipping and Nick Tiratsoo (eds) *Americanisation in Twentieth Century Europe: Business, Culture, Politics*, Lille, University of Lille Press: 309–23.

Booth, Alan (2003). "The Manufacturing Failure Hypothesis and the Performance of British Industry during the Long Boom', *Economic History Review* 56/1: 1–33.

Booth, Alan (2004). "Technical Change in Branch Banking at the Midland Bank, 1945–75", *Accounting, Business and Financial History* 14: 277–300.

Booth, Alan and Joseph Melling (eds) (2007). *Workplace Cultures and Industrial Performance: British Labour Relations and Industrial Output in Comparative Perspective*, Aldershot, Ashgate.

Booth, Alan, Joseph Melling and Christoph Dartmann (1997). "Institutions and Economic Growth: The Politics of Productivity Growth in West Germany, Sweden and the United Kingdom, 1945–55", *Journal of Economic History* 57: 416–44.

Bordo, Michael, Angela Redish and Hugh Rockoff (1995). "A Comparison of the United States and Canadian Banking Systems in the Twentieth Century: Stability versus Efficiency?", in Michael Bordo and Richard Sylla (eds) *Anglo-American Financial Systems: Institutions and Markets in the Twentieth Century*, New York, Irwin: 11–40.

Bowonder, B. and T. Miyake (1994). "Creating and Sustaining Competitiveness: The Japanese Robotics Industry", *International Journal of Technology Management* **9**: 575–601.

Boyer, Richard O. and Herbert M. Morais (1955). *Labor's Untold* Story, New York, Cameron Associates.

Bradley, Keith and Stephen Hill (1983). "'After Japan': The Quality Circle Transplant and Productive Efficiency", *British Journal of Industrial Relations* **21**: 291–311.

Brady, Robert (1993). *The Rationalisation Movement in Germany*, Berkeley, University of California Press.

Braun, Ernest and Stuart MacDonald (1982). *Revolution in Miniature: The History and Impact of Semiconductor Electronics*, Cambridge, Cambridge University Press, 2nd edn.

Braverman, Harry (1974). *Labor and Monopoly Capital: The Degradation of Work in the Twentieth Century*, New York, Monthly Review Press.

Brech, M. and M. Sharp (1984). *Inward Investment: Policy Option for the United Kingdom*, Chatham House Papers, 21, London, Routledge.

Bright, James R. (1958). *Automation and Management*, Boston MA, Division of Research, Graduate School of Business Administration, Harvard University.

Brittan, Samuel (1971). *Steering the Economy: The Role of the Treasury*, Harmondsworth, Penguin.

Broadberry, S.N. (1993). "Manufacturing and the Convergence Hypothesis: What the Long-run Data Show", *Journal of Economic History* **53**/4: 772–95.

Broadberry, S.N. (1997a). *The Productivity Race: British Manufacturing in International Perspective, 1850–1990*, Cambridge, Cambridge University Press.

Broadberry, S.N. (1997b). "Forging Ahead, Falling Behind and Catching-Up: A Sectoral Analysis of Anglo-American Productivity Differences, 1870–1990", *Research in Economic History* **17**: 1–37.

Broadberry, S.N. (1998). "How Did the United States and Germany Overtake Britain? A Sectoral Analysis of Comparative Productivity Levels, 1870–1990", *Journal of Economic History* **58**: 375–407.

Broadberry, S.N. and N.F.R. Crafts (1990). "Explaining Anglo-American Productivity Differentials in the Mid-twentieth Century", *Bulletin of the Oxford University Institute of Statistics* **52**/4: 375–402.

Broadberry, S.N. and N.F.R. Crafts (1996). "British Economic Policy and Industrial Performance in the Early Postwar Period", *Business History* **38**/4: 65–91.

Broadberry, S.N. and N.F.R. Crafts (2001). "Competition and Innovation in 1950s Britain", *Business History* **43**/1: 97–118.

Broadberry, S.N. and Peter Howlett (1998). "The United Kingdom: "Victory at all Costs", in Harrison 1998: 43–80.

Brody, David (1980). *Workers in Industrial America: Essays on the Twentieth Century Struggle*, New York, Oxford University Press.

Brody, David (1993). *In Labor's Cause: Main Themes on the History of the American Worker*, New York, Oxford University Press.

Brooke, Stephen (1991). "Problems of 'Socialist Planning': Evan Durbin and the Labour Government of 1945", *Historical Journal* **34**: 687–702.

Brooke, Stephen (1992). *Labour's War: The Labour Party During the Second World War*, Oxford, Clarendon Press.

Brown, John Seely and Paul Duguid (1991). "Organisational Learning and Communities-of-practice: Toward a Unified View of Working, Learning and Innovation", *Organisation Science* **2**/1: 40–57.

Brown, John Seely and Paul Duguid (2001). "Knowledge and Organisation: A Social Practice Perspective", *Organisation Science* **12**/2: 198–213.

Brown, W.A. (1973). *Piecework Bargaining*, London, Heinemann.

Bufton, Mark W. (2004). *Britain's Productivity Problem, 1948–1990*, Basingstoke, Palgrave.

Bullock, Alan (1983). *Ernest Bevin: Foreign Secretary, 1945–1951*, London, Heinemann.

Burn, D.E. (ed.) (1961a). *The Structure of British Industry: A Symposium*, volume 1, Cambridge, Cambridge University Press.

Burn, D.E. (ed.) (1961b). *The Structure of British Industry: A Symposium*, volume 2, Cambridge, Cambridge University Press.

Burn, D.E. (1961c). "The Oil Industry", in Burn 1961a: 156–217.

Burn, D.E. (1961d). "Steel", in Burn 1961a: 260–308.

Burns, Tom and G.M. Stalker (1994). *The Management of Innovation*, Oxford, Oxford University Press, 3rd edn.

Butler, David and Donald Stokes (1969). *Political Change in Britain: Forces Shaping Electoral Choice*, London, Macmillan.

Cain, P.J. and A.G. Hopkins (1993). *British Imperialism: Crisis and Deconstruction, 1914–1990*, Harlow, Longman.

Cairncross, Alec (1987). *Years of Recovery: British Economic Policy, 1945–51*, London, Methuen.

Calder, Kent (1988). *Crisis and Compensation: Public Policy and Political Stability in Japan, 1949–1986*, Princeton, Princeton University Press.

Calmfors, Lars and John Driffil (1988). "Bargaining Structure, Corporatism and Macroeconomic Performance", *Economic Policy* **6**: 13–62.

Campbell, Alan, Nina Fishman and John McIlroy (eds) (1999a). *British Trade Unions and Industrial Politics: The Postwar Compromise, 1945–64*, Aldershot, Ashgate.

Campbell, Alan, Nina Fishman and John McIlroy (1999b). "The Postwar Compromise: Mapping Industrial Politics, 1945–64", in Campbell *et al.* 1999a: 69–113.

Campbell, D.P (1953). "Dynamic Behaviour of Linear Production Processes", *Mechanical Engineering*, **75**: 279–83.

Campbell-Kelly, Martin (1989). *ICL: A Business and Technical History*, Oxford, Clarendon.

Campbell-Kelly, Martin (1992). "Large-scale Data Processing in the Prudential, 1850–1930", *Accounting, Business and Financial History* **2**: 117–39.

Campbell-Kelly, Martin and William Aspray (1996). *Computer: A History of the Information Machine*, New York, Basic Books.

Capie, Forrest and Mark Billings (2001). "Accounting Issues and the Measurement of Profits: English Banks 1920–68", *Accounting, Business and Financial History* **11** (2001): 225–51.

Carew, Anthony (1987). *Labour under the Marshall Plan: the Politics of Productivity and the Marketing of Management Science*, Manchester, Manchester University Press.

Carr, Fergus (1993). "Cold War: The Economy and Foreign Policy", in Fyrth 1993: 135–47.

Chandler, A.D. (1990). *Scale and Scope: the Dynamics of Industrial Capitalism*, Cambridge MA, Belknap Press.

Chester, D.N. (1952a). "Machinery of Government and Planning", in Worswick and Ady 1952: 336–64.

Chester, D.N. (ed.) (1952b). *Lessons of the British War Economy*, Cambridge, Cambridge University Press.

Chick, Martin (1992). "Private Industrial Investment", in Mercer *et al.* 1992: 74–90.

Chick, Martin (1998). *Industrial Policy in Britain, 1945–1951: Economic Planning, Nationalisation and the Labour Governments*, Cambridge, Cambridge University Press.

Church, R.A. (1994). *The Rise and Decline of the British Motor Industry*, Basingstoke, Macmillan.

Clark, Ian (1999). "Institutional Stability in Management Practice and Industrial Relations: The Influence of the Anglo-American Council for Productivity, 1948–52", *Business History* 41/3: 64–92.

Clegg, H.A. (1994). *A History of British Trade Unions Since 1889: Volume III, 1934–1951*, Oxford, Clarendon Press.

Clegg, H.A. and Rex Adams (1957). *The Employers' Challenge: A History of the National Shipbuilding and Engineering Disputes of 1957*, Oxford, Blackwell.

Cline, Peter (1982). "The Winding Down of the War Economy: British Plans for Peacetime Recovery, 1916–19", in Kathleen Burk (ed.) *War and the State: the Transformation of British Government, 1914–1919*, London, Allen and Unwin: 157–81.

Cockerill, Anthony (1988). "Steel", in Peter Johnson (ed.) *The Structure of British Industry*, London, Unwin Hyman, 2nd edn.

Cohen, I.B. (1988). "The Computer; A Case Study of Support by Government, Especially the Military, of a New Science and Technology", in E. Mendelsohn *et al.* (eds) *Science, Technology and the Military*, Amsterdam, Kluwer.

Cohn, Samuel Ross (1985). "Clerical Labor Intensity and the Feminisation of Clerical Labor in Great Britain, 1857–1937", *Social Forces* 63: 1060–8.

Cole, Robert E. and Tazio Yakushiji (eds) (1984). *The American and Japanese Auto Industries in Transition*, Ann Arbor, University of Michigan Center for Japanese Studies.

Coleman, D.C. (1987). "The Uses and Abuses of Business History", *Business History* 29/2: 141–56.

Coopey, Richard (1993). "Industrial Policy", in R. Coopey, S. Fielding and N. Tiratsoo (eds) *The Wilson Governments, 1964–1970*, London, Pinter: 102–22.

Coopey, Richard (1999). "Management and the Introduction of Computing to British Industry, 1945–70", *Contemporary British History* 13: 59–71.

Coopey, Richard (2004). "A Passing Technology? The Automatic Teller Machine", in Peter Lyth and Helmuth Trischler (eds) *Wiring Prometheus: Globalisation, History and Technology*, Aarhus, Aarhus University Press: 175–92.

Cortada, James W. (2000). *Before the Computer: IBM, NCR, Burroughs and Remington Rand and the Industry they Created, 1865–1956*, Princeton, Princeton University Press.

Crafts, N.F.R. (1988). "The Assessment: British Economic Growth over the Long Run", *Oxford Review of Economic Policy* **4**/1: i–xxi.

Crafts, N.F.R. and Gianni Toniolo (eds) (1996). *Economic Growth in Europe since 1945*, Cambridge, Cambridge University Press.

Crandall, R.W. (1981). *The US Steel Industry in Recurrent Crisis*, Washington DC, Brookings Institution.

Crompton, Rosemary (1997). *Women and Work in Modern Britain*, Oxford, Oxford University Press.

Crompton, Rosemary and Gareth Jones (1984). *White Collar Proletariat: Deskilling and Gender in Clerical Work*, London, Macmillan.

Crompton, Rosemary and Kay Sanderson (1990). *Gendered Jobs and Social Change*, London, Unwin Hyman.

Cronin, James E. (1979). *Industrial Conflict in Modern Britain*, London, Croom Helm.

Croucher, Richard (1982). *Engineers at War, 1939–1945*, London, Merlin.

Cusumano, Michael A. (1986). *The Japanese Automobile Industry: Technology and Management at Nissan and Toyota*, Cambridge MA, Harvard University Press.

Daniel, W.W. (1987). *Workplace Industrial Relations and Technical Change*, London, Frances Pinter.

David, Paul A. (1990). "The dynamo and the computer: An historical perspective on the modern productivity paradox", *American Economic Review* **80**: 355–61.

Davies, S. and R.E. Caves (1987). *Britain's Productivity Gap*, Cambridge, Cambridge University Press.

Davis Smith, Justin (1990). *The Attlee and Churchill Governments and Industrial Unrest, 1945–55*, London, Pinter.

Davison, J.F., P. Sargant Florence, Barbara Gray and N.S. Ross (1958). *Productivity and Economic Incentives*, London, Allen and Unwin.

Denison, E.F. (1967). *Why Growth Rates Differ: Postwar Experience in Nine Western Countries*, Washington DC, Brookings Institution.

Dex, Shirley (1985). *The Sexual Division of Labour: Conceptual Revolutions in the Social Sciences*, Brighton, Wheatsheaf.

Dobson, Alan P. (1986). *US Wartime Aid to Britain, 1940–1946*, Beckenham, Croom Helm.

Dore, Ronald (1986). *Flexible Rigidities: Industrial Policy and Structural Adjustment in the Postwar Japanese Economy*, London, Athlone Press.

Dore, Ronald (1973 and 1990). *British Factory – Japanese Factory: The Origins of National Diversity in Industrial Relations*, Berkeley, University of California Press.

Dorf, Richard C. (1989). *Modern Control Systems*, Reading MA, Addison-Wesley, 5th edn.

Dosi, Giovanni, Christopher Freeman, Richard Nelson, Gerald Silverberg and Luc Soete (eds) (1988). *Technical Change and Economic Theory*, London, Pinter.

Dow, J.C.R. (1964). *The Management of the British Economy, 1945–60*, Cambridge, Cambridge University Press.

Dow, J.C.R. and L. Dicks-Mireaux (1958). "The Excess Demand for Labour: A Study of Conditions in Great Britain, 1946–1956", *Oxford Economic Papers* **10**: 1–33.

Dunnett, Peter (1980). *The Decline of the British Motor Industry: The Effects of Government Policy, 1945–1979*, London, Croom Helm.

Dunning, John (1958). *American Investment in British Manufacturing Industry*, London, Allen and Unwin.

Dunning, John (1986). *Japanese Participation in British Industry*, London, Croom Helm.

Dunning, John (1998a). *American Investment in British Manufacturing Industry: Revised and Updated Edition*, London, Routledge.

Dunning, John (1998b). "US-owned Manufacturing Affiliates and the Transfer of Managerial Techniques: The British Case", in Kipping and Bjarnar 1998: 74–90.

Dupree, Marguerite (1992). "The Cotton Industry: A Middle Way Between Nationalisation and Self-Government?", in Mercer *et al.* 1992: 137–61.

Durbin, Elizabeth (1985). *New Jerusalems: The Labour Party and the Economics of Democratic Socialism*, London, Routledge.

Durcan, J.W., W.E.J. McCarthy and G.P. Redman (1983). *Strikes in Postwar Britain: A Study of Stoppages of Work due to Industrial Disputes, 1946–73*, London, Allen and Unwin.

Edgerton, David (1991) "The Prophet Militant and Industrial: The Peculiarities of Correlli Barnett", *Twentieth Century British History* **2**: 359–79.

Edgerton, David (1996a). "The 'White Heat' Revisited: The British Government and Technology in the 1960s", *Twentieth Century British History* **7**/1: 53–82.

Edgerton, David (1996b). *Science, Technology and the British Industrial "Decline"*, Cambridge, Cambridge University Press.

Edwards, P.K and Colin Whitson (1991). "Workers are Working Harder: Effort and Shopfloor Relations in the 1980s", *British Journal of Industrial Relations* **29**: 593–601.

Edwards, Paul N. (1996). *The Closed World*, Cambridge MA, MIT Press.

Edwards, Richard (1979). *Contested Terrain: The Transformation of the Workplace in the Twentieth Century*, New York, Basic Books.

Eichengreen, Barry (1996). "Institutions and Economic Growth: Europe after World War II", in Crafts and Toniolo 1996: 38–72.

Eklund, Jon (1994). "The Reservisor Automated Airline Reservation System: Combining Communications and Computing", *Annals of the History of Computing* **16**: 62–9.

Elbaum, Bernard and William Lazonick (eds) (1986). *The Decline of the British Economy*, Oxford, Clarendon Press.

Fagerberg, Jan, David C. Mowery and Richard R. Nelson (eds) (2005). *The Oxford Handbook of Innovation*, Oxford, Oxford University Press.

Feilden, G.B.R. (1995). "David Theodore Nelson Williamson. 15 February 1923–10 May 1992", *Biographical Memoirs of Fellows of the Royal Society* **41**: 516–32.

Feinstein, C.H. (1972). *National Income, Expenditure and Output of the United Kingdom, 1855–1965*, Cambridge, Cambridge University Press.

Feinstein, C.H. (1990). "Benefits of Backwardness and Costs of Continuity", in Andrew Graham and Anthony Seldon (eds) *Government and Economies in the*

Postwar World: Economic Policies and Comparative Performance, 1945–85, London, Routledge: 284–94.

Ferguson, Michael (2002). *The Rise of Management Consulting in Britain*, Aldershot, Ashgate.

Fisher, Amy Weaver and J.L. McKenney (1993). "The Development of the ERMA Banking System: Lessons from History", *Annals of the History of Computing* 15 (1993): 44–57.

Fishman, Nina (1999). "The Most Serious Crisis since 1926: The Engineering and Shipbuilding Strikes of 1957", in Campbell *et al.* 1999a: 242–67.

Flamm, Kenneth (1987). *Targeting the Computer: Government Support and International Competition*, Washington DC, Brookings Institution.

Flamm, Kenneth (1988). *Creating the Computer: Government, Industry and High Technology*, Washington DC, Brookings Institution.

Flanders, Allan (1964). *The Fawley Productivity Agreements: A Case Study of Management and Collective Bargaining*, London, Faber.

Floud, Roderick and D.N. McCloskey (eds) (1994). *The Economic History of Britain since 1700, volume 3, 1939–1992*, Cambridge, Cambridge University Press, 2nd edn.

Floud, Roderick and Paul Johnson (eds) (2004). *The Cambridge Economic History of Modern Britain: Volume II, Economic Maturity, 1860–1939*, Cambridge, Cambridge University Press.

Foreman-Peck, James, Sue Bowden and Alan McKinlay (1995). *The British Motor Industry*, Manchester, Manchester University Press.

Freeman, Christopher (1988). "Japan: A New National System of Innovation?", in Dosi *et al.* 1988: 330–48.

Freeman, Christopher, A.B. Robertson, P.J. Whittaker, R.C. Curnow and J.K. Fuller (1968). "Chemical Process Plant: Innovation and the World Market", *National Institute Economic Review* 45: 29–57.

Freeman, Christopher and Carlotta Perez (1988). "Structural Crises of Adjustment, Business Cycles and Investment Behaviour", in Dosi *et al.* 1988: 38–66.

Freeman, Christopher, C.J.E. Harlow, J.K. Fuller and R.C. Curnow (1965). "Research and Development in Electronic Capital Goods", *National Institute Economic Review* 34: 40–91.

Freeman, Christopher, John Clark and Luc Soete (1982). *Unemployment and Technical Innovation: a Study of Long Waves in Economic Development*, London, Pinter.

Freeman, Richard B. (1995). "The Future of Unions in Decentralised Collective Bargaining Systems: US and UK Unionism in an Era of Crisis", *British Journal of Industrial Relations* 33: 519–36.

Friedman, A. (1990). "Managerial Strategies, Activities, Techniques and Technology: Towards a Complex Theory of the Labour Process", in D. Knights and H. Willmott (eds) *Labour Process Theory*, London, Macmillan: 177–208.

Friedman, Milton and Anna J. Schwartz (1982). *Monetary Trends in the United States and the United Kingdom: their Relation to Income, Prices and Interest Rates, 1867–1975*, Chicago, University of Chicago Press.

Fyrth, Jim (ed.) (1993). *Labour's High Noon: The Government and the Economy, 1945–51*, London, Lawrence and Wishart.

Gaddis, John Lewis (2001). "Dividing the World", in Larres and Lane 2001: 41–64.

Gallagher, James D. (1961). *Management Information Systems and the Computer*, New York, American Management Association.

Gallie, Duncan, Michael White, Yuan Cheng and Mark Tomlinson (1998). *Restructuring the Employment Relationship*, Oxford, Oxford University Press.

Garrahan, Philip and Paul Stewart (1992). *The Nissan Enigma: Flexibility at Work in a Local Economy*, London, Mansell.

Garside, W.R. (1990). *British Unemployment, 1919–1939: A Study in Public Policy*, Cambridge, Cambridge University Press.

Gebhardt, A. and O. Hatzold (1974). "Numerically Controlled Machine Tools", in Nabseth and Ray 1974: 22–57.

Gemelli, Guiliana (ed.) (1998). *The Ford Foundation and Europe (1950s–1970s): Cross-Fertilisation of Learning in Social Sciences and Management*, Brussels, European Interuniversity Press.

Glucksmann, Miriam (1990). *Women Assemble: Women Workers and the New Industries in Interwar Britain*, London, Routledge.

Goldfield, Michael (1987). *The Decline of Organised Labor in the United States*, Chicago, University of Chicago Press.

Gospel, Howard F. (1992). *Markets, Firms and the Management of Labour in Modern Britain*, Cambridge, Cambridge University Press.

Gould, J.D. (1969). "Hypothetical history", *Economic History Review* 22/2: 195–207.

Grant, Robert M. (1996). "Toward a Knowledge-based Theory of the Firm", *Strategic Management Journal* 17 (Winter special issue): 109–22.

Grant, Wyn and David Marsh (1977). *The Confederation of British Industry*, London, Hodder.

Gregg, Paul and Jonathan Wadsworth (1995). "A Short History of labour Turnover, Job Tenure and Job Security, 1975–93", *Oxford Review of Economic Policy* 11: 73–90.

Griffiths, Brian (1973). "The Development of Restrictive Practices in the UK Monetary System", *Manchester School* XLI: 3–18.

Griliches, Zvi (1994). "Productivity, R&D and the Data Constraint", *American Economic Review* 84: 1–23.

Guest, David E. (1990). "Have British Workers been Working Harder in Thatcher's Britain? A Reconsideration of the Concept of Effort", *British Journal of Industrial Relations* 28: 293–312.

Guest, David E. and Philip Dewe (1991). "Company or Union? Which Wins Workers' Allegiances?", *British Journal of Industrial Relations* 29: 75–96.

Haigh, Thomas (2001). "Inventing Information Systems: The Systems Men and the Computer, 1950–69", *Business History Review* 75/1: 15–61.

Hamel, Gary and C.K. Prahalad (1996). *Competing for the Future*, Boston MA, Harvard Business School Press.

Hamilton, Ross (1995). "Despite the Best Intentions: The Evolution of the British Minicomputer Industry", *Business History* 38: 81–104.

Hancock, W.K. and M.M. Gowing (1949). *British War Economy*, London, HMSO and Longman.

Hanieski, John F. (1973). "The Airplane as an Economic Variable: Aspects of Technical Change in Aeronautics, 1903–55", *Technology and Culture* 14/4: 535–52.

Hannah, Leslie (1976). *The Rise of the Corporate Economy*, London, Methuen, 2nd edn 1983.

Harris, Howell (1982). *The Right to Manage: Industrial Relations Policies of American Big Business in the 1940s*, Madison, University of Wisconsin Press.

Harris, Howell (1985). "The Snares of Liberalism? Politicians, Bureaucrats and the Shaping of Federal Labour Relations Policy in the United State, ca. 1915–47", in Tolliday and Zeitlin 1985: 148–91.

Harris, Jose (1991). "Enterprise and Welfare States: A Comparative Perspective", in Terry Gourvish and Alan O'Day (eds) *Britain since 1945*, Basingstoke, Macmillan: 39–58.

Harrison, Mark (ed.) (1998). *The Economics of World War II: Six Great Powers in International Comparison*, Cambridge, Cambridge University Press.

Hartley, Keith (1996). "The Defence Economy", in Richard Coopey and Nicholas Woodward (eds) *Britain in the 1970s: The Troubled Economy*, London, UCL Press: 212–35.

Hasegawa, Shin (2004). "The Americanisation and Japanisation of Electronics firms in Postwar Japan", in Kudo *et al.* (eds) 2004a: 138–60.

Haynes, Michelle and Steve Thompson (2000). "Productivity, Employment and the 'IT paradox': Evidence from Financial Services", in Barrell *et al.* (eds) 2000: 93–116.

Hays, S., M.F.W. Hemming and G.F. Ray (1967). "The Office Machinery Industry in the UK", *National Institute Economic Review* 49: 52–74.

Hays, William Orchard (1984). "History of Mathematical Programming Systems", *Annals of the History of Computing* 6: 296–312.

Heath, Anthony and Sarah K. Macdonald (1987). "Social Change and the Future of the Left", *Political Quarterly* 58: 364–77.

Heims, Steve J. (1980). *John von Neumann and Norbert Wiener: From Mathematics to the Technologies of Life and Death*, Cambridge MA, MIT Press.

Henderson, P.D. (1952). "Development Councils: An Industrial Experiment", in Worswick and Ady 1952: 452–62.

Henderson, P.D. (1962). "Government and Industry", in Worswick and Ady 1962: 326–77.

Hendry, John (1987). "The Teashop Computer Manufacturer: J. Lyons, LEO and the Potential and Limits of High-tech Diversification", *Business History* 29/1: 73–103.

Herding, Richard (1972). *Job Control and Union Structure: A Study on Plant-level Industrial Conflict in the United States with a Comparison with West Germany*, Rotterdam, Rotterdam University Press.

Hill, Stephen (1991). "Why Quality Circles Failed but TQM Might Succeed", *British Journal of Industrial Relations* 29: 541–68.

Hinton, James (1994). *Shopfloor Citizens: Engineering Democracy in 1940s Britain*, Aldershot, Elgar.

Hirschman, Albert O. (1970). *Exit, Voice and Loyalty: Responses to Decline in Firms, Organizations and States*, Cambridge MA, Harvard University Press.

Hogan, Michael J. (1987). *The Marshall Plan: America, Britain and the Reconstruction of Western Europe, 1947–1952*, Cambridge, Cambridge University Press.

Hogan, Michael J. (1998). *A Cross of Iron: Harry S. Truman and the Origins of the National Security State*, Cambridge, Cambridge University Press.

Holland, Max (1989). *When the Machine Stopped: A Cautionary Tale from Industrial America*, Boston MA, Harvard Business School Press.

Holmes, A.R. and E.H. Green (1986). *Midland: 150 Years of Banking Business*, London, Batsford.

Horne, Alistair (1989). *Harold Macmillan, 1957–86: Volume II of the Official Biography*, London, Macmillan.

Horner, D. (1993). "The Road to Scarborough: Wilson, Labour and the Scientific Revolution", in R. Coopey, S. Fielding and N. Tiratsoo (eds) *The Wilson Governments, 1964–1970*, London, Pinter: 48–71.

Hounshell, David A. (1995). "Planning and Executing 'Automation' at Ford Motor Company, 1945–65: The Cleveland Engine Plant and its Consequences", in Shiomi and Wada 1995: 49–86.

Howell, David (1999). "Shut Your Gob! Trade Unions and the Labour Party, 1945–64", in Campbell *et al.* 1999a: 119–44.

Howson, Susan (1993) *British Monetary Policy, 1945–51*, Oxford: Clarendon Press.

Howson, Susan (1994). "Money and monetary policy in Britain, 1945–1990", in Floud and McCloskey 1994: 221–54.

Hunsacker, J.C. (1955). "Forty Years of Aeronautical Research", *Smithsonian Report for 1955*, Washington DC, Smithsonian Institution: 238–74.

Hunter, Laurie, Alan McGregor, John MacInnes and Alan Sproull (1993). "The 'Flexible Firm': Strategy and Segmentation", *British Journal of Industrial Relations* 31: 383–407.

Hyman, Richard (1993). "Praetorians and Proletarians: Unions and Industrial Relations", in Fyrth 1993: 165–94.

ICBH [Institute of Contemporary British History] (1988). "Symposium: The Trade Unions and the Fall of the Heath Government", *Contemporary Record* 2/1: 36–46.

Industrial Relations Journal (1988). 19/1, special issue on Japanisation.

Jacobsson, Staffan (1986). *Electronics and Industrial Policy: The Case of Computer Controlled Lathes*, London, Allen and Unwin.

James, B. (1989). *Trojan Horse: the Ultimate Japanese Challenge*, London, Mercury.

Jeremy, David J. (1998). *A Business History of Britain, 1900–1990s*, Oxford, Oxford University Press.

Johnson, Chalmers A. (1982). *MITI and the Japanese Miracle: The Growth of Industrial Policy, 1925–75*, Stanford, Stanford University Press.

Jones, Bryn (1985). "Controlling Production on the Shopfloor: The Role of State Administration and Regulation in the British and American Aerospace Industries", in Tolliday and Zeitlin 1985: 219–55.

Jones, Bryn (1991). "Technological Convergence and Limits to Managerial Control: Flexible Manufacturing Systems in Britain, the USA and Japan", in Tolliday and Zeitlin 1991: 231–55.

Jones, Russell (1987). *Wages and Employment Policy, 1936–1985*, London, Allen and Unwin.

Jorgenson, D. and K. Stiroh (1995). "Computers and Growth", *Economics of Innovation and New Technology* 3: 295–333.

Kamata, Satoshi (1983). *Japan in the Passing Lane: An Insider's Account of life in a Japanese Auto Factory*, London, Allen and Unwin.

Katz, Harry C. (1984). "The US Automobile Collective Bargaining System in Transition", *British Journal of Industrial Relations* 22/2: 205–17.

Katz, Richard (1998). *Japan the System that Soured: the Rise and Fall of the Japanese Economic Miracle*, Armonck, NY, M.E. Sharpe.

Kay, John (1993). *Foundations of Corporate Success*, Oxford, Oxford University Press.

Keefe, Jeffrey H. (1991). "Numerically Controlled Machine Tools and Worker Skills", *Industrial and Labor Relations Review* 44/3: 503–19.

Kelly, John (1999). "Social Democracy and Anti-Communism: Allan Flanders and British Industrial Relations in the Early Post-War Period", in Campbell *et al.* 1999: 192–221.

Kelly, Scott (2002). *The Myth of Mr. Butskell: The Politics of British Economic Policy, 1950–55*, Aldershot, Ashgate.

Kenney, Martin and Richard Florida (1988). "Beyond Mass Production: Production and the Labour Process in Japan", *Politics and Society* 16: 121–58.

Kessler, Sid and Fred Bayliss (1992). *Contemporary British Industrial Relations*, Basingstoke, Macmillan.

Kevles, Daniel J. (1975). "Scientists, the Military and the Control of Postwar Defense Research: The Case of the Research Board for National Security, 1944–46", *Technology and Culture* 16/1: 20–47.

Kinch, Nils (1995). "The Road from Dreams of Mass Production to Flexible Specialisation: American Influences on the Development of the Swedish Automobile Industry, 1920–39", in Shiomi and Wada 1995: 107–36.

Kipping, Matthias (1997). "Consultancies, Institutions and the Diffusion of Taylorism in Britain, Germany and France, 1920s to 1950s", *Business History* 39/4: 66–82.

Kipping, Matthias (1998). "'Operation Impact': Converting European Employers to the American Creed", in Kipping and Bjarnar 1998: 55–73.

Kipping, Matthias (1999). "American Management Consulting Companies in Western Europe, 1920 to 1990: Products, Reputation and Relationships", *Business History Review* 73/2: 190–220.

Kipping, Matthias (2000). "A Slow and Difficult Process: The Americanisation of the French Steel-Producing and Using Industries after the Second World War", in Zeitlin and Herrigel 2000: 209–35.

Kipping, Matthias and Ove Bjarnar (eds) (1998). *The Americanisation of European Business: The Marshall Plan and the Transfer of US Management Models*, London, Routledge.

Klingender, F.D. (1935). *The Condition of Clerical Labour in Britain*, London, Martin Lawrence.

Kochan, Thomas and Marc Weinstein (1994). "Recent Developments in US Industrial Relations", *British Journal of Industrial Relations* 32: 483–504.

Kogut, Bruce and Udo Zander (1992). "Knowledge of the Firm, Combinative Capabilities and the Replication of Technology", *Organisation Science* 3/3: 383–97.

Korpi, Walter and Michael Shalev (1979). "Strikes, industrial relations and class conflict in capitalist societies", *British Journal of Sociology* 30/2: 164–87.

Kudo, Akira, Matthias Kipping and Harm G. Schröter (eds) (2004a). *German and Japanese Business in the Boom Years: Transforming American Management and Technology Models*, London, Routledge.

Kudo, Akira, Matthias Kipping and Harm G. Schröter (2004b). "Americanisation: Historical and Conceptual Issues", in Kudo *et al.* 2004a: 1–29.

Kuisel, Richard F. (1981). *Capitalism and the State in Modern France*, Cambridge, Cambridge University Press.

Kunz, Diane B. (1991). *The Economic Diplomacy of the Suez Crisis*, Chapel Hill, University of North Carolina Press.

Kurtzman, Joel (1988). *The Decline and Crash of the American Economy*, New York, Norton.

Kynaston, David (2001). *The City of London*, volume IV. *A Club No More, 1945–2000*, London, Chatto and Windus.

Lamb, Richard (1995). *The Macmillan Years, 1957–63: The Emerging Truth*, London, John Murray.

Lane, C. (1988). "New Technology and Clerical Work", in Duncan Gallie (ed.) *Employment in Britain*, Oxford, Blackwell.

Langlois, Richard N. (1992). "External Economies and Economic Progress: The Case of the Microcomputer Industry", *Business History Review* 66: 1–50.

Larres, Klaus and Ann Lane (eds) (2001). *The Cold War: Essential Readings*, Oxford, Blackwell: 21–41.

Lave, Jean C. and Etienne Wenger (1991). *Situated Learning: Legitimate Peripheral Participation*, New York, Cambridge University Press.

Lazonick, William (1990). *Competitive Advantage on the Shop Floor*, Cambridge MA, Harvard University Press.

Lazonick, William (1991). *The Myth of the Market Economy*, Cambridge, Cambridge University Press.

Lazonick, William (2005). "The Innovative Firm", in Fagerberg *et al.* 2005: 29–55.

Lee, C.H. (1990). "Corporate Behaviour in Theory and History, 1: The Evolution of Theory", *Business History* 32/1: 17–31.

Leffler, Melvyn P. (1984). "The American Conception of National Security and the Beginnings of the Cold War, 1945–48", *American Historical Review* 89: 346–81.

Leffler, Melvyn P. (1992). "National Security and US Foreign Policy", in Melvyn P. Leffler and David S. Painter (eds) *Origins of the Cold War: an International History*, London, Routledge: 15–52.

Leffler, Melvyn P. (1994). *A Preponderance of Power: National Security, the Truman Administration and the Cold War*, Stanford CA, Stanford University Press.

Leffler, Melvyn P. (2001). "Economics, Power and National Security: Lessons of the Past", in Larres and Lane 2001: 21–41.

Leruez, Jacques (1975). *Economic Planning and Policies in Britain*, London, Martin Robertson.

Lewchuk, Wayne (1986). "The Motor Vehicle Industry", in Elbaum and Lazonick 1986: 135–61.

Lewchuk, Wayne (1987). *American Technology and the British Vehicle Industry*, Cambridge, Cambridge University Press.

Leyshon, Andrew and Jane Pollard (2000). "Geographies of Industrial Convergence: The Case of Retail Banking", *Transactions of the Institute of British Geographers* 25: 203–20.

Leyshon, Andrew and Nigel Thrift (1999). "Lists Come Alive: Electronic Systems of Knowledge and the Rise of Credit Scoring in Retail Banking", *Economy and Society* 28: 434–66.

Lichtenstein, Nelson (1982). *Labor's War at Home: The CIO in World War II*, Cambridge, Cambridge University Press.

Lichtenstein, Nelson (1983). "Conflict over Workers' Control: The Automobile Industry in World War II", in Michael H. Frisch and Daniel J. Walkowitz (eds)

Working Class America: Essays on Labour, Community and American Society, Chicago, University of Illinois Press: 284–311.

Lichtenstein, Nelson (1986). "Reutherism on the Shop Floor: Union Strategy and Shop-floor Conflict in the USA, 1946–70", in Tolliday and Zeitlin 1986: 121–43.

Lillrank, Paul (1995). "The Transfer of Management Innovations from Japan", *Organisation Studies* 16: 971–90.

Locke, Robert R. (1996). *The Collapse of the American Management Mystique,* New York, Oxford University Press.

Lockwood, David (1986). "Class, Status and Gender", in Rosemary Crompton and Michael Mann (eds) *Gender and Stratification,* Cambridge, Polity Press: 11–22.

Lockwood, David (1989). *The Blackcoated Worker: A Study in Class Consciousness,* Oxford, Clarendon Press, 1st edn. London, Allen and Unwin, 1958.

Loveman, G.W. (1994). "An Assessment of the Productivity Impact of Information Technology", in T.J. Allen and M.S. Scott Morton (eds) *Information Technology and the Corporation of the 1990s: Research Studies,* Cambridge MA, MIT Press: 84–110.

Lowe, Graham S. (1987). *Women in the Administrative Revolution: The Feminisation of Clerical Work,* Cambridge, Polity Press.

Lupton, Tom (1963). *On the Shopfloor: Two Studies of Workshop Organisation and Output,* Oxford, Pergamon.

Lyddon, Dave (1983). "Workplace Organisation in the British Car Industry. A Critique of Jonathan Zeitlin", *History Workshop* 15: 131–40.

Lyddon, Dave (1996). "The Car Industry, 1945–1979: Shop Stewards and Workplace Unionism", in Chris Wrigley (ed.) *A History of British Industrial Relations, 1939–1979: Industrial Relations in a Declining Economy,* Cheltenham, Elgar: 186–211.

Lynk, E.L. (1986). "On the Economics of the Oil Refining Industry in the UK", *Applied Economics* 18: 113–26.

Maddison, Angus (1991). *Dynamic Forces in Capitalist Development: A Long-run Comparative View,* Oxford, Oxford University Press.

Maddison, Angus (1995). *Monitoring the World Economy, 1820–1992,* Paris, OECD.

Maielli, Giuliano (2007). "Technical Change and Industrial Relations at Fiat, 1969–85: A Critical Re-examination", in Booth and Melling 2007.

Malerba, Franco (2005). "Sectoral Systems of Innovation: How and Why Innovation Differs across Sectors", in Fagerberg *et al.* 2005: 380–406.

Mansfield, Edwin (1993). "The Diffusion of Flexible Manufacturing Systems in Japan, Europe and the United States", *Management Science* 39: 149–59.

Marrison, Andrew (1996). *British Business and Protection, 1903–1932,* Oxford, Clarendon Press.

Marsden, David (1983). "Wage Structure", in Bain 1983: 263–90.

Marsden, David, Timothy Morris, Paul Willman and Stephen Wood (1985). *The Car Industry: Labour Relations and Industrial Adjustment,* London, Tavistock.

Marshall, J.N. and R. Richardson (1996). "The Impact of 'Telemediated' Services on Corporate Structures: The Example of 'Branchless' Retail Banking in Britain", *Environment and Planning A* 28: 1843–58.

Mason, Geoff, Brent Kellner and Karin Wagner (2000). "Productivity and Service Quality in Banking: Commercial Lending in Britain, the United States and Germany", in Barrell *et al.* 2000: 117–48.

Matthews, R.C.O., C.H. Feinstein and J.C. Odling-Smee (1982). *British Economic Growth, 1856–1973*, Oxford, Clarendon Press.

Maxcy, George and Aubrey Silberston (1959). *The Motor Industry*, London, Allen and Unwin.

Mayes, David and Soterios Soteri (1994). "Does Manufacturing Matter?", in Tony Buxton, Paul Chapman and Paul Temple (eds) *Britain's Economic Performance*, London, Routledge: 373–96.

McCarthy, W.E.J. and S.R. Parker (1968). *Shop Stewards and Workshop Relations*, Royal Commission on Trade Unions and Employers' Associations, Research Paper 10, London, HMSO.

McGlade, Jacqueline (1998). "From Business Reform to Production Drive: The Transformation of US Technical Assistance to Western Europe", in Kipping and Bjarnar 1998: 18–34.

McGlade, Jacqueline (2000). "Americanisation: Ideology or Process? The Case of the United States Technical Assistance and Productivity Programme", in Zeitlin and Herrigel 2000: 53–75.

McIlroy, John and Alan Campbell (1999). "The High Tide of Trade Unionism: Mapping Industrial Politics, 1964–79", in McIlroy *et al.* 1999: 93–130.

McIlroy, John, Alan Campbell and Nina Fishman (1999b). "Introduction: Approaching Postwar Trade Unionism", in Campbell *et al.* 1999a: 1–19.

McIlroy, John, Nina Fishman and Alan Campbell (eds) (1999). *British Trade Unions and Industrial Politics: The High Tide of Trade Unionism, 1964–79*, Aldershot, Gower.

McKenney, James L., Duncan C. Copeland and Richard O. Mason (1995). *Waves of Change: Business Evolution through Information Technology*, Boston MA, Harvard Business School Press.

McKinlay, Alan and Joseph Melling (1999). "The Shopfloor Politics of Production: Work, Power and Authority Relations in British Engineering, c.1945–57", in Campbell *et al.* 1999a: 222–41.

McNally, Fiona (1979). *Women for Hire: A Study of the Female Office Worker*, London, Macmillan.

Melling, Joseph (1996). "Management, Labour and the Politics of Productivity: Strategies and Struggles in Britain, Germany and Sweden", in Melling and McKinlay 1996: 1–24.

Melling, Joseph (2007). "Fordism and the Foreman: Labour Relations and Supervisory Trade Unionism in the American and British Automobile Companies, c., 1939–1970", in Booth and Melling 2007.

Melman, Seymour (1958). *Decision-Making and Productivity*, Oxford, Blackwell.

Mensch, Gerhard (1979). *Stalemate in Technology: Innovations Overcome the Depression*, New York, Ballinger.

Mercer, Helen (1995). *Constructing a Competitive Order: The Hidden Story of British Antitrust Policies*, Cambridge, Cambridge University Press.

Mercer, Helen, Neil Rollings and Jim Tomlinson (eds) (1992) *Labour Governments and Private Industry: The Experience of 1945–1951*, Edinburgh, Edinburgh University Press.

Merchant, M.E. (1973). "The Future of Batch Production [and Discussion]", *Philosophical Transactions of the Royal Society of London. Series A, Mathematical and Physical Sciences* 275/1250: 357–72.

Meyer, David G. and William N. Cooke (1993). "US Labour Relations in Transition: Emerging Strategies and Company Performance", *British Journal of Industrial Relations* 31: 531–52.

Meyer, J.R. and G. Herregat (1974). "The Basic Oxygen Steel Process", in Nabseth and Ray 1974: 146–99.

Middlemas, R.K. (1979). *Politics in Industrial Society: The Experience of the British System since 1911*, London, Andre Deutsch.

Middlemas, R.K. (1986). *Power, Competition and the State, Volume 1: Britain in Balance, 1940–61*, Basingstoke, Macmillan.

Middlemas, R.K. (1990). *Power, Competition and the State, Volume 2: Threats to the Postwar Settlement in Britain, 1961–74*, London, Macmillan.

Millward, Robert (2004). "The Rise of the Service Economy", in Roderick Floud and Paul Johnson (eds) *The Cambridge Economic History of Modern Britain*, volume 3: *Structural Change and Growth, 1939–2000*, Cambridge, Cambridge University Press, 3rd edn: 238–66.

Milward, Alan S. (1977). *War, Economy and Society, 1939–1945*, London, Allen Lane.

Milward, Alan S. (1984). *The Reconstruction of Western Europe, 1945–51*, London, Methuen.

Milward, Alan S. and George Brennan (1996). *Britain's Place in the World: A Historical Enquiry into Import Controls, 1945–60*, London, Routledge.

Mobley, Lou and Kate McKeown (1989). *Beyond IBM*, Harmondsworth, Penguin Books.

Moggridge, D.N. (ed.) (1979). *The Collected Writings of John Maynard Keynes*. Volume XXIV, *Activities, 1944–1946: The Transition to Peace*, London, Macmillan for the Royal Economic Society.

Moos, S. (1957). "The Scope of Automation", *Economic Journal* **67**: 26–39.

Moran, Michael (1986). *The Politics of Banking: The Strange Case of Competition and Credit Control*, Basingstoke, Macmillan, 2nd edn.

Morgan, Carol E. (2001). *Women Workers and Gender Identities, 1835–1913: The Cotton and Metal Industries in England*, London, Routledge.

Morgan, Kenneth O. (1984). *Labour in Power, 1945–1951*, Oxford, Clarendon.

Morishima, Michio (1982). *Why has Japan "Succeeded"? Western Technology and the Japanese Ethos*, Cambridge, Cambridge University Press.

Morrison, Catherine J. (1997). "Assessing the Productivity of Information Technology Equipment in US Manufacturing Industries", *Review of Economics and Statistics* **79**: 471–81.

Mowery, D.C. (2003). "50 years of Business Computing: LEO to Linux", *Journal of Strategic Innovation Systems* **12**: 295–308.

Mroczkowski, Tomasz (1984). "Is the American Labour-management Relationship Changing?", *British Journal of Industrial Relations* **22**: 47–62.

Mumford, Lewis (1934). *Technics and Civilization*, London, Routledge and Kegan Paul.

Nabseth, L. and G.F. Ray (1974). *The Diffusion of New Industrial Processes: An International Study*, Cambridge, Cambridge University Press.

Nelson, Richard R. (1988). "Institutions Supporting Technical Change in the United States", in Dosi *et al.* 1988: 312–29.

Nelson, Richard R. and S. Winter (1982). *An Evolutionary Theory of Economic Change*, Cambridge MA, Belknap Press.

Neuschel, Richard F. (1950). *Streamlining Business Procedures*, New York, McGraw-Hill.

Nevins, Allan and Frank T. Hill (1962). *Ford: Decline and Rebirth, 1932–62*, New York, Scrivener.

Nicholas, Tom (2004). "Enterprise and Management", in Floud and Johnson 2004a: 227–52.

Nichols, Theo (1986). *The British Labour Question: A New Look at Workers and Productivity in Manufacturing*, London, Routledge.

Noble, David F. (1979). "Social Choice in Machine Design: The Case of Automatically Controlled Machine Tools", in A. Zimbalist (ed.) *Case Studies in the Labor Process*, New York, Monthly Review Press: 18–50.

Noble, David F. (1984). *Forces of Production: A Social History of Industrial Automation*, New York, Oxford University Press.

Nolan, Mary (1994). *Visions of Modernity: American Business and the Modernisation of Germany*, New York, Oxford University Press.

Nonaka, Ikujiro and Hirotaka Takeuchi (1995). *The Knowledge-creating Company: How Japanese Companies Create the Dynamics of Innovation*, New York, Oxford University Press.

Nottage, Raymond (1954). "Organisation and Methods in the Smaller Public Authority", *Public Administration* **XXXII**: 143–64.

Nottage, Raymond (1955). "O&M in the Nationalised Industries", *Public Administration* **XXXIII**: 395–400.

O'Brien, James A. (1968). *The Impact of Computers in Banking*, Boston MA, Bankers' Publishing Company.

Okimoto, Daniel (1989). *Between MITI and the Market: Japanese Policy for High Technology*, Stanford CA, Stanford University Press.

Okumura, A. (1989). "The Globalisation of Japanese Companies", in K. Shibagaki, M. Trevor and T. Abo (eds) *Japanese and European Management: Their International Adaptability*, Tokyo, University of Tokyo Press: 31–40.

Oliver, Nick and Barry Wilkinson (1989). "Japanese Manufacturing Techniques and Personnel and Industrial Relations Practice in Britain: Evidence and Implications", *British Journal of Industrial Relations* **27**: 73–91.

Oliver, Nick and Barry Wilkinson (1992). *The Japanisation of British Industry: New Developments in the 1990s*, Oxford, Blackwell.

Olson, Mancur (1996). "The Varieties of Eurosclerosis: The Rise and Decline of Nations since 1982", in Crafts and Toniolo 1996: 73–94.

Owen, Geoffrey (1999). *From Empire to Europe: The Decline and Revival of British Industry since the Second World War*, London, Harper-Collins.

Pagnamenta, Peter and Richard Overy (1984). *All Our Working Lives*, London, BBC.

Paish, F.W. (1966). *Studies in an Inflationary Economy*, London, Macmillan.

Panitch, Leo (1976). *Social Democracy and Industrial Militancy: The Labour Party, the Trade Unions and Incomes Policy, 1945–1974*, Cambridge, Cambridge University Press.

Paqué, Karl-Heinz (1996). "Why the 1950s and not the 1920s? Olsonian and non-Olsonian Interpretations of Two Decades of German Economic History", in Crafts and Toniolo 1996: 95–106.

Parkin, Frank (1971). *Class Inequality and Political Order: Social Stratification in Capitalist and Communist Societies*, London, MacGibbon and Kee.

Pascale, Richard Tanner (1996). "The Honda Effect", *California Management Review* **38**: 80–91, 112–17.

Pascale, Richard Tanner and Anthony G. Athos (1982). *The Art of Japanese Management*, Harmondsworth, Penguin.

Patrick, Hugh and Henry Rosovsky (1976). *Asia's New Giant*, Washington DC, Brookings Institute.

Pavitt, Keith and Luc Soete (1980). "Innovative Activities and Export Shares: Some Comparisons Between Industries and Countries", in Keith Pavitt (ed.) *Technical Innovation and British Economic Performance*, London, Macmillan.

Peck, Merton J. (1968). "Science and Technology", in Richard E. Caves (ed.) *Britain's Economic Prospects*, London, Allen and Unwin: 448–84.

Peters, Thomas J. and Robert H. Waterman (1982). *In Search of Excellence: Lessons from America's Best-run Companies*, New York, Harper and Row.

Pettigrew, Andrew M. (1985). *The Awakening Giant: Continuity and Change in Imperial Chemical Industries*, Oxford, Blackwell.

Pimlott, Ben (1992). *Harold Wilson*, London, Harper-Collins.

Piore, Michael J. (1968). "The Impact of the Labour Market upon the Design and Selection of Productive Techniques within the Plant", *Quarterly Journal of Economics* 82/4: 602–20.

Piore, Michael J. and Charles F. Sabel (1984). *The Second Industrial Divide: Possibilities for Prosperity*, New York, Basic Books.

Polanyi, Michael (1966). *The Tacit Dimension*, Garden City, NY, Doubleday.

Pollard, Sidney (1989). *Britain's Prime and Britain's Decline: the British Economy, 1870–1914*, London, Edward Arnold.

Porter, Michael E. (1990). *The Competitive Advantage of Nations*, London, Macmillan.

Porter, Michael E. and Victor E. Millar (1985). How information Gives You Competitive Advantage", *Harvard Business Review* 63/4: 149–74.

Posner, Michael and Andrew Steer (1978). "Price Competitiveness and the Performance of Manufacturing Industry", in Frank Blackaby (ed.) *De-industrialisation*, London, Heinemann: 141–65.

Powell, Walter W. and Stine Grodal (2005). "Networks of Innovators", in Fagerberg *et al.* 2005: 56–85.

Prahalad, C.K. and Gary Hamel (1990). "The core competence of the corporation", *Harvard Business Review* 68: 79–91.

Prais, S.J. (1981). *Productivity and Industrial Structure: A Statistical Study of Manufacturing Industry in Britain, Germany and the United States*, Cambridge, Cambridge University Press.

Prandy, K., A. Stewart and R.M. Blackburn (1983). *White Collar Unionism*, London, Macmillan.

Pratten, C.F. (1976). *Labour Productivity Differentials within International Companies*, Cambridge, Cambridge University Press.

Pressnell, L.S. (1986). *External Economic Policy since the War*, vol. 3: *The Postwar Financial Settlement*, London, HMSO.

Price, R. (1983). "White Collar Unions: Growth, Character and Attitudes in the 1970s", in R. Hyman and R. Price (eds) *The New Working Class? White Collar Workers and their Organisations*, London, Macmillan: 147–83.

Public Administration (1951). "O&M in Local Government", *Public Administration* XXIX: 1–2.

Public Administration (1954). "Coventry and Organisation and Methods", *Public Administration* XXXII: 52–94.

Pugh, Emerson R., Lyle R. Johnson and John H. Palmer (1991). *IBM's 360 and Early 370 Systems*, Cambridge MA, MIT Press.

Purcell, John (1991). "The Rediscovery of the Management Prerogative: The Management of Labour Relations in the 1980s", *Oxford Review of Economic Policy* 7: 33–43.

Purcell, John and Keith Sisson (1983). "Strategies and Practice in the Management of Industrial Relations", in Bain 1983: 95–120.

Ramsden, John (1977). "From Churchill to Heath", in Norman Gash, Donald Southgate, David Dilks and John Ramsden (ed. Lord Butler), *The Conservatives: A History from their Origins to 1965*, London, Allen and Unwin.

Ranieri, Ruggero (1993). "Inside or Outside the Magic Circle? The Italian and British Steel Industries Face to Face with the Schuman Plan and the European Coal and Steel Community", in Alan Milward, Frances M.B. Lynch, Ruggero Ranieri, Frederico Romero and Vibeke Sørensen, *The Frontier of National Sovereignty: History and Theory, 1945–1992*, London, Routledge: 117–54.

Ranieri, Ruggero (1998). "Learning from America: The Re-modelling of Italy's Public Sector Steel Industry in the 1950s and 1960s", in Kipping and Bjarnar 1998: 208–28.

Rayback, Joseph G. (1966). *A History of American Labor: Expanded and Updated*, New York, Free Press.

Reader, W.J. (1975). *Imperial Chemical Industries: A History*. Volume 2: *The First Quarter Century, 1926–1952*, London, Oxford University Press.

Redmond, Kent C. and Thomas M. Smith (1980). *Project Whirlwind: The History of a Pioneer Computer*, Bedford MA, Digital Press.

Reich, Robert B. (1992). *The Work of Nations: Preparing Ourselves for 21st-century Capitalism*, New York, Knopf.

Renshaw, Patrick (1991). *American Labour and Consensus Capitalism*, Basingstoke, Macmillan.

Revell, Jack (1983). *Banking and Electronic Fund Transfers: A Study of the Implications*, Paris, OECD.

Rhys, D.G. (1972). *The Motor Industry: An Economic Survey*, London, Butterworth.

Richter, Irving (1984). "The Decline of Organised Labour from 1945", *Papers in the Social Sciences* 4.

Ringe, Astrid and Neil Rollings (2000). "Responding to Relative Decline: The Creation of the National Economic Development Council", *Economic History Review* 53/2: 331–53.

Roach, S.S. (1991)."Services under Siege: The Restructuring Imperative", *Harvard Business Review* 69/5: 82–9.

Rockoff, Hugh (1998). "The United States: From Ploughshares to Swords", in Harrison 1998: 81–121.

Roeber, Joseph (1975). *Social Change at Work: The ICI Weekly Staff Agreement*, London, Duckworth.

Rogers, Everett M. (1995). *Diffusion of Innovations*, New York, Free Press, 4th edn.

Rogow, A.A. and Peter Shore (1955). *The Labour Government and British Industry*, Ithaca, NY, Cornell University Press.

Rollings, Neil (1988). "British Budgetary Policy, 1945–54: A Keynesian Revolution?", *Economic History Review* 41/2: 283–98.

Rollings, Neil (1994). "Poor Mr. Butskell: A Short Life Wrecked by Schizophrenia?", *Twentieth Century British History* 5/2: 183–205.

Rolt, L.T.C. (1965). *Tools for the Job: A Short History of Machine Tools*, London, Batsford.

Rose, E. and T. Wooley (1992). "Shifting Sands? Trade Unions and Productivity at Rover Cars", *Industrial Relations Journal* **23**: 257–67.

Rose, Mary E. (2000). *Firms, Networks and Business Values: The British and American Cotton Industries since 1750*, Cambridge, Cambridge University Press.

Rosen, Michael and Jack Baroudi (1992). "Computer-based Technology and the Emergence of New Forms of Managerial Control", in Andrew Sturdy, David Knights and Hugh Willmott, eds. *Skill and Consent. Contemporary Studies in the Labour Process*, London, Routledge: 213–34.

Rosenberg, Nathan (1994). *Exploring the Black Box: Technology, Economics and History*, Cambridge, Cambridge University Press.

Routh, Guy (1980). *Occupation and Pay in Great Britain, 1906–1979*, London, Macmillan.

Ryle, Gilbert (1949). *The Concept of the Mind*, London, Hutchinson.

Sabel, Charles and Jonathan Zeitlin (1985). "Historical Alternatives to Mass Production: Politics, Markets and Technology in Nineteenth Century Industrialisation", *Past and Present* **108**: 133–76.

Sampson, Anthony (1967). *Macmillan: A Study in Ambiguity*, Harmondsworth, Penguin.

Samuels, Richard J. (1987). *The Business of the Japanese State: Energy Markets in Comparative and Historical Perspective*, Ithaca, Cornell University Press.

Saul, S.B. (1960). "The American Impact on British Industry, 1895–1914", *Business History* **3**: 19–38.

Saunders, Christopher (1978). *Engineering in Britain, West Germany and France: Some Statistical Comparisons of Structure and Competitiveness*, Falmer, University of Sussex European Research Centre.

Sayers, R.S. (1956). *Financial Policy, 1939–1945*, London, HMSO and Longman.

Schenk, Catherine R. (1994). *Britain and the Sterling Area: From Devaluation to Convertibility in the 1950s*, London, Routledge.

Schils, Edward B. (1963). *Automation and Industrial Relations*, New York, Holt, Rinehart and Winston.

Scientific American (1952). Special issue on automatic control (September).

Scranton, Philip (1997). *Endless Novelty: Specialty Production and American Industrialisation, 1865–1925*, Princeton, Princeton University Press.

Searle, G.R. (1971). *The Quest for National Efficiency: A Study in British Politics and Political Thought*, Oxford, Basil Blackwell.

Seldon, Anthony (1981). *Churchill's Indian Summer: The Conservative Government, 1951–55*, Sevenoaks, Hodder and Stoughton.

Shani, A.B., Robert M. Grant, R. Krishnan and Eric Thompson (1992). "Advanced Manufacturing Systems and Organisational Choice: A Sociotechnical System Approach", *California Management Review* **34**: 91–111.

Shanks, Michael (1961). *The Stagnant Society*, Harmondsworth, Penguin.

Sherry, Michael S. (1977). *Preparing for the Next War: American Plans for Postwar Defense, 1941–45*, New Haven, Yale University Press.

Sherwin, Martin J. (1973). "The Atomic Bomb and the Origins of the Cold War: US Atomic Energy Policy and Diplomacy, 1941–45", *American Historical Review* **78**: 945–68.

Shiomi, Haruhito and Kazuo Wada (eds) (1995). *Fordism Transformed: The Development of Production Methods in the Automobile Industry*, Oxford, Oxford University Press.

Shonfield, Andrew (1958). *British Economic Policy Since the War*, Harmondsworth, Penguin.

Sichel, Daniel E. (1997). "The Productivity Slowdown: Is a Growing Unmeasurable Sector the Culprit?", *Review of Economics and Statistics* **79**: 367–70.

Siebert, W.S. and J.T. Addison (1991). "Internal Labour Markets: Causes and Consequences", *Oxford Review of Economic Policy* **7**: 76–92.

Silverstone, Rosalie (1976). "Office Work for Women: An Historical Review", *Business History* **18**: 98–110.

Sisson, Keith (1993). "In Search of HRM", *British Journal of Industrial Relations* **32**: 201–10.

Sisson, Keith and William Brown (1983). "Industrial Relations in the Private Sector: Donovan Revisited", in Bain 1983: 139–54.

Slichter, Sumner H. (1941). *Union Policies and Industrial Management*, Washington DC, Brookings Institution.

Smith, A.D. (1989). "New Measures of British Service Outputs", *National Institute Economic Review* **128**: 75–88.

Smith, Harold (ed.) (1986). *War and Social Change: British Society in the Second World War*, Manchester, Manchester University Press.

Smith, Keith (1984). *The British Economic Crisis: Its Past and Future*, Harmondsworth, Penguin.

Smith, Thomas M. (1976). "Project Whirlwind: An Unorthodox Development Project", *Technology and Culture* **17**/3: 447–64.

Sobel, Robert (1981). *IBM: Colossus in Transition*, London, Sidgwick and Jackson.

Soffer, Jonathan (2001). "The National Association of Manufacturers and the Militarization of American Conservatism", *Business History Review* **75** (Winter): 775–805.

Starkey, Ken and Alan McKinlay (1989). "Beyond Fordism? Strategic Choice and Labour Relations in Ford UK", *Industrial Relations Journal* **20**: 93–100.

Stephenson, Carol (1996). The Different Experience of Trade Unionism in Two Japanese Transplants", in Ackers *et al.* 1996a: 210–39.

Stern, Nancy (1981). *From ENIAC to UNIVAC: An Appraisal of the Eckert-Mauchly Computers*, Bedford MA, Digital Press.

Stern, Nancy (1982). "The Eckert-Mauchly Computers: Conceptual Triumphs, Commercial Tribulations", *Technology and Culture* **23**/4: 569–82.

Stevens, Richard (1999). "Cold War Politics: Communism and Anti-Communism in Trade Unions", in Campbell *et al.* 1999: 168–91.

Stewart, A., K. Prandy and R.M. Blackburn (1980). *Social Stratification and Occupations*, London, Macmillan.

Stout, D.K. (1976). *International Price Competitiveness, Non-price Factors in International Trade*, London, NEDO.

Strange, Roger (1993). *Japanese Manufacturing Investment in Europe: Its Impact on the UK Economy*, London Routledge.

Strange, Susan (1971). *Sterling and British Policy: A Political Study of an International Currency in Decline*, London, Oxford University Press.

Supple, Barry (1962). "The Uses of Business History", *Business History* **4**/2: 81–90.

Supple, Barry (1994). "British Economic Decline since 1945", in Floud and McCloskey 1994: 318–46.

Taylor, Robert (1993). *The Trade Union Question in British Politics: Government and the Unions since 1945*, Oxford, Blackwell.

Taylor, Robert (1997). "The Heath Government and Industrial Relations: Myth and Reality", in Stuart Ball and Anthony Seldon (eds) *The Heath Government, 1970–74*, Harlow, Longman: 161–90.

Taylor, Robert (1999). "What are we here for? George Woodcock and trade union reform", in McIlroy *et al.* 1999: 187–215.

Taylor, Robert (2000). *The TUC: From the General Strike to New Unionism*, Maidenhead, Palgrave.

Temin, Peter (2002). "The Golden Age of European Growth Reconsidered", *Review of European Economic History* 6: 3–22.

Terry, Michael (1983). "Shop Steward Development and Managerial Strategies", in Bain 1983: 67–91.

Thompson, Paul (1989). *The Nature of Work: An Introduction to Debates on the Labour Process*, London, Macmillan, 2nd edn.

Thoms, David and Tom Donnelly (1985). *The Motor Car Industry in Coventry since the 1890s*, Beckenham, Croom Helm.

Thorpe, D.R. (1989). *Selwyn Lloyd*, London, Jonathan Cape.

Tiratsoo, Nick (1995). "Standard Motors and the Postwar Malaise of British Management", in Youssef Cassis, Francois Crouzet and Terry Gourvish (eds) *Management and Business Practice in Britain and France: The Age of the Corporate Economy*, Oxford, Clarendon Press: 88–108.

Tiratsoo, Nick (1998). "What you need is a Harvard: American Influence on British Management Education, c. 1945–65", in T.R. Gourvish and N. Tiratsoo (eds) *Missionaries and Managers: American Influences on European Management Education, 1945–60*, Manchester, Manchester University Press: 140–56.

Tiratsoo, Nick (1999). "Cinderellas at the Ball: Production Managers in British Manufacturing, 1945–80", *Contemporary British History* 13/3: 105–20.

Tiratsoo, Nick (2003). "Materials handling in British industry: anatomy of a manufacturing fundamental", *Business History* 45/4: 52–72.

Tiratsoo, Nick and Jim Tomlinson (1993). *Industrial Efficiency and State Intervention: Labour, 1939–51*, London Routledge.

Tiratsoo, Nick and Jim Tomlinson (1997). "Exporting the 'Gospel of Productivity': US Technical Assistance and British Industry, 1945–60", *Business History Review* 71: 41–81.

Tiratsoo, Nick and Jim Tomlinson (1998a). "Americanisation beyond the Mass Production Paradigm: The Case of British Industry", in Kipping and Bjarnar 1998: 115–32.

Tiratsoo, Nick and Jim Tomlinson (1998b). *The Conservatives and Industrial Efficiency: Thirteen Wasted Years?*, London, Routledge.

Tiratsoo, Nick and T.R. Gourvish (1996). "'Making it like in Detroit': British Managers and American Productivity Methods, 1945–c.1965", *Business and Economic History* 25: 206–16.

Titmuss, R.M. (1950). *Problems of Social Policy*, London, HMSO and Longman.

Tolliday, Steven (1985). "Government, Employers and Shopfloor Organisation in the British Motor Industry, 1939–69", in Tolliday and Zeitlin 1985: 108–47.

Tolliday, Steven (1986). "High Tide and After: Coventry Engineering Workers and Shopfloor Bargaining, 1945–80", in Bill Lancaster and Tony Mason (eds) *Life and Labour in a Twentieth Century City: The Experience of Coventry*, Coventry, Cryfield Press: 204–45.

Tolliday, Steven (1991). "Ford and 'Fordism' in Postwar Britain: Enterprise Management and the control of Labour, 1937–87", in Tolliday and Zeitlin 1991: 81–114.

Tolliday, Steven (2000). "Transplanting the American Model? US Automobile Companies and the Transfer of Technology and Management to Britain, France and Germany, 1928–1962", in Zeitlin and Herrigel 2000: 76–119.

Tolliday, Steven and Jonathan Zeitlin (eds) (1985). *Shopfloor Bargaining and the State: Historical and Comparative Perspectives*, Cambridge, Cambridge University Press.

Tolliday, Steven and Jonathan Zeitlin (eds) (1986a). *The Automobile Industry and its Workers: Between Fordism and Flexibility*, Cambridge, Polity Press.

Tolliday, Steven and Jonathan Zeitlin (1986b). "Introduction: Between Fordism and Flexibility", in Tolliday and Zeitlin 1986a: 1–25.

Tolliday, Steven and Jonathan Zeitlin (1986c). "Shop-floor Bargaining, Contract Unionism and Job Control: An Anglo American Comparison", in Tolliday and Zeitlin 1986a: 99–120.

Tolliday, Steven and Jonathan Zeitlin (eds) (1991). *The Power to Manage? Employers and Industrial Relations in Comparative-Historical Perspective*, London, Routledge.

Tomayko, James E. (1983). "The Stored-Program Concept: National Computer Conference, Houston, Texas, June 9, 1982", *Technology and Culture* **24**/4: 660–3.

Tomlins, Christopher L. (1985). *The State and the Unions: Labor Relations, Law, and the Organised Labor Movement in America*, New York, Cambridge University Press.

Tomlinson, Jim (1991a). "The 1945 Labour Government and the Trade Unions", in Nick Tiratsoo (ed.) *The Attlee Years*, London: Pinter: 90–105.

Tomlinson, Jim (1991b). "The Failure of the Anglo-American Council on Productivity", *Business History* **33**: 82–92.

Tomlinson, Jim (1994a). *Government and the Enterprise since 1900*, Oxford, Oxford University Press.

Tomlinson, Jim (1994b). "The Politics of Economic Measurement: The Rise of the 'Productivity Problem' in Britain in the 1940s", in A.G. Hopwood and P. Miller (eds) *Accounting as a Social and Institutional Practice*, Cambridge, Cambridge University Press: 168–89.

Tomlinson, Jim (1996). "Inventing 'Decline': The Falling Behind of the British Economy in the Postwar Years", *Economic History Review* **49**/4: 731–57.

Tomlinson, Jim (1997a). "Correlli Barnett's History: The Case of Marshall Aid", *Twentieth Century British History* **8**: 222–38.

Tomlinson, Jim (1997b). *Democratic Socialism and Economic Policy: The Attlee Years, 1945–51*, Cambridge, Cambridge University Press.

Tomlinson, Jim (2001). *The Politics of Decline: Understanding Postwar Britain*, Harlow, Longman.

Trevor, M. and I. Christie (1988). *Manufacturers and Suppliers in Britain and Japan: Competitiveness and the Growth of Small Firms*, London, Policy Studies Institute.

Tsuru, Shigeto (1993) *Japan's Capitalism: Creative Defeat and Beyond*, Cambridge, Cambridge University Press.

Tuke, A.W. and R.J.H. Gillman (1972). *Barclays Bank Limited, 1926–1969*, London, Barclays Bank.

Turnbull, Paul (1986). "The Japanisation of Production and Industrial Relations at Lucas Electrical", *Industrial Relations Journal* **17**: 193–206.

Turner, Graham (1971a). *The Leyland Papers*, London, Eyre and Spottiswoode.

Turner, Graham (1971b). *Business in Britain*, Harmondsworth, Penguin.

Turner, H.A., Garfield Clack and Geoffrey Roberts (1967). *Labour Relations in the Motor Industry: A Study of Industrial Unrest and an International Comparison*, London, Allen and Unwin.

Turner, Louis, A. Asakura, R. Hild, M. Hodges, R-D. Mayer, Y. Miyanaga, K. Tomisawa and M. Toriihara (1987). *Industrial Collaboration with Japan*, Chatham House Papers, 34, London, Routledge.

Tweedale, Geoffrey (1987). *Sheffield Steel and America*, Cambridge, Cambridge University Press.

Tweedale, Geoffrey (1992). "Marketing in the Second Industrial Revolution: A Case Study of the Ferranti Computer Group, 1949–63", *Business History* **34**/1: 96–127.

Ueda, Hirofumi (2004). "Americanisation with the Japanese Supplier System in the Japanese Automobile Industry, 1950–65", in Kudo *et al.* (eds) 2004a: 93–115.

Vaizey, John (1974). *The History of British Steel*, London, Weidenfeld and Nicolson.

Vig, N. (1968). *Science and Technology in British Politics*, Oxford, Pergamon.

Vinen, Richard C. (1991). *The Politics of French Business, 1936–1945*, Cambridge, Cambridge University Press.

Vries, M.G. de (1987). *Balance of Payments Adjustment, 1945–1986: The IMF Experience*, Washington, IMF.

Walker, Charles R. (1950). *Steeltown: An Industrial Case History of the Conflict Between Progress and Security*, New York, Harper and Brothers.

Walker, Charles R. (1957). *Toward the Automatic Factory: A Case Study of Men and Machines*, New Haven, Yale University Press.

Wardley, Peter (2000). "The Commercial Banking Industry and its Part in the Emergence of the Corporate Economy in Britain before 1940", *Journal of Industrial History* **3**: 71–97.

Watt, D.C. (1984). "Britain, the United States and the Opening of the Cold War", in Ritchie Ovendale (ed.) *The Foreign Policy of the British Labour Governments, 1945–51*, Leicester, Leicester University Press: 43–60.

Weiss, Andrew (1984). "Simple Truths of Japanese Manufacturing", *Harvard Business Review* **62**/4: 119–25.

Wheelwright, Steven C. (1981). "Japan: Where Operations really are Strategic", *Harvard Business Review* **59**/4: 67–74.

Whelan, Karl (2001). "Computers, Obsolescence and Productivity", *Review of Economics and Statistics* **84**: 445–61.

Whisler, Timothy R. (1995). "Design, Manufacture and Quality Control of Niche Products: The British and Japanese Experiences", in Shiomi and Wada 1995: 87–106.

Whisler, Timothy R. (1999). *The British Motor Industry, 1945–1994: A Case Study in Industrial Design*, Oxford, Oxford University Press.

Whybrow, R. (1989). *Britain Speaks Out, 1937–87: A Social History as Seen Through the Gallup Data*, Basingstoke, Macmillan.

Wiener, Norbert (1947). *Cybernetics: or Control and Communication in the Animal and the Machine*, New York, Wiley.

Wiener, Norbert (1950). *The Human Use of Human Beings: Cybernetics and Society*, Boston, Houghton Mifflin.

Wiener, Norbert (1953). "The Automatic Factory", *Mechanical Engineering* **184**.

Wigham, Eric (1961). *What's Wrong with the Unions?*, Harmondsworth, Penguin.

Wigham, Eric (1973). *The Power to Manage: A History of the Engineering Employers' Federation*, London, Macmillan.

Wilkie, Tom (1991). *British Science and British Politics Since 1945*, Oxford, Blackwell.

Wilkins, Mira (1974). *The Maturing of Multinational Enterprise: American Business Abroad from 1914 to 1970*, Cambridge, MA, Harvard University Press.

Wilkinson, Barry (1983). *The Shopfloor Politics of New Production Technology*, London, Heinemann.

Wilks, Stephen (1984). *Industrial Policy and the Motor Industry*, Manchester, Manchester University Press.

Williams, Karel, Colin Haslam, Sukhdev Johal and John Williams (1994). *Cars: Analysis, History, Cases*, Oxford, Berghahn Books.

Williams, Karel, John Williams and Dennis Thomas (1983). *Why are the British bad at Manufacturing?*, London, Routledge.

Williams, Karel, John Williams and Colin Haslam (1987a). *The Breakdown of Austin Rover: A Case-study in the Failure of Business Strategy and Industrial Policy*, Leamington Spa, Berg.

Williams, Karel, Tony Cutler, John Williams and Colin Haslam (1987b). "The end of mass production?", *Economy and Society* **16**: 405–39.

Williams, Mari E.W. (1984). "Choices in Oil Refining: The Case of BP, 1900–60", *Business History* **26**/3: 307–29.

Willman, P. and G. Winch (1987). *Innovation and Management Control: Labour Relations at BL Cars*, Cambridge, Cambridge University Press.

Wilson, John F. (1995). *British Business History, 1720–1994*, Manchester, Manchester University Press.

Winton, J.R. (1982). *Lloyds Bank, 1918–1969*, Oxford, Oxford University Press.

Wolf, M. (1985). *The Japanese Conspiracy*, Sevenoaks, The New English Library.

Womack, James P., Daniel T. Jones and Daniel Roos (1990). *The Machine that Changed the World*, New York, Rawson Associates.

Wong, V., J. Saunders and P. Doyle (1987). "Japanese Marketing Strategies in the United Kingdom", *Long Range Planning* **20**: 54–63.

Woodward, N.C. (1991). "Inflation", in N.F.R. Crafts and N.C. Woodward (eds) *The British Economy since 1945*, Oxford, Clarendon Press: 180–211.

Worswick, G.D.N. and P.H. Ady (eds) (1952). *The British Economy, 1945–1950*, Oxford, Clarendon Press.

Worswick, G.D.N. and P.H. Ady (eds) (1962). *The British Economy in the Nineteen-Fifties*, Oxford, Clarendon Press.

Wrigley, Chris (1997). *British Trade Unions, 1945–1995*, Manchester, Manchester University Press.

Yamamura, Kozo (1982). "Success that Soured: Administrative Guidance and Cartels in Japan", in Kozo Yamamura (ed.) *Policy and Trade Issues of the Japanese Economy: American and Japanese Perspectives*, Tokyo, Tokyo University Press: 77–112.

Yavitz, Boris (1967). *Automation in Commercial Banking, its Process and Impact: A Case Study and Conceptual Analysis*, New York, Free Press.

Yonekura, Seiichiro (1997). "Internalisation and Externalisation: Organisational Structures for Fuji Denki, Fujitsu and Fanuc", in Abé and Gourvish 1997: 237–59.

Young, Kelvin (1986). "The Management of Craft Work: A Case Study of an Oil Refinery", *British Journal of Industrial Relations* 24: 363–80.

Zeitlin, Jonathan (1995). "Americanisation and its Limits: Theory and Practice in the Reconstruction of Britain's Engineering Industries", *Business and Economic History* 24/1: 277–86.

Zeitlin, Jonathan (2000a). "Introduction: Americanisation and its Limits: Reworking US Technology and Management in Postwar Europe and Japan", in Zeitlin and Herrigel 2000: 1–50.

Zeitlin, Jonathan (2000b). "Americanising British Engineering? Strategic Debate, Selective Adaptation and Hybrid Innovation in Post-War Reconstruction, 1945–60", in Zeitlin and Herrigel 2000: 123–52.

Zeitlin, Jonathan (2000c). "Reconciling Automation and Flexibility? Technology and Production in the Postwar British Automobile Industry", *Enterprise and Society* 1/1: 9–62.

Zeitlin, Jonathan and Gary Herrigel (eds) (2000). *Americanisation and its Limits: Reworking American Technology and Management in Postwar Europe and Japan*, Oxford, Oxford University Press.

Zysman, John (1994). "How Institutions Create Historically Rooted Trajectories of Growth", *Industrial and Corporate Change* 3: 243–83.

Theses

Gandy, A. (1992). The Entry of Established Electronics Companies into the Early Computer Industry in the UK and USA, University of London, PhD.

Hamilton, Ross (1997). Continuous Path: the Evolution of Process Control Technology in Post-War Britain, University of Warwick, PhD, Department of Computer Science.

Koerner, Steven (1995). The British Motor Cycle Industry, 1935–75, University of Warwick, PhD.

O'Hara, Glenn (2002). British Economic and Social Planning, 1959–70, University of London, PhD.

Index